INDIA'S FREEDOM STRUGGLE AND THE URDU POETRY

Poetry, mainly Urdu poetry, played a very significant role in India's freedom struggle. This book explores the poetic contributions going back centuries of colonial rule, which became songs of freedom and captured both the poignancy and fervor of revolution, protest, and hope.

Urdu became one of the essential languages in colonial India, used by both political leaders and many young revolutionaries in speeches and writings as slogans for freedom and a call to action. Poets such as Josh Malihabadi, Firaq Gorakhpuri, Sahir, Makhdoom, Kaifi Azmi, Majaz, Majrooh, and Faiz Ahmad Faiz wrote highly patriotic poetry which was used not only to inspire and help mobilize people but also to offer criticism of existing socio-cultural practices in India and promote reform and equality. This work – a creative and selective translation of the book *Hindustan Ki Tahriik-e Aazadi aur Urdu Shaa'yiri* by Professor Gopi Chand Narang – includes English translations of poems from rare historical manuscripts as well as banned and witnessed poetry confiscated by the British. It looks at key events in India's struggle for freedom through the prism of literature, language, poetry, and culture while also delving into the lives of poets who became the voice of their generation.

This book is an essential read for students and researchers of colonial and postcolonial literature, cultural studies, comparative studies, history, and South Asian literature and culture.

Gopi Chand Narang (1931–2022) won awe-inspiring recognition all around the world for his outstanding contribution to literature. He authored numerous pathbreaking scholarly books, and he was the Indira Gandhi Memorial Fellow of the IGNCA (2002–2004) and Rockefeller Foundation Fellow for Residency at

Bellagio Study Centre, Italy (1997). He was also Professor Emeritus at University of Delhi and Jamia Millia Islamia University, New Delhi, India.

Surinder Deol is the author of *SAHIR: A Literary Portrait*, published in 2019. His translations of books on poets such as Ghalib, Mir Taqi Mir, and the Urdu Ghazal have received critical acclaim. He has also published a poetical biography of Faiz Ahmed Faiz. He lives in Potomac, Maryland.

INDIA'S FREEDOM STRUGGLE AND THE URDU POETRY

Awakening

Gopi Chand Narang
Translated by Surinder Deol

Routledge
Taylor & Francis Group

LONDON AND NEW YORK

Designed cover image: Surinder Deol

First published in English 2023
by Routledge
4 Park Square, Milton Park, Abingdon, Oxon OX14 4RN

and by Routledge
605 Third Avenue, New York, NY 10158

Routledge is an imprint of the Taylor & Francis Group, an informa business

Translated by Surinder Deol

The Urdu edition of the book titled *Hindustan Ki Tahriik-e Aazadi aur
Urdu Shaa'yiri* was published by the National Council for the Promotion
of Urdu Language, New Delhi, in 2003.

Published in Urdu by National Council for the Promotion of Urdu
Language, New Delhi 2003

British Library Cataloguing-in-Publication Data
A catalogue record for this book is available from the British Library

ISBN: 978-1-032-24818-9 (hbk)
ISBN: 978-1-032-42403-3 (pbk)
ISBN: 978-1-003-36084-1 (ebk)

DOI: 10.4324/9781003360841

Typeset in Bembo
by codeMantra

For the Moths of the Flame of Freedom.
For Poets, Writers, Thinkers, Artists, Journalists,
who helped nurture the feelings of Patriotism,
prepared the ground for opposing the colonial rule,
and who played a crucial role in awakening
the longing for freedom.
For those who answered the call for the highest sacrifice.

This approach to ensuring the growth of a language is wrong. To think that the progress of one language will retard the development of another is equally erroneous. Our approach should not oppose any language but persuade others to learn the language they did not know. As far as Urdu's growth is concerned, I am not much worried about it. It will undoubtedly flourish and develop gradually. Any language with vitality and liveliness will grow, and Urdu has these qualities. It cannot be suppressed. In the past, passions had been roused in the name of the language. It was thought that the state could either help or suppress the growth of a language. It was not so. Sometimes state suppression of a speech has the reverse effect. No language could depend on outside help for its growth. Of course, state help clears the way for progress and vitality. Urdu too, if it has these qualities, I think it has very much of them, will have its place. It is one of the fourteen languages the constitution recognizes, and it or any other will not be suppressed.

Jawaharlal Nehru
All India Urdu Conference
February 15–17, 1958
Delhi

CONTENTS

PREFACE

Every great movement and every significant social or political revolution in human history has seen behind the scenes the presence of poets who spoke for justice, freedom, or whatever other altruistic motive moved them. Their words inspired ordinary people and provided a new language to describe their struggle. Poetic language is very effective in exposing the nature of evil that is confronted. It also empowers participants in a struggle to clarify the objectives of their resistance. Literature played a vital role in the French revolution of 1799, a turning point in world history. It is impossible to understand the Russian Revolution of 1917 without appreciating the impact of poets like Anna Akhmatova, Boris Pasternak, and Vladimir Mayakovsky on peoples' consciousness. Poetry played an essential part during the Civil Rights Movement in the USA. There is no doubt that the lyrical speeches of Dr. Martin Luther King Jr. greatly inspired the activists. But the poetry of Langston Hughes, Amiri Baraka, and Dudley Randall was also responsible for creating awareness of the injustice and prejudice that the black people had to live with daily. Similarly, the anti-war movement of the sixties had poets like Allen Ginsberg, Bob Dylan, Galway Kinnell, W.S. Merwin, and Adrienne Rich who provided lyrics for the resistance.

There is an impressive body of literature on India's freedom movement, yet it is hard to find a book on how Indian poets influenced the struggle. There is very little recognition that Urdu, out of all the Indian languages, played a more significant role in making people aware of exploitation by colonial power and the need to gain total freedom from foreign rule. Such Urdu poets number dozens, if not hundreds, and their poetic contributions are spread over the past several centuries. The central theme of this book is to shed light on this little-known facet of the role of the Urdu language, especially its verse, in India's freedom struggle.

The battle for freedom started decades before the Rebellion of 1857. We often forget rulers like Siraj ud-Daula, Nawab of Murshidabad, Bengal, who fought to block the British advance into North India. His military general, Mir Jafar, betrayed him in the Battle of Plassey (1757), and the young Nawab was later executed at the orders of the British East India Company. Mir Jafar's betrayal was so grave that it has turned into an idiom of treachery in Urdu and Hindi. This tragic episode was captured by Raja Ram Narain Mauzoon, a subedar in the local militia, in a poignant couplet that is considered the first nationalistic couplet of the Urdu ghazal.

> *ghazallaan tum to vaaqif ho kaho majnuun ke marne ki*
> *divaana mar gaya aakhir ko viraane p kya guzri*

O gazelles of devastated lands,
you for sure have been a witness
to what happened to ill-fated Majnuun –
the mad lover lost his life, of course,
but what happened to the rampaged state?

The couplet was addressed to Bengal's citizens (ghazallaan), reminding them of their ruler's death, the one who loved his state in the same manner as crazy Majnun loved his beloved Laila. The freedom struggle gained momentum during the First World War when Mahatma Gandhi returned from South Africa and practiced his revolutionary idea of satyagraha (peaceful civil disobedience). At the same time, the nation was shocked by the brutal massacre of innocent citizens in Jallianwala Bagh. This sad event led to the first non-cooperation movement and, eventually, the demand for purna swaraj (India's independence).

The campaign to free India from the yoke of slavery involved thousands upon thousands of citizens, who participated in protest marches, filled the jails, and many brave souls who willingly climbed the hanging posts to make the highest sacrifice. These freedom fighters came from all parts of India, and they belonged to all castes and classes, rich and poor, farmers and workers, men and women, and spoke various languages. But interestingly, Urdu emerged as the core language of the freedom movement. There were several reasons why this happened.

First, Urdu was the most popular language, probably more in circulation than English, which provided a common forum for sharing ideas among people from different parts of India. From Peshawar to Patna, from Kashmir to Kanyakumari, all major Indian cities had at least one widely read Urdu daily newspaper. Second, many freedom movement leaders like Motilal Nehru, Jawaharlal Nehru, Jinnah, Maulana Azad, and others knew Urdu well and addressed the masses using this language. Even Gandhi mostly spoke in a mix of Hindi and Urdu, called Hindustani. Packed with Urdu words, phrases, and idioms, orations for the country's freedom made a strong impression on audiences. Third, several revolutionary activists who inspired the younger generation knew Urdu so well that they composed famous verses in the language. Ram Prasad Bismil, who gave his life for the cause of freedom, comes to mind. His words *sarfroshi ki tamanna ab hamaare dil mein hai* summed up the people's mood, exasperated with British oppression and ready to sacrifice their lives. Even other revolutionary figures and martyrs like Bhagat Singh used Urdu as the medium for inspiring their younger followers while using verses like *mera rang de basanti chola*. Fourth, Urdu was fortunate in having great poets, early in the freedom struggle, who composed poems that quickly became songs of freedom. We can mention the early work of Allama Iqbal and his *Tarana-e Hindi* like *saare jahaan se achha hindostaan hamaara*. This short poem became the song that was most sung during protest marches. Every great movement has a slogan, and the main slogan of India's freedom movement, *Inqilaab Zindabaad*, was coined by Hasrat Mohani, a leading Urdu poet and freedom fighter. Many Urdu poets were part of the progressive writers' movement, especially poets like Josh Malihabadi, Firaq Gorakhpuri, Sahir, Makhdoom, Sardar Jafri, Kaifi Azmi, Majaz, Majrooh, and Faiz Ahmad Faiz, who wrote highly inspirational patriotic poetry. It is also important to mention that Hindi poets, who wrote patriotic songs, published their work in Urdu newspapers using Urdu script. It happened because there were very few Hindi newspapers in the urban areas, and their circulation was relatively small. Therefore, the work of Hindi poets became indistinguishable from those writing in Urdu.

Hindustan Ki Tahreek-e-Azadi Aur Urdu Shayari was initially written in Urdu, and the National Council for the Promotion of Urdu Language published it in 2003. As several reviewers noted, the book was the first well-documented proof of what was commonly known. Still, the historians did not explicitly recognize that Urdu was indeed the language of India's freedom struggle. This English edition is not a straightforward translation of the Urdu book. It has been carefully designed, keeping in view the demands and preferences of English readers. We describe the most significant events of the freedom struggle and explain how they appear to the reader through the Urdu verse's lens. We do not consider these two things separate and distinct, but as points of interest on the same continuum, since Urdu and *Aazaadi* (the idea of freedom) merge into one whole and become one.

The work is divided into two parts. Part I contains the evolution of concepts like nationalism and freedom over the past several centuries, the origins of the freedom struggle, key markers in this journey, and their culmination. The banned and witnessed poetry confiscated by the British appears here for the first time in English translation. Part II highlights the poetic contributions of four leading poets of the freedom movement: Durga Sahai Suroor Jahanabadi, Josh Malihabadi, Tilok Chand Mehroom, and Firaq Gorakhpuri.

My deep association with Surinder Deol, a highly innovative writer and translator, lasting over several years and resulting in the publication of three previous substantive literary works, goes beyond customary words of appreciation. Surinder used his poetic skills and translated all Urdu and Persian poems included in this volume that beautifully conveyed the flair of the original work. I am grateful to the personnel of libraries who generously provided me access to rare historical manuscripts and documents. Many scholars whose insights were of great value are acknowledged in the footnotes throughout the book. I am grateful to all those who helped me accomplish this vital task, including my family members, my wife, Manorma, and my sons, Arun and Tarun, and their families. They unflinchingly provided me with the emotional support that made it possible to pursue these academic interests. I am also thankful to Mohammad Musa Raza, who has helped me prepare this and several other books.

India's freedom struggle is the most significant part of its modern history. Historians and political commentators have described how various events unfolded in lucid detail and how the geopolitical game was played out. This book is unique because we look at the freedom movement and its key landmarks through the prism of literature, language, poetry, culture, fine arts, and emotional states of key actors in this drama that unfolded over hundreds of years. We hope that the book will not only offer a great reading but also find a place in the hearts and minds of the readers, reminding us of Urdu's maxim in Ghalib's dynamic words.

bakhshe hai jalva-e gul zauq-e tamaasha Ghalib
chashm ko chaahiye har rang mein va ho jaana

The splendor of flowers, Ghalib,
makes us appreciate beauty.
The eye should be able to see reality
in the colors in which it reveals itself.

Gopi Chand Narang
Charlotte, North Carolina
May 2022

PART I

Prison and the Hanging Post

1

THE PATRIOTIC TRADITION

From Amir Khusrau to 1857

Life in South Asia was defined by the tension between center and periphery in a variety of senses. In both the Delhi Sultanate and the Mughal Empire, centralized authority was legitimized by appeals to transcendent principles, and yet practical power was built around local negotiation, patronage, tribal power, and mundane networks of influence (and armed strength). For most, central power was distant, and yet its presence was dramatized through a variety of connecting links, sacred genealogies, rituals, and architectural sites that suggested the power and pull of the "center, " even on local life. In this context Sufis (and their shrines), like Christian holy men, made locally manifest the principles of central Islamic power on which transcendent power was based—and in the process helped to legitimize the Islamic state. Yet at the very same time, the particularity of Sufi power (with its powerful local associations) dramatized the periphery's inescapable particularity and intractability. For rulers Sufis were thus, as the writings of many historians have made clear, simultaneously instruments of legitimation and figures of potential political subversion.[1]

David Gilmartin

The development of Urdu poetry occurred in the complex web of social and cultural relations and interactions, and it is not something that flowered in isolation in a fancy mirror house. Even in its early days, this language showed social, cultural, and nationalistic aspirations. We need to remember that the definition of 'national' or 'nationalistic' changed over time. Urdu never stayed detached from its surroundings and the march of history. Doubts arose because Urdu borrowed from elements that were local and nonlocal and from places inside and outside the country. Therefore, nationalism exhibited by Urdu poets has no grave and stable grounding in the Indian soil. This assertion lacks evidence.

DOI: 10.4324/9781003360841-2

The truth is that Urdu is the fruition of the interaction between people belonging to two different cultural traditions and linguistic backgrounds. Since the communication was creative, the elements blossomed as the ever-flowing fountain of a unique pluralistic *Ganga–Jamuni* civilization. This profuse cultural fusion happened on Indian soil, which is why the basic structure of Urdu remained Indo-Aryan. The presence of alien influences in the language is customary and formal. They are metaphoric and suggestive. Any force emanating from a foreign source can shape the surface structure, but it can't determine the configuration of the inner core. We can concede that Persian poets, who were residing in India at the time when the Urdu language was in its early stages of development, acted as role models on how to use different genres of poetry (ghazal, qasida, rubai, etc.). These genres were not native to the Indian literary tradition. But, during the seventeenth and eighteenth centuries, when Urdu poetry emerged as a distinctive innovation, Muslims had been residents of the country for a considerable time. These people had no other country other than India to call their own. Since the Persian language was the measure of intellectual and cultural excellence, Urdu visibly accepted its influence. Both Muslims and Hindus were equal partners in learning Persian language and adopting Persianized styles of writing. It is one thing to borrow what is best in a foreign language, and it is another to stay immersed in the colorful beauty of one's native land, accepting its historical traditions and cultural distinctiveness. Therefore, we should not mix these two elements when we talk about Urdu poetry. The Indian artistic genius takes and naturalizes what is suited to its core. The rest it rejects and sets aside.

We should realize that the concept of nationalism during the middle ages was different from its current interpretation. The limitations of cultural and historical consciousness of those times did not allow for concepts such as contemporary national unity. Nationalism, as a broadly shared modern-day political ideal, took several centuries to emerge as a distinct idea. The idea of *Bharata* of the sacred texts while passing through the degeneration period and alien invasions had remained an indistinct part of the cumulative memory, an idea that was erased. Evident at that time were patriotic feelings that were more or less personal, which were expressed at a local level, and their scope was limited. There was no shared consciousness of these ideas at a broader societal level. Therefore, when we talk about early Urdu poetry and its expression as a love of the land, we should keep these considerations in view.

Amir Khusrau (1253–1325), the first poet of the Hindavi language, took great pride in calling himself Indian. He called India, 'My origin, my place of birth, and my land.' Although his ethnic roots were Turkish, he neither used this fact in defining himself nor took any pride in it. On the contrary, he derived great pleasure in calling himself Indian. His father was a Turk courtier, and his mother, a Rajput. He wrote masnavi *Nuh Sipihr* (Nine Skies) in 1318, including a chapter regarding his vivid perceptions of India and its culture. In his first masnavi *Qiran us-Sa'dain* (Meeting of the Two Auspicious Stars), written in 1289, he included several couplets eulogizing the sheer beauty of his birthplace, and in doing so, he showed his preference for the Indian sites and locations over cities like Balkh and Bukhara from where his ancestors had come. When Khusrau talks about India, he praises, in particular, its gardens overflowing with abundant fruits and flowers, the physical appearance and beauty of its men and women, the ability of its people to learn foreign languages quickly, and the artistic ability of its artisans. There is hardly any aspect of India's religious, social, and ethical life that he fails to appreciate. He liked Indian winters, which were comfortable and enjoyable compared with places like Khurasan. He had words of praise for the Sanskrit language, which, when spoken, he thought was like a clustering of pearls, and in its eminence, it was better than Persian. He was India's true lover and a patriot. Whenever he talks about India in his poetry, he becomes ecstatic, raining flowers. In *Nu Sipihr,* a couplet gives Hindavi a higher place over his paternal languages like Persian and Turkish. In his third divan, called *Ghurrat ul-Kamaal* (The Prime of Perfection), written in 1294, he wrote:

turk-e hindos-taanem man hindavi goyem javaab
shakar misri nadaaram kaz arab goyem sukhan

As a Turkish-Indian, I can speak in Hindavi.
I do not have the Egyptian (rock candy)
so that I could speak in Arabic.

There was a pun in the original text.
    In the Preface, he wrote:

chu man tuuti-e hindam ar raast pursi
z man hindavi purs ta naghz goyam

I am a 'Parrot of India,'[2]
please speak to me in Hindavi
to hear my musical speech.

One exciting aspect of Khusrau's patriotism is his praise for customs and manners, which many foreigners and Indians look upon with great disapproval, such as Sati and Jauhar, which he thought were excellent symbols of self-worth and personal pride during those difficult times. He suggests that if such actions were not prohibited in Islam, many Muslims would engage in them to show their love either for an ideal or for a person.

Urdu poetry had its humble beginnings in the South. The part played by early kingdoms (Bahmani, Qutub Shahi, Aadil Shaahi, etc.) in the early years of Urdu's growth is part of history. Urdu poetry explicitly recognized the physical surroundings in which it was growing and the customs and pastimes of early users of this language. The verse composed by Sultan Quli Qutub Shah (1470–1543), the founder of Qutub Shahi dynasty of Golconda, who ruled from 1512 to 1543, is a good example. He had the same temperamental affinity with the Indian culture as Khusrau or Akbar. Like Khusrau, his mother was an Indian woman having no foreign genetic association. He had inherited ideas of communal harmony and fairness from his elders. He was the first king of Dakan who adopted a typical Indian style of living, including his royal wardrobe. His poetry is filled with praise for different places and sites, and he had a great appreciation of the Indian civilization and its traditions. Because of his highly romantic temperament, he admired Indian beauty. He described in his verse the aspects of Indian feminine glamor in a language filled with exquisite metaphors and similes. He also provided delightful descriptions of Indian gardens, fruits, flowers, Indian seasons like Basant, and the rainy season. He actively participated in these festivals and the people he ruled.

Several other Dakani poets showed great poetic appreciation for local customs and places of interest. They expressed satisfaction with everything that belongs to their land, including natural beauty, birds and animals, and products created by the local artisans. They used metaphors and similes that best demonstrated their feelings of utmost endearment, especially for the female beauty. The bun, a hairstyle in which a woman draws back her hair into a tight coil, was likened to black clouds ready to rain. Her cheeks were similar to a lotus flower. Her nose was the same as a bud of *champa* flower. She walked like a drunken elephant. Her whole body was as charming as a *madan baan,* sweet-smelling creeper. We don't need to debate whether this recognition of the allure of living and nonliving objects was conscious or unconscious. There is no doubt that this was the sincere expression of the sentiments that resided in the hearts of these poets.

Another distinctive contribution of Dakani poets was recreation in beautiful words of love stories from traditional Indian sources. Up until that point, it was common among poets to refer to love stories like Laila–Majnun, Yusuf–Zulaikha, and Shirin–Farhad that were inherited from Persian and other foreign sources. Nizami, Ghawaasi, and Nusrati wrote and revived epic love stories of *Kadam Rao Padam Rao, Tota Kahani,* and *Manohar-Malti,* respectively. *Padmavat* was translated into Urdu by Vali Vilori and Ghulam Ali. Mir Mohammad Kazim Hussain brought out the hidden beauty in *Ruup-Kam Lata* fable, while Arif Ulddeen Ajiz composed *Lal-o-Gauhar* that concerned God Indra's exploits.[3]

From the political perspective, this was the time when the Mughals ruled in the North, while the South was divided between several small self-governing states. Because of the long distances and travel constraints, there was no collective Indian consciousness. This kind of broader awareness was nearly impossible. Under the circumstances, there was scope for patriotic sentiment at the local level that was felt strongly by some individuals but would, unfortunately, lack depth and broad acceptance. A new kind of shared consciousness came much later. Poets found comfort in singing songs about the region or city they lived in. Here is poet Vajahi expressing his love for Dakan.

> dhakan sa nahien thaar sansaar mein
> panch fazillan ka hai is thaar mein
> dhakan hai nagiina anguuthi hai jag

anguuthi kon hurmat nagiina hai lag
dhakan mulk kon dhan a'jab saaj hai
k sab mulk sar aur dhakan taaj hai
dhakan mulk bho-tij khaasa aahe
tlingaana is ka khulaasa aahe

There is no country in the world like Dakan.
The land is full of talented, gifted people.
If the world could be compared to a ring,
then Dakan is the precious garnet set in the ring,
And the value of the ring is because of the garnet.
O my ladylove, Dakan is a beautiful place
If other countries are heads, Dakan is the crown.
It undoubtedly is a lovely place
And Telangana is its pulsating throbbing heart!

There was another poet named Tab'ii Golkandavi, who lived during late 1600s and was Qutub Shah's contemporary and his court poet. He wrote the following couplet.

je-koi yaad karta na-ien apna vatan
o murda hai peran hai us ka kafan[4]

If there is someone
who does not love his land,
he is dead from within,
and his apparel is his coffin.

Poet Mohammad Nusrat Nusrati, in his masnavi *Ali Nama,* is ecstatic in his praise for the city of Surat and its harbor. This city, according to him, is like a garden, and its bloom is unlike any other city in the world. It has not been hit yet by the autumn's flurry of wind.[5] In his masnavi *Diipak-Patang,* poet Syed Mohammad Khan I'shrati expresses his admiration for India, as a country, in the following moving words:

a'jab saaz hai hind ka soznaak
k karta hai naghme son je-on jaan raakh
hindustaan hai deval butaan us mein mast
kai haat son aa'shqaan but parast
bhariya hind mein daat kar yuun jamaal
k tis saamne zuhd o taqva muhaal

India is like a musical instrument
that produces melodies filled with pathos.
These songs touch the listener so that he is burned to ashes.
India is like a temple, filled with idols
and the hands of hundreds of lovers who worship these idols.

There is so much beauty in India
that it is a challenge to remain a pious believer.

Along with Surat, Bijapur is another city that caught the attention of poet Syed Aa'lam Bijapuri. After the city's fall in 1685, he moved to Kurnool but could not bear the separation from the city he loved. He wrote the following couplets.

bijapur hai shahr-e sahib jamaal
zamiin vaan ki hai sakht aahan misaal
zamiin kon yuun nit vaan ki taasiir hai
hava lag ke hue javaan jo piir hai

Bijapur's grandeur stands out among other cities.
Its soil is as hard as metal, and there is nothing to compare.
Not only the land but its climate is also life-giving.
If an older man gets a puff of its air,
he would undoubtedly regain his youth.

Wali Mohammad Wali Dakani (1667–1707) wrote a qat'a consisting of 13 couplets to Gujarat, his home state. He did it when he was away from Gujarat, visiting places in Punjab along with his friend, Syed Abu-Al'muaali. Here are two couplets from that qat'a.

gujaraat ke firaaq son hai khaar khaar dil
betaab hai siine mein aatish bahaar dil
lekin hazaar shukr wali haq ke faiz son
phir us ke dekhne ka hai umiidvaar dil

My heart is full of grief because of the separation from Gujarat.
My heart is uneasy like the sparks going up in flames.
But Wali, thanks to the Almighty and His Grace,
my heart expects to see what it wishes very soon.

Wali was also full of praise for the city of Surat, and he loved this city dearly. Look at the following couplets.

a'jab shahraan mein hai purnuur yak shahr
bila shak vo hai jag mein maqsad-e dahr
ahe mashuur is ka naam suurat
k jaave jis ke dekhe son kaduurat

Strange among the cities, luminous, one-of-a-kind city.
Without a doubt, it is present in the world as its symbol.
Its name, famous as it is, is Surat.
If we look at it, our maladies will go away.

About the presence of various religious groups in the city and the color they add to the city's grandeur, Wali says

vahaan saakin itte hain ahl-e mazhab
k ginti mein n aavein in ke mashrab

agarche sab hain vo ibnaaye aadam
avval-e biinash mein ranga rang aa'lam

There is so much religious diversity
that it is hard to count their faiths.
Although they are all born of Adam,
temperamentally they are diverse and thus
they create a world of many colors and hues.

About Surat's beauty and glamor, Wali wrote the following lines in a masnavi.

bhari hai siirat o suurat son suurat
har ik suurat hai vaan un-mol muurat
sabha inder ki hai har ik qadam mein
chhupa inder sabha kon le a'dam mein
kishan ki gopiyaan ki naiien hai ye nasl
rahiin sab gopiyaan vo naql ye asl
nazar bhar kar dikho har gul badan kon
k hai parde son be parva inan kon[6]

Surat is filled with people of pleasant disposition and beauty.
Every face you see is unique, like a portrait.
Every step of the way, there is God Indra's court.
That might be fake; this one is real.
It is not the lineage of Lord Krishna's companions.
Those were untrue. You will find the real here.
Look carefully at every feminine body made of flowers!
Who wants to be without their veil?

Lahore was another city that was well-known for its picturesque monuments and gardens. Here are few lines by the poet Hazrat Murad Shah.[7]

khuubi is ki thi shohra-e aafaaq
husn ka is ke tha jahaan mushtaaq
khuubru the haya se sab mausuuf
aur aashiq vafa mein the ma'ruuf
jo k aalam tamaam dekh aata
so n dekh is ko phir kahien jaata
rashk-e aabaadi-e jahaan tha ye
al-gharaz khuub hi makaan tha ye

Its uniqueness was famous all over the world.
The people everywhere were desirous of its beauty.
The ones who lived here were beautiful and earned praise for their modesty.
And its lovers were famous for their fidelity.
Anyone who went around the world,
after seeing it, never thought of going to any other place.
All the people around the globe were envious –
what a place, what a city this was.

Urdu poetry had its formal materialization in North India after Wali's Divan reached Delhi. We can say that Emperor Mohammad Shah to Shah Alam II was the golden age of poetry. We saw the emergence of such gifted master poets as Mirza Jan-e Jaanaan Mazhar, Shah Hatim, Sauda, and Mir during this period. These were also poets who considered India as their motherland. Mazhar was a Sufi. They did not see any differences between Hindus and Muslims and respected the spiritual traditions of both these religions. The old practice of labeling non-Muslims as Kafirs (nonbelievers) found little support. Hatim wrote masnavis and poems in which he celebrated India's geographic diversity and its cultural mélange. Let us see some couplets by Shah Hatim (1699–1783) praising Delhi as a city.

> *nahien hai shahr dehli hai gulistaan*
> *chaman se jis ka khushtar hai biyaabaan*
> *jidhar dekho tidhar har kuucha bazaar*
> *hua hai gul-rukhaan se sahn gulzaar*
> *vo be-shak vaqt ka shah-e jahaan hai*
> *jo koi mutavatan-e hindostaan hai*
> *rahe taa-hashar qaayem is ki bunyaad*
> *rakhe haq shahjahaan aabaad aabaad*

Delhi is more like a garden than a city.
Even its barren parts look better than a garden.
Wherever you look, each alley and the bazaar
is a stack of flowers revealing the beauty of loved ones.
He is a king of the world,
the one who is a resident of India.
May its foundations last until the day of judgment!
May God keep and preserve this kingdom forever!

Indian temperament is also revealed in the poetry of Mohammad Rafi Sauda (1713–1781). His imagination had been so Indianized that he even presented the traditional Islamic characters in the Indian flavoring. We get a good sense of different facets of Indian culture from Sauda's poetry. He wrote masnavis on topics such as changing Indian seasons and marital customs.

About Mir Taqi Mir (1723–1810), there is a famous saying that he didn't write ghazals, but elegies for his *dil* (heart) and *dilli* (the city). He spent 60 years of his life in the city. He described every street corner as *haft-aqliim* (equal to seven worlds) and *auraaq-e mussavvar* (pages of an album). Let us delve into some Mir couplets about Delhi.

> *dilli ke n the kuuche auraaq-e mussavvar the*
> *jo shakl nazar aaii tasviir nazar aaii*

The alleys of Delhi
were like pages from an album.

Each face that I saw
was like a framed beauty.

har roz naya ek tamaasha dekha
har kuuche mein so javaan ra'na dekha
dilli thi talismaat k har jaagah mir
in aankhon se aah ham ne kya kya dekha

Each day I was charmed by recreation.
In each alley, I found a hundred handsome people.
Delhi was a magical place so Mir everywhere
what I saw with my eyes is difficult to describe.

haft-aqliim har gali hai kahien
dille se bhi dayaar hote hain

Every street equal seven worlds.
Is there another place like Delhi?

These patriotic sentiments were primarily individual, and they were indeed not based on a shared or collective national consciousness. But at the same time, we can't call them too restrictive, and by using the term 'individual,' we can't reject them as insignificant. These sentiments may not be nationalistic, as the term is understood today, but they were authentic expressions of the social fabric that bound and inspired people together at that time. For example, Delhi was not merely loved for its buildings, monuments, and artifacts. It was indeed love for the people, their way of life, what they valued, and how they connected. It is a strange coincidence that this period of Urdu poetry's early years was also a period of considerable political and economic hardships. Therefore, while Urdu poets sang songs of praise for the city and its surroundings, they expressed their grief for the sufferings of the habitat and people.

The fall of the Mughal Empire started quickly after the death of Aurangzeb in 1707. Many emperors occupied the thrones, but their reigns were limited (Table 1.1). There was much infighting among the princes and cruelty. Added to this was the devastation caused by Nader Shah's invasion of Delhi in 1739. A poet named Syed Ja'far Zatalli, known for his mocking and sarcastic poetry, wrote that the days of peace and stability were gone. Wherever you looked, you saw death and destruction. People could not sleep at night because the sound of gunfire was a constant distraction. Everything was in great turmoil.

A poet named Mohammad Shakir Naji, who witnessed the humiliating defeat of Mughal forces at the hands of Nader Shah, expressed his feelings in a long poem. He stated that the Mughals had not fought a battle for a long time. They were like breastfed lads who spent time in drinking and merry making. They wore all kinds of ornaments, but they were amateurs in the art of fighting. The reign of Ahmad Shah Bahadur (1748–1754) was primarily known for lawlessness, plundering, and pillage. A poet named Ashraf Ali Fughan, a close friend of the emperor has captured in his verse the sad situation of the Mughal court. Things

TABLE 1.1 Mughal Emperors after the Death of Aurangzeb

Name	Reign	Major Events
Bahadur Shah	1707–1712	Tried to build good relations with Marathas, Rajputs, and Sikhs
Jahandar Shah	1712–1713	
Farrukhsiyar	1713–1719	He granted trading rights to the East India Company. This meant that the British could import goods into Bengal without paying any duty to the Mughal administration.
Rafi ud-Darajat Rafi ud-Daulah (also known as Shah Jahan II)	1719–1719	They were power brokers, and their reign lasted about 200 days.
Muhammad Shah	1719–1748	He fought a long war against Marathas and suffered the invasion of Nader Shah in 1739.
Ahmad Shah Bahadur	1748–1754	The Marathas defeated Mughal forces in the battle of Sikandarabad.
Alamgir II	1754–1759	
Shah Jahan III	1759–1760	
Shah Alam II (Saani)	1760–1806	Defeated in the battle of Buxar. He was blinded by a Rohaila who too later met a deadly end.
Akbar Shah II	1806–1837	Titular figurehead under British protection. British 'Resident' takes control in Delhi.
Bahadur Shah II (Zafar)	1837–1857	Last Mughal Emperor. Defeated and deposed by the British and exiled to Rangoon till death.

did not improve with Shah Alam Sani. Although he ruled for 46 years, there was no functioning government, and the grand Mughal Empire was now breaking into small pieces. The nobles were busy fighting one another. There was no shortage of conspiracies. Because of the economic decline, everything was in free fall. Soldiers were not getting their salaries. Rohillas and Jats were at war, and their fighting adversely affected the Delhi residents. The emperor had become a toy and was tossed around by different factions. The financial constraint was such that the emperor had no ride available for going to Eidgah for his prayers. No food was cooked in the royal kitchen for several days at a time. Begums and princesses of the palace spent time looking for morsels of food. Mus-hafi Ghulam Hamdani (1747–1824), a leading poet, captured the sad condition in the following words:

> kahti hai ise khalq-e jahaan sab shah-e aa'lam
> shaahi jo kuchh us ki hai so aa'lam p aa'yaan hai
> atraaf mein dilli ke ye lath maaron ka hai shor

jo aave hai bahar se vo ba-shikasta dahaan hai
but-khaana o masjid mein jo phaili hai kharaabi
na-quus ka naala n muazzan ka azaan hai
ae mus-hafi! is ka karuun mazkuur kahaan tak
hai saaf to ye gulshan-e dilli mein khizaan hai[8]

People call him the world's ruler,
but whatever royalty is left is just a name.
The fact is that Delhi is a city of those with strength.
Whosoever comes to the city from outside
comes with injuries and broken bones.
Both the idol-house and the mosque are in bad shape.
There is no sound of a conch shell from the temple and
no call to prayer from the mosque.
O Mus-hafi! What more can I say about this state?
The garden of Delhi is devastated by autumn.

Shah Alam Sani suffered the worst fate than his predecessor. A Rohilla chief not only dishonored the emperor, but he also sat on his chest and, with a sharp knife, gouged his eyes and left him to lead the rest of his life in great misery. Mirza Jafar Ali Hasrat, who witnessed this horrific scene, described it in painful detail in one of his poems.[9]

The country was in terrible shape, and it remained a better part of the eighteenth century. Emperors ascended the throne, but soon they were either removed with force or killed and dishonored in many ways. One could imagine the fate of ordinary people under these circumstances. Urdu poets who witnessed this carnage expressed their horror and disappointment in their verses. Here is a selection of couplets from some of the leading poets of that time.

Aabru (1685–1733)

ab zamaana hai be-taraah bigra
kya bane rozgaar ki suurat

zabaani hai shujaa'at in sabhon ki
amiir is jang ke hain sher-e qaaliin

We are living in terrible times.
There is no way left to make a living.
It is a futile effort to show one's courage.
In this fight, the nobles are like tigers
woven into royal carpets.

Sauda

luti hai mai uth gaaya saaqi mara bhi pur hua paimaana
ilaahi is taraah dekhuun main kin aankhon se mai-khaana

Wine has been looted, Saqi has given up, the glass is empty.
O, God! I don't have eyes to look at the devastated wine-house.

Hatim (1699–1783)

haatim yahi hamesha zamaane ki chaal hai
shikva baja nahien hai tujhe inqilaab ka

Hatim, this is trick the world plays with you.
You can't complain about the state of affairs.

khair o barkat hind se sab ur gaaii
sab ki dhaar-e tegh himmat mur gaaii

Generosity and affluence, found in India
in the olden days, are things of the past.
The courage that was once sharp as a sword
has been twisted, deformed, and warped.

chaman kharaab hua ho khizaan ka khaana kharaab
n gul raha hai n bulbul hai baaghbaan tanha

The garden is destroyed woe betide autumn.
No rose, no nightingale, and the gardener is lonely.

Mir

shahaan k kohl-e javaahir thi khaak-e pa jin ki
unhien ki aankhon mein phirti salaaiiyaan dekhein

Royals whose eyes were decorated with kohl once,
I saw in those very eyes, needles piercing and
turning them blind.

dilli mein aaj bhiik bhi milti nahien unhein
tha kal talak damaagh jinhein takht o taaj ka

In the city of Delhi, they can't get even alms if they begged,
who until yesterday adorned the crown and kingship.

jis sar ko gharuur aaj hai yaan taaj-vari ka
kal us p yahiin shor hai phir nauha gari ka

The head that is filled with vanity today of lordship,
tomorrow will be the subject of mourning and elegies.

ab kharaaba hua jahaan aabaad
varna har ik qadam p yaan ghar tha

The places where devastation resides today
had a humming home, each step of the way.

jis ja k khas o khaak ke ab dher lage hain
vaan ham ne inhi aankhon se dekhi hain bahaarein

The places where we now find mounds of rubble,
I have seen springs bloom with these very eyes.

ya qaafila dar qaafila in raston mein the log
ya aise gaye yaan se k phir khoj n paaya

There were caravans of people on these pathways.
They vanished that one could not find them again.

Dard (1721–1785)

haif! kahte hain hua gulzaar taaraaj-e khizaan
aashna apna bhi vaan ik sabza-e begaana tha

Alas, they say the autumn destroyed that spring.
Greenery, my friend, didn't belong to me anymore.

guzruun huun jis kharaabe p kahte hain vaan ke log
hai koi din ki baat y ghar tha y baagh tha

When I pass by the ruined places, I heard —
this was a home, and this was a garden.

jag mein koi n tuk hansa ho ga
k n hansne mein ro diya ho ga

No one would have smiled in this world.
For not smiling, he would have cried.

Mus-hafi

mujhe rahm aaye hai hasrat p aah us murgh-e be par ki
k ur sakta n ho aur ho vo zer-e aashiyaan baitha
n tanha mus-hafi hi us ke haathon se hai aavaara
koi bhi chain se yaaro na ziir aasmaan baitha

I pity for the aspiration of the bird without feathers.
It can't fly and is sitting still near its nest.
It is not only Mus-hafi who is troubled,
no one is living at ease under this cruel sky.

kauri kauri bikte hain gul-e kishvaraan dehli ke biich
husn ke maalik jo the vo aise arzaan ho gaye

Rose-like beauties are selling
for pennies in the city of Delhi.
Those who presented themselves as paragons
of beauty are going for a song.

Urdu poets did not just witness the downfall of Delhi; they lived through it, suffering great hardships along with others. The disintegration of civil society and its institutions had a profound psychological impact on their consciousness and creativity. They were themselves victims of poverty and adverse economic circumstances. The only way they could respond to this situation was through their verse, which they did. Here are some essential collections of poetry that are significant for their lyrical content and are consequential as documents of tragic historical value.

Shah Hatim[10]
Poem *Nairangi-e Jahaan* and Makhammus (five liner stanza poem) *Shahr Aashob*

Sauda[11]
Qasida Shahr Aashob, Qasida Tazhiik-e Rozgaar, Masnavi Dar Hajv Shiidi Faulaad Khan Kotvaal, Makhammus Shahr Aashob

Mir[12]
Masnavi *Darbiyaan-e Kizb,* Makhammas *Dar Hajv Lashkar, Shahr Aashob, Zikr-e Mir*

Mus–hafi[13]
Shahr Aashob

Rasikh Azimabadi
Shahr Aashob

Hafiz Abdul Rahman Khan Ahsaan
Shahr Aashob

Nawab Zuvulqadr Dargah Quli Khan
Qasida Salar Jung

We can add even more names to this list. *Shahr Aashobs* generally provide mournful narration of the destruction and disintegration of a city, including loss of trade and commerce, widespread fear, the indifference of the upper classes to the sufferings of the ordinary people, corruption of people with authority, and maltreatment of animals. The reader is overcome with sadness while reading these accounts. Deep within the words of anguish, we find hidden meaning expressing a love of the country.

The more substantial part of Delhi's population could not bear the impact of these adverse circumstances and fell apart. People moved to new places to find safety and means for sustenance. Poets who had a high standing in the areas where they were born became drifters and wanderers. Look at the following couplets.

Sauda
bulbul ko kya tarapte mein dekha chaman se duur
yaarab n kiijio tu kisi ko vatan se duur

What a heartbreaking scene when
I saw a nightingale languishing
away from the garden. O, God!
Do not separate anyone
from their native place.

Mir

jaata hai aasmaan liye kuuche se yaar ke
aata hai ji bhara dar o diivaar dekh kar

My circumstances are separating me
from the alley of my beloved.
I am overcome with broken heartedness
on seeing these doors and walls.

Yaqeen (1727–1755)

ham to chale hain yaarab aabaad rakhiio in ko
in baaghichon mein kya kya dhuumein machaaiiyaan hain

We are leaving this place, but please God
take care of these gardens where we had
loud and boisterous assemblies.

Khaliiq

muddat se baham rahte the jis ghar mein ham aur yaar
ab dekh ke khaali vo makaan aankh bhar aaii

The place where my beloved and I
had lived for a very long time,
now looking at that empty hearth
my eyes are filled with tears.

Hidayat (1768–1801)

hazaar haif k dilli sa shahr viiraan kar
kiya hai yaaron ne aabaad mulk puurab ko

Alas! After the devastation of a city like Delhi,
friends have found comfort in Avadh.

Avadh had one great advantage over Delhi. There was peace and the semblance
of a civilized society. That was one reason that Lucknow attracted some of the
best Delhi poets, including Mir. According to a resident of the city, not only
poets and men of good taste, but even prostitutes found Lucknow a better place
for their trade. Besides law and order, Lucknow offered avenues for recreation
such as assemblies and gatherings that offered a variety of entertainment such
as dances, singing, and poetic competitions. But the memory of Delhi was a

spike stuck in the hearts of poets who were forced by the circumstances to leave the city of their unbounded love. Mohammad Husain Azad[14] narrates an incident about Mir that best describes that feeling. When Mir reached the outskirts of Lucknow, and he was spending the night in a caravanserai, he came to know about a mushaira that was taking place in the evening. Dressed in the traditional Agra-Delhi style, he reached the venue. His appearance in the dress he was wearing was a matter of some amusement to other poets and the audience because it violated the more polished and sophisticated Lucknow dress code for such a gathering. When he was asked to recite his poetry, Mir chose the following words that reveal his inner pain for being forced to leave the city he loved.

> kya buud o baash puuchho ho puurab ke saakino
> ham ko ghariib jaan ke hans hans pukaar ke
> dilli jo ek shahr tha aa'lam mein intikhaab
> rehte the muntakhab hi jahaan rozgaar ke
> us ko falak ne luut ke viraan kar diya
> ham rahne vaale hain usi ujre diyaar ke

How can I tell you my whereabouts, O residents of the East?
You consider me an alien, as you laughingly inquire about my whereabouts.
Delhi was once considered one of the most beautiful cities in the world, and only cultured, and highly sophisticated people lived there.
The heavens robbed it, and the devastation followed.
I am a resident of the same ruined and abandoned place.

In another couplet, Mir says

> kharaaba dilli ka dah chand behtar lucknow se tha
> vahiin main kaash mar jaata sarasiima n aata yaan

But for its destruction, Delhi was a better place than Lucknow.
I wish I had died there.
I should not have come here heart broken.

Mus-hafi wrote a poem in the flowing style of Mir Hasan.

> mera ji jaanta hai ya ise khud main hi jaanuun huun
> jo gham guzre hai mujh par mere gham khawaaron se mat puuchho
> hasan ka she'r hai miyaan mus-hafi kya hasb-e haal apne
> suno tum ham se is ko khaanmaan daaron se mat puuchho
> "gaye vo din jo rehte the jahaan aabaad mein ham bhi
> kharaabi shahr ki sahra ke aavaaron se mat puuchho"

I know it, and this is something I alone can describe it.
The way I'm suffering,
don't ask about it from others who were distressed.
There is a couplet by Hasan

that best describes Mus-hafi's state of mind.
You should listen to it from me,
don't ask others who have been afflicted.
"Those days are gone when I used to live
in a world filled with people.
How the city was wrecked and ruined,
don't ask the pilgrims who left in great misery."

Mir Hasan suffered a great deal when he was forced to leave Delhi. In his masnavi
Gulzar-e Irm, there is a poem with a title *aavaara shudan az dyaar o haal-e zaar*
(departing as a vagrant, without a place, in a terrible state of mind).

hua aavaara-e hindstaan jab se
qaza puurab mein laaii mujh ko tab se
chala gaari mein yuun main laachaar
qafas mein jis tarah said-e griftaar
kare hai zikr dilli ka koi jab
meri aankhon se girta hai lahuu tab
jab aaya main dyaar-e lucknow mein
n dekha kuchh bahaar-e lucknow mein

Since the day I lost my home in India,
my death brought me to Avadh.
I left in a bullock-cart strangely,
like a bird being taken away in a cage.
My eyes have been raining blood
since the day I arrived in Lucknow, and
I have seen no springtime in this city.

Mir Hasan lived in Lucknow for a short time and then moved to Faizabad, the
capital of Avadh. He wrote masnavis to praise religious gatherings in Surajkund
and Muslim shrines. But even after a passage of time, the memory of Delhi and
its sights and sounds, especially the royal processions, stayed fresh in his mind.

Around this time of migration of Delhi poets to Avadh, something unusual
was happening in the Agra-Mathura region. Nazeer Akbarabadi (1735–1830)
was born in Agra, but he was free from stereotypical influences. He was very
prolific and wrote thousands of verses, of which 6,000 survive, including 600
ghazals. His concept of beauty was quite playful like Braj poets and without any
inhibitions. Sometimes, he cleverly changed gender descriptions, and thus he
was the only Urdu poet of his time who looked at each situation from a woman's
perspective. He also had a great affinity with the Hindu religion and its mythol-
ogies, especially the legendary Radha–Krishna relationship of ancient times in
this region of Mathura and Brindavan. Look at the following lines where Nazeer
playfully depicted Krishna's multiple names.

main kya vasf kahuun yaaro, us shaam baran avtaari ke
sii kishan kanhaiya, murlidhar, manmohan, kunj bihaari ke

> *gopal, manohar, saanvalia, ghanshaam, atal banvaari ke*
> *nandlal dulaare, sunder chhab, brij chand, mukat jhalkari ke*

[The sheer charm and imagery of these lines cannot be captured in translation. Therefore, no translation has been provided for this text. These are all names and epithets of Lord Krishna lovingly used.]

The spirit of nationalism that we find in Nazeer is based on Indian spirituality and the physical attributes of the land. He was also the first Urdu poet who wrote a poem in praise of the Taj Mahal.[15] He mentioned that the Taj came into being because of the imagination of an emperor as well as the collective physical contribution of Indian artisans and laborers, a point that Sahir Ludhianvi made in his poem more than 100 years later. He also wrote a mukhammas in praise of Agra city and called it *Shahr-e Sukhan* (the city of verse). The economic situation in Agra was no better than in Delhi and neighboring places. Shopkeepers, artisans, service providers – they were all suffering because of pillage and plunder of invaders, wrecked law and order, and the lack of work. Nazeer captured the prevailing mood of helplessness in the following mukhammas:

> *aa'shiq kaho asiir kaho aagrey ka hai*
> *mulla kaho dabiir kaho aagrey ka hai*
> *muflis kaho faqiir kaho aagrey ka hai*
> *shaa'yir kaho nazeer kaho aagrey ka hai*
> *is vaaste ye us ne likhe paanch chaar band*

> Call one a lover or a slave; he belongs to Agra.
> Call one a Mulla or a bookkeeper; he belongs to Agra.
> Call one poor or a beggar; he belongs to Agra.
> Call one a poet or Nazeer; he belongs to Agra.
> That is why he has written these five four stanzas.

Going back to Lucknow, we encounter Imam Baksh Nasikh (1772–1838), who was born in Faizabad, but he later moved to Lucknow, where he set up his school with scores of followers. He claimed that he had 'cleansed' Delhi's raw Urdu idiom and he set a new standard for Lakhnavi poets. We give below a sample of verse by the Lucknow poets as they shower all kind of compliments and go into raptures about the beauty of their city.

Nasikh

> *ham safiir apna vatan hai lucknow*
> *ham to bulbul hain chaman hai lucknow*

> Our friend, our companion, our land is Lucknow.
> We are the nightingales; the garden is Lucknow.

> *aasmaan ki kya hai taaqat jo chhuraaye lucknow*
> *lucknow mujh par fida hai main fidaaye lucknow*
> *tu ne dekhe hain kahaan rangiin adaaye lucknow*
> *laala o gul ke chaman hain kuucha haae lucknow*

What power the unknown must take away Lucknow from us?
Lucknow is in love with me, and I'm in love with Lucknow.
Where have you seen such colorful trifling ways as you see in Lucknow?
The alleys and gardens of Lucknow are filled with blossoming tulips and roses.

Saher

ye shahr mohabbat ka bazaar hai
yahaan jo hai ji ka kharidaar hai
a'jab shahr hai kuchh a'jab log hain
bahut hain magar muntkhab log hain[16]

This city is a bazaar of love.
Every buyer here is looking for the heart.
Fantastic city and beautiful people.
A lot of people, but they are top of the range.

Munir Shikohabadi

Munir fought in the 1857 war. The British brought a false case against him, and he was sent to Port Blair, Andaman Islands, for the rest of his life.

pesh-e nazar hai sair gulistaan-e lucknow
har ek samt nuur ka jalva hai dekh lo
jalse mushai'ron ke hain yaaron ki sohbatein
har ek fan-e sh'er mein yakta hai dekh lo
pariyon ki diid hai sar-e bazaar raat din
har kuuche mein talism ka mela hai dekh lo[17]

I am thinking of a walk in the gardens of Lucknow.
Wherever you look, you will find a splendor of light.
There are poetical symposia and gathering of friends.
Each one is uniquely competent in the art of verse.
You can see it for yourself.
You can see fairies in the bazaar each day and night.
In every alley, there is an element of magic that you see.

Shiv Parshad Vahbi (Died 1877)

ye vaz'a ye libaas ye husn-e butaan kahaan
kion kar hamaare dil ko n ho lucknow pasand

This style, this apparel, this beauty of the idols –
where will you find it?
Give me the reason why our hearts should not yearn
and love Lucknow?

Amir Minai (1829–1900)

kahaan hon gi amiir aisi adaayein huur o ghilman mein
rahe ga khuld mein bhi yaad ham ko lucknow barson

Amir, such attractions will not be found
among fairies and the young ones.
Even in paradise, I will continue to remember
Lucknow for years.

Love for Lucknow among the poets was an article of faith. They were obsessed with every bit of thing that existed in the city. They talked about the gardens, fairs, meetings, and processions and wrote qasidas about them. In the Salar Jung Library, there are two masnavis about Lucknow. For one of them, the name of the author is not known. It consists of 14 pages, and it was written during the reign of Asif Ud-Daula. Mohammad Bakhsh Shahid wrote the second masnavi in 1839, and it consists of 37 pages. Not much is known about the author's life. This was the time when the poets had started to focus their attention on the beauty of the local places rather than following the Persian poets praising non-Indian, mainly Iranian, towns and cities. The dominance of the Persian that peaked during the time of Shah Hatim and Mazhar was now fading. Urdu as a language was starting to get the respect that was equal to Persian. The roots of the Urdu language had spread over areas that were centers of Hindu culture for hundreds of years. Urdu absorbed local customs, belief systems, and sensibilities in cities like Lucknow and Agra. The subject of Urdu masnavis was invariably an Indian folk story. The poets gained the option of using the names of Indian lovers in places where references to Laila Majnu and Shiiriin-Farhaad were routine. Here is the partial list of Indian masnavis written in Avadh based on Indian folklore.

Heer-Ranjha
Munshi Mool Chand, Najiib Uddin Najiib

Nal-Daman
Niaz Ali Beg Nikhat, Bhagwant Rai Raahat

Shakuntla
Syed Mohammad Taqi and Inayat Singh composed poems based on a translation by Nawaz.

Singhasan Battiisi Masnavi
A disciple wrote them of Khwaja Mir Dard. Rang Lal Chaman and Makhan Lal transformed it into a poem.

Ruup Basant
Kanwar Kaam and Kala Kaam

Different authors

Padmavat
Zia Uddin Ibrat

When Ibrat started to write Padmavat, some people raised objections about a story that involved an Indian king and his consort. Ibrat responded in the following words:

> My land is India, and there is nothing dearer to me than my land. What I find in my land, I can find nowhere else. Then, why should I leave my country aside, and repeat the already repeated stories of foreign countries? To ignore one's cultural heritage is against the spirit of patriotism.

Notice the lines Ibrat wrote in praise of India.

a'jam se hind ka hai i'shq khuunkhwaar
qayaamat hind ki kaate hai talvaar
hai sho'la i'shq-e hindi ka sharar-rez
k hai ga aaftaab is ja nipat tez
likhuun hindostaan ki gar main taa'riif
to daftar ho juda ik aur tasniif

Compared to Iran, the love of India is bloodthirsty.
But the apocalyptic sword of India is sharp.
The flame of India burns its attackers
because sun rays are pungent when they fall here.
If I have to describe India's qualities,
I would need volumes to elaborate on what I have to say.

Munshi Mool Chand writes in his masnavi *Heer-Ranjha*.

tamaasha hai iqliim-e hindostaan
b-khuubi o lutf intikhaab-e jahaan
jise diikhiye so tarah-daar hai
pari chehra o maah rukhsaar hai

The realm of India is fascinating
Everything which is best in the world is found here.
Every person you look here is beautiful –
the facial glamor of a fairy and cheeks like the moon.

Bhagwant Rai and Rahat Kakorvi, authors of the highly acclaimed and most popular masnavi *Nal-Daman*, pay their respects to their native land in the following words:

a'jab nuzhat faza hindostaan hai
k har shahr is ka rangiin bostaan hai
ghazab hain but vahaan ke shokh o be-baak
k hain zaahid ka dil lene mein chalaak

vo kaafir zulf rakhte hain kamar tak
phanse jis mein dil-e islaam be-shak
a'jab vo mulk hai ruu-e zamiin par
nahien koi vilayaat is ke ham sar

Strangely delightful is India's spaciousness
because every city is like a colorful garden.
Profusely attractive and wooing are idols here,
and they cleverly steal the heart of the virtuous.
These non-believers keep their tresses long to touch their waists,
without paying attention to the plight of the sacred hearts.
Strange land that exists among all realms,
and no foreign domain is truly equal.

During the reign of Bahadurshah Zafar (1837–1857), several great Urdu poets had taken residence in Delhi despite political uncertainties and economic difficulties. These poets included big names like Zauq, Momin, Ghalib, Sahbai, Azurdah, and Shefta – the poets who were the heart and soul of every literary gathering in the city. Although Ghalib took pride in his Turkish ancestry, he showed great affection for India and the Indian way of life. Ghalib was indeed obsessed with the idea of gaining recognition as a leading Persian poet; his soul found solace in his Urdu verse, the alleys of Delhi, and the people of Delhi. His Persian masnavi *Chiraagh-e Dair* in praise of Benaras is well known where he wished he could have spent his whole life there. Ghalib's love for India is best expressed in the letters to his patrons, friends, and disciples.

hindostaan saaya-e gul paaye takht tha
jaah o jalaal-e ahd-e visaal-e butaan n puuchh

The throne of India stood on the top
which was like the reflection of a garden.
The grandeur and beauty of meeting with the idols
was such that it could not be described in words.

Ghalib wrote several verses about India's festivals, especially Diwali and Holi.

hai tamaasha gaah-e soz-e taaza har yak uzv-e tan
juun chiraaghaan-e divaali saf b saf jalta huun main

In this spectacle of light,
my body is filled with new wounds.
I am burning like the lights of Diwali
arrayed one after another.

Pyare Lal Aashob, who hailed from Todar Mal family of Akbar's time and occupied a high-ranking position in the education department, was a close friend of Ghalib. He was also secretary of the Literary Society of Delhi. He published

Mirza's following qat'a in the society's magazine in 1857 as his latest composition that had not been previously published.

hindostaan ki bhi a'jab sar zamiin hai
jis mein vafa o mehr o mohabbat ka hai vufuur
jaisa k aaftaab nikalta hai sharq se
ikhlaas ka hua hai isi mulk se zuhuur
hai asl tukhm-e hind se aur is zamiin se
phaila hai sab jahaan mein ye meyva duur duur

What a great country India is
where you will find love,
compassion and tolerance
in great abundance everywhere.
As the sun rises in the East,
love is spread around from this land.
The seed of love sown here in this land
became a sweet-tasting fruit
that reached far and wide.[18]

Although Ghalib considered himself to be of foreign descent, his love for India was deep. He believed in *dehli v agara shiraz v isfahaan-e manist* (Delhi and Agra are like Shiraz and Isfahan for me). He considered Hindus, Muslims, and Christians as brothers. He looked upon his disciples, Hargopal Tafta and Jauhar Singh Jauhar, as his children, and called Tafta out of affection for him as 'Mirza,' his own epithet.

Mohammad Husain Azad writes that Zauq's poetry gained such fame that the Divan of Hyderabad Chandu Lal Shaadaan sent an invitation to the poet along with 500 rupees and royal regalia. Zauq declined the invitation but sent a ghazal instead.[19]

aaj kal garche dakan mein hai bari qadr-e sukhan
kaun jaaye zauq par dilli ki galiyaan choor kar

Although these days Urdu verse in Dakan
is held in very high esteem,
Zauq, who would leave the alleys of Delhi
for something else.

Shefta too was filled with patriotic sentiments. Notice his verse in praise of India.

hind ki vo zamiin hai ishrat khez
k n zaahid karein jahaan parhez
vajd karte hain pi ke mai suufi
mast sote hain sub-h tak shab khez
rind kya yaan to shaahid o mai se
paarsa ko nahien gurez gurez[20]

India's land is so full of delightful attractions
that even preachers can't control themselves.
Sufis are in a state of rapture after a drink
and they sleep deeply until the morning.
Not just the drinkers, even the spiritual devout love the wine.
And the temperate can't control themselves.

The reign of Nawab Wajid Ali Shah came to an end in 1856, a year before the Mughal Empire saw its demise. The fall of Avadh resulted not only from the machinations of the British but it had also much to do with the incompetence of rulers. People loved the Nawab. They also loved poetry and drama. But they were not prepared and ready to fight. When Wajid Ali Shah was taken to Calcutta, the hearts of the citizens were broken. They had not anticipated such a calamity. Poets wrote ghazals expressing their shock and dismay. Singers roamed the streets, singing melodies of despair.

waajid ali payara kalkatte ko sidhaara
sadkein nikal rahi hain suuni gali gali hai

Wajid Ali, the loved one, has been taken to Calcutta.
The roads and alleys are abandoned and forsaken.

The economy of Avadh was destroyed after the British takeover. Millions lost their employment. Many Urdu poets were severely hit, and they suffered great hardships. Poet Qalaq wrote a long *Safr Aashob* about the king's journey from Avadh to his confinement. His description of the miserable condition of much-adored Nawab touched the heart of every Avadh resident. The celebratory mood of the bazaars filled with people vanished. The streets were deserted, and people lived in great fear of the unknown.

Poet Saher, who was more vocal about his love for Lucknow than the other poets, captured the mood of absolute desolation in the following lines:

a'jiib majm'a-e ahl-e kamaal tha afsoos
hazaar haif vo sohbat falak n dekh saka
n chauthi ka kahien jalsa n tiije ki sohbat
jahaan mein shaadi o gham donon ka maza n raha
sada vo danke ki kaanon se phir sunein yaarab
chalein salaami ki topein khuda kare aisa

It was a gathering of ingenious people, alas!
It is so sad that Heaven could not bear this.
There is no meeting of the fourth or an assembly of the third.
The enchantment of both the wedding and the wake is gone.
I would like to hear the sounds once again.
I want to hear ceremonial guns, God willing!

Poet Mir Anis was disheartened by the excessive use of force by the British. He wrote:

kiyon kar dil-e gham zada n fariyaad kare
jab mulk ko yon ghaniim barbaad kare
mango ye dua k phir khudavand-e kareem
ujri hui saltanat ko aabaad kare

Why shouldn't my grief-filled heart cry for help
when are the British destroying this land?
Let us pray that merciful God once again
re-establish the devastated empire!

The occupation of Avadh was the culmination of a long chain of secret plans and intrigues on the part of the British. Their ultimate goal was to control the whole of India. This development scared the ordinary people and the rulers of different states who got the painful message that what the British did to Avadh could very well be their fate. Their first reaction against this threat took the form of what is known as the 'First War of Independence.' Not all historians agree whether this was the proper description. There was no well-organized movement that drove the events one after the other of 1857. Its core was the conspiracy by small groups of soldiers, and its support came from rulers and theologians who felt threatened and faced the risk of losing their power. There was no country-wide centralized national movement behind this fight. On the positive side, this was the first common front for Hindus and Muslims to fight as comrades for a shared goal. Although this effort failed, it sowed the seeds of the birth of national con-sciousness and the eventual struggle for India's independence. We shall discuss the events of 1857 in some detail in the next chapter.

Notes

1 David Gilmartin, 'Sufism, Exemplary Lives, and Social Science in Pakistan' in *Rethinking Islamic* Studies: *From Orientalism to Cosmopolitanism* (Columbia: University of South Carolina Press, 2010), p. 106. Reproduced with permission.
2 *Tuuti-e Hind* (the Parrot of India) – this is how Khusrau was known among his contemporaries.
3 Gopi Chand Narang (Khurshid Alam, trans.) *Bharatiya Lok Kathaon Par Aadharit Urdu Masnaviyan* (New Delhi: Bharatiya Jnanpith, 2016).
4 Tab'ii Golkandvi, *Masnawi Bahram o Gul-e Andam* (New Delhi: Qaumi Council Bara-e Farogh-e Urdu, 1999).
5 Maulvi Abdulhaq (Muallafa), *Nusrati* (New Delhi: Anjuman'e Tarraqi Urdu), p. 131.
6 Nurul Hasan Hashmi, ed. *Divan-e Wali* (Karachi: Anjuman Press, 1954), pp. 324–326.
7 He was the son of a Sufi named Pir Karam Shah, also known as Masiita Shah. He died during his youth in 1800.
8 Mas-hafi, *Third Divan of Mas-hafi*, Manuscript (Rampur: Raza Library, 1211 Hijri), p. 109.
9 Abu-aliis Siddiqi, ed. *Lucknow Ka Dabistan's Shaa'yiri* (Lahore, 1955), p. 102.

10 See *Divan Zaadah* (Manuscript) Shah Hashim (Patna: Kutab Khana Khuda Baksh, 1188 Hijri), p. 359.
11 Sauda, Compiled by Aasi *Kulliyaat-e Sauda*, Vol. I (Lucknow: Naval Kishore, 1932), pp. 363–367, 373–378.
12 Mir, Taqi Mir. Compiled by Abdulbari Aasi, *Kulliyaat-e Mir* (Lucknow: Naval Kishore, 1941).
13 *Divan-e Mus-hafi* (Vol III, MS) (Rampur, Raza Library).
14 Muhammad Husain Azad, *Aab-e Hayaat* (Lucknow: Uttar Pradesh Urdu Academy, 1982), p. 204.
15 Nazeer Akbarabadi, *Gulzar-e Nazeer*, Compiled by Salim Ja'far (Allahabad, 1951), p. 75.
16 Hasrat Mohani, ed. *Intikhaab Urdu-e Mualla*, 1903–1908 (Aligarh), p. 26.
17 Ul-aa'm, ed. *Divan-e Munir*, Vol. 1 (Rampur: Syedi, 1264 Hijri), p. 301.
18 Gopi Chand Narang, trans. Surinder Deol, *Ghalib: Innovative Meanings and the Ingenious Mind* (New Delhi: Oxford University Press, 2017), pp. 435–436.
19 Muhammad Husain Azad, *Aab-e Hayaat*, p. 476.
20 Mustafa Khan Shefta, *Divan-e Shefta* (Lahore: Akademi Punjab), p.108.

2

THE 1857 UPRISING AND THE URDU POETRY

Some historians of colonialist persuasion called it *ghadar* (Rebellion). This fire initially started in Meerut, and it slowly spread to entire North India. The restlessness of our national conscience lit it. Our soldiers were not merely fighting for the *cartridges*. Their unease was reflective of the feelings shared by the state rulers, rajahs, nawabs, nobles, elites, traders, religious preachers, artisans, and ordinary people who made their living by their daily labor. Maharani Lakshmibai, Tantia Tope, Nana Sahib, Gen. Bakht Khan, Maulvi Ahmed Shah, Kanwar Singh, Amar Singh, and others were becoming conscious of the nefarious activities of British, who were planning to extend their colonial control to the whole country. These leaders, encouraged by the support of the people for protecting our national freedom, were ready to sacrifice everything they owned in this fight. In a real sense, this was our "war of freedom," and the people who were entering this fight were aware of the risks involved. Thousands were savagely killed; tied to the barrels of canons, many were brutally blown to the winds. From Calcutta to Allahabad, the grand trunk road had dead bodies hanging from the trees. Not only many a hearth and home were destroyed, but the whole habitats and neighbourhoods were also shattered. It was not a conventional war. Uttar Pradesh took an essential part in this movement. Many centers of this fight, Delhi, Meerut, Bareilly, Farrukhabad, Kanpur, Lucknow, Azamgarh, Benares, Allahabad down to the jungles of Madhya Pradesh and Maharashtra, many places were fiercely involved. If we had the organizational unity and shared understanding that was needed for an undertaking of such magnitude, India would have gained its freedom one hundred years ago.[1]

Ali Jawad Zaidi

A modern interpretation of nationalism is hard to find until the first half of the nineteenth century. Until then, the prevalent concept was different from our

DOI: 10.4324/9781003360841-3

understanding of the same in today's parlance. As we move into the second half of the nineteenth century, we find an emergence. This awakening was the direct result of the social and political enlightenment ignited by the struggle of 1857. It was the start of a new era. We can call this period the time of the beginning of the Indian Renaissance. The old concept of nationalism had its roots in certain historical developments and social forces operating locally. Its foundation was ethical and religious and not political or economic. It was more personal and local than collective. Of course, it was filled with feelings of sacrifice, bravery on the battlefield, and manliness. But in these times of social disorder, that included petty rivalries among nawabs, sultans, rajas, and princes of small states, besides Muslims, Rajputs, Marathas, and Rohillas, the idea of a unified India as one nation was hard to conceptualize. This situation changed with the expansion of British power. Their broader interests collided with local interests, and the feelings of enslavement and powerlessness took concrete shape. Over time, these feelings were shared by all classes of people, rich and poor, higher castes and lower castes, coupled with a deep sense of religious and cultural alienation.

Urdu poetry started to reflect this change. Poets with names like Mus-hafi, Jurrat, and Momin entered the scene, and they began to convert the people's hidden feelings into lyrical and inspirational words. Because of their passion, they captured the imagination of the masses. The concept of freedom still primarily operated with local castes, tribes, religion, and religious practices. Therefore, the opposition to the British rule was premised on the idea that the new rulers were a threat to the fundamentals of Islam and age-old local religious practices. It was the fuel that helped ignite the fires of the 1857 conflict. The British failed to judge the intensity of peoples' feelings on religious practices such as what was prohibited (taboo) and what was permitted. Since this movement originated in emotionally charged individual responses, its sudden outburst and outward appearance were destructive rather than constructive. Efforts were made to subvert British rule, but since this revolutionary zeal had no productive side and broader participation of people across the regional, tribal, and religious boundaries, it failed to realize its purpose. Administratively, the states under the local rule were performing poorly, and there was deep-seated hate and animosity between neighboring petty kingdoms. The British, therefore, as a strategy, exploited the mutual rivalries of local actors by playing one against the other, using all sorts of unfair manners, even bribing the feudal titleholders and army chieftains. Thus, eventually annihilating the opposition and resistance one by one, they had become, in a short period, a formidable colonial power from the South to the whole of North India.

The Urdu poetry of the time perceptively reflects conflicting aspirations and many historical forces crashing into one another. It is, therefore, important that as we look at the poetry written in this period, we should keep in mind differences and divergences, both religious and nonreligious.

From Lord Clive, who was Governor of the Presidency of Fort William in Bengal (1757–1760), to Lord Dalhousie, who was Governor-General of India

(1848–1856), it is pretty clear that the East India Company aimed to bring the entire subcontinent under their rule. Earlier, they had smashed the mighty kingdom of the brave Tipu Sultan and had won over the support of the fabulously wealthy but meek Nizam of Dakan. In the Battle of Plassey in 1757, Robert Clive won against Bengal's Nawab Siraj-ud-Daula by unethically buying over and managing the wicked betrayal of the latter's commander in chief, Mir Jafar Ali Khan. The Battle of Buxar in 1764 was a decisive victory for the East India Company that paved the way for the fall of Oudh and the growth of the British influence over the Mughal Emperor Shah Alam. Oudh's annexation was a formality. Nawab Wajid Ali Shah was deposed without resistance and mercilessly exiled to the British citadel, Fort William.[2] After Oudh, Delhi was the next logical step. The British managed it clandestinely under Lord Lake in the early 1800s. A Resident was appointed to keep control of the administration and help the Crown. When the last king, Bahadur Shah Zafar, ascended the throne in 1837, the British imposed several conditions, including requiring that his successor would have the title of a prince and not a king. He will have a reduced pension, and the Fort will be vacated. The end of the Mughal rule in India was thus predestined.

The East India Company was slowly swallowing small kingdoms. Gov. Gen. Warren Hastings (1773–1785) had reduced Bengal, Benares, and Rohel Khund to a pile of dust. Gov. Gen. Richard Wellesley captured Mysore, Puna, Sitara, and many other states. Therefore, there was fear and a rising tide of hatred for the British among small-state rulers and estate holders. Gov. Gen. Lord Dalhousie (1848–1856), due to his excesses, further inflamed loathing, and detestation. The British used petty excuses to extend the boundaries of their rule. By 1849, Punjab came under the Company's control. This sudden expansion of foreign rule had a devastating impact on indigenous manufacturers, artisans, traders, and farmers. The political take over paved the way for widespread economic control, tax increases, and opening of new markets for British imports.

At the social level, there were several red signals. The British dreamed of converting large numbers of locals into the Christian faith. As a result, several movements aimed at reform started within the Muslim community. The rise of Shah Waliullah Dehlavi with a large following, a well-respected theologian; Maulvi Ahmed Shah Madrasi; and Maulana Liaqat Ali are worth mentioning in this regard. Their work was responsible for arousing hatred and distrust for the British Raj. Nana Rao Peshwa and Azeem Ullah started weaving a web of conspiracies in the states. In Bengal, Ali Naqi Khan used faqirs and sanyasis to influence Indian soldiers working for the Company. Secret meetings were organized within military cantonments.

At the start of 1857, there were isolated incidents, such as setting fires on the Company's assets. The Rebellion of sepoys started in the Meerut cantonment on May 10, 1857. They took Delhi by surprise and killed hundreds of British men and women. The uprising spread like wildfire to several places in East and North India. The Rebellion was fueled by several factors, including the high-handed style of functioning by the British, imposition of western-style social reforms, harsh land taxation, and the humiliating treatment of the Indian rulers. Because this Rebellion was not centrally planned and executed, the British got the time to prepare and hit back. When a peace treaty was signed with Iran, the British forces on the Iran–India border were brought to North India to suppress the revolt. The troops that were headed to China were stopped in Calcutta. The solidarity of soldiers from the state of Punjab and Patiala broke the back of the Rebellion. The British took advantage of the deep enmity between the Sikhs and the Mughals, and they succeeded in separating Sikhs from the rebels. This left the rebels helpless and vulnerable, and eventually, the uprising failed, the core was broken, and Delhi once again came under the control of the British on September 18, 1857.

Meanwhile, fighting and sporadic resistance continued until November 1858, and the local leaders and commanders who played an important role included Nana Sahib Peshwa, Maharani Lakshmibai of Jhansi, and Tantia Tope. In Lucknow, the young prince Barjees Qadr was recognized as the new ruler, but the British attacked the city for the third time, and due to the differences among the ranks of the rebels, they succeeded. Begum Hazrat Mahal and her young son, prince Barjees Qadr, ruefully fled and vanished in the forests of Nepal.

It was common to distribute leaflets (because there were no newspapers) containing revolutionary verses of the poets during those days. Notice the following three couplets, drawn from a news leaflet distributed in Allahabad.

> *jo rah-e haq mein hue tukre nahien marte hain*
> *balke vo jiite hain jannat mein khushi karte hain*
> *kab talak ghar mein pare juutiyaan chatkhaao ge*
> *apni susti ka juz afsoos n phal paao ge*
> *baat ham kaam ki kahte hain suno ae yaaro*
> *vaqt aaya hai k talvaar ko barh kar maaro*

Those who die defending God's path do not die.
They continue to live; they spread happiness in paradise.
How long will you rot in your homes, wasting time?
Your laziness, sad to say, will not bear any fruit.
We say something vital; friends, please listen.
A time has come to pick up the sword and to use it fiercely.

By June 1858, Maulvi Ahmed Shah Madrasi and Rani Lakshmibai, too, were demolished. Although Nana Sahib Peshwa continued to keep attacking for some more time, the Rebellion had lost its momentum after the fall of Bareilly. Bahadur Shah Zafar had an orchestrated court trial in Delhi, and in October 1858, the unfortunate sad king was exiled to a faraway place, Rangoon, in Burma.

Urdu poets were severely caught up in this conflict. Some of them entered the fray as warriors to prove their love of the land. They were not part of the movement, but they were saddened by the fall of the Mughal Empire, one of the three great empires of the world. They were also not fans of the new rulers; they were treated as enemies determined to destroy the social and religious environment they had grown up in. When the Company entered India as a trading enterprise, Urdu poetry was in the embrace of Sufism (*tasavvuf*). The poets were used to expressing all kinds of thoughts in spiritual vocabulary. That is why we find anti-British feelings in places expressed not as political statements but as metaphysical pronouncements.

Looking at the utter helplessness of the nobles and the so-called nawabs, who were leaders in that period of decay and degeneration, poet Jurrat wrote:

samjhein n amiir inko aur n vaziir
angrezon ke haath se qafas mein hain asiir
jo kuchh vo parhaayen voh ye munh se bolein
bangaale ki maina hain ye puurab ke amiir

Don't call them nobles or nawabs.
They are miserable in the hands of the British
and are captives in their clutches.
Whatever they tutor them, they utter with their tongues.
These nobles of the East are like Bengal's mimicking birds.

Regarding India's economic collapse, poet Mus-hafi said:

hindostan ki daulat o hashmat jo kuchh k thi
kaafir firangiyon ne batadbiir khench li

India's wealth and its prestige,
which was there for everyone to see,
was diplomatically stolen and undercut
by these non-believers white firangiis.

laa'nat hai aise sikke aur zar ke chalaane mein
sar company ka kat ke bika sola aane mein

This currency of gold and silver be damned,
For sixteen *aanaas,* the severed head of the Company
is being sold.

Shah Kamaluddin Kamal wrote a *Shahr Ashob* poem. Here is a stanza that reflects the extreme misery and desolation of the people.

jahaan k naubat o shahnaai jhaanjh ki thi sada
firangiyon ka hai us ja p tum-tum ab bajta
isi se samjho raha saltanat ka kaya rutba
ho jabke mahal- saraaon mein bhi goron ka pahra
na shah hai n waziir ab firangi hain mukhtaar

Where delightful music
of our instruments was played,
now we can only hear
the nonsensical English tum-tum.
You can understand
how the empire lost its glory
when the guards of white men
are guarding ladies' quarters.
There is no king or ministers.
You find goras taking charge.

Of the many religious and secular movements that got started against occupation by the British, the one with Shah Waliullah Dehlvi in the lead was most effective. Poet Momin was much impressed by this movement. We have discovered the following couplet in which a leading Urdu poet uses the word *inqilaab* in an apparent political sense for the first time. It is generally believed that poet Hasrat Mohani was the first to coin the famous slogan of the freedom struggle '*Inqilaab Zindabaad*' (Long Live Revolution), which became part of the nation-wide struggle's vocabulary at the start of the twentieth century. Momin beat him by more than half a century.

ae hashr jald kar tah o baala zamiin ko
kuchh bhi n ho ummiid to hai inqilaab mein

O the day of judgment!
Raise the turmoil quickly.
Maybe nothing concrete
will be achieved by the bloodshed,
but there certainly is hope
for the **revolution**!

Khwaja Ahmad Faruqi has stated that Momin looked upon *jihad* against the foreign rulers as an expression of his faith, and he considered his willingness to sacrifice his life in this fight as an expression of his devotion. Here are few selected couplets from his masnavi *Jehaadiya*.

a'jab vaqt hai ye jo himmat karo
hayaat-e abd hai jo is dam maro
ilaahi mujhe bhi shahaadat nasiib
ye afzal se afzal i'baadat nasiib
ye daa'vat ho maqbuul dargaah mein
meri jaan fida ho teri raah mein
main ganj-e shahiidaan mein masruur huun
isi fauj ke saath mahshuur huun

This is the time if you try,
eternal life is available to you if you die now.

O God, please grant me the honor of martyrdom!
This is the most exceptional devotion one could obtain.
If You accept my request in Your shrine,
I'll sacrifice my life in Your cause
I'm happy in the cherished company of the martyrs,
I belong to this band; I want to be one with them.

Notice the sparks of hate bursting out in yet another couplet by Momin:

momin hasad se karte hain samaan jehaad ka
tarsa sanam ko dekh ke nusraaniyon mein ham

Momin, filled with jealousy,
is ready for Jihad, after seeing
the helpless beloved
in the fold of Christians.

We can say that Urdu poetry was anti-British even before the Rebellion. The events of 1857 hit hard the city of Delhi, which was also the prime center of Urdu poetry and literature. Although the town had borne the brunt of attacks by ruthless invaders like Nader Shah, Ahmed Shah Abdali, and many others, poetical gatherings had returned under the rule of Mohammad Shah Rangila. By the time Bahadur Shah Zafar ascended the throne, the city had dozens of highly celebrated poets. These included Sheikh Imam Bakhsh Sahbai, Sheikh Ibrahim Zauq, Munshi Sadruddin Aazurdah, Mirza Asad Ullah Khan Ghalib, Nawab Mustafa Khan Shefta, Hakim Agha Jaan A'ish, and many others. The next generation of poets comprising Mohammad Husain Azad, Hali, Dagh, Qaadir Bakhsh Saabir, Shahabuddin Saaqib, Saalik, Mir Mehdi Majrooh, Mirza Anwar, and Baqir Ali Kaamil was young. Still, it was getting ready to take the place of the old.

Tazkirah Gul-e Raa'na is right in saying, 'When these people assembled, even Heavens must have felt a pint of envy.' That is why the distinguished history of this period by leading historian Percival Spear is titled, *Twilight of the Mughals: Studies in Late Mughal Delhi* (Oxford in Asia Historical Reprints), published in 1982. It is a fact that almost everyone belonging to different classes and tribes in the city was crazy about poetry and art. Be it royalty or nobles, businessmen or workers, Sufis or drunks – everyone had surrendered to the magical charms of the Urdu Muse.

Tazkirah-e Gulistaan-e Sukhan (written in 1854) mentioned 375 poets who lived in Delhi. Few great poets like Shah Nasir, Momin, and Zauq had passed away a few years before 1857, but most of the others, experienced first-hand the destruction and bloodshed of innocent lives, each day and night. The ruination of the Red Fort felt like everyone's tragic story. Among these, some refused to be simply witnesses of this annihilation; they took up arms and died fighting the alien forces. Some of them used their pen as a sword and wrote extremely charged anti-British poems.

Although there were widespread desolation and suffering, some poets and their families were afflicted more than others. Among these horror stories is what happened to the respected poet Imam Bakhsh Sahbai. According to Khwaja Hasan Nizami, 21 members of his family, including his young son Abdul Karim Soz, were mercilessly butchered. Aazurdah captured this calamitous killing in the following couplet.

> *kiyon k aazurdah nikal jaaye n saudaaii ho*
> *qatl is tarah se be jurm jo sahbai ho*[3]

Why shouldn't Aazurdah feel the outrage and lose his mind,
watching the cruel killing of innocent Sahbai?

Aazurdah was *Mufti,* the city magistrate of Delhi at that time. He supported the rebels and signed the Fatwa of Jihad against the British.[4] He was removed from his high position, his properties were confiscated, and his precious book collection was destroyed. The madrasa where he used to impart education on religious and metaphysical topics was rampaged and demolished. Notice a few other couplets of the stanza poem that was quoted above.

> *roz vahshat mujhe sahra ki taraf laati hai*
> *sar hai aur josh-e junuun sang hai aur chhaati hai*
> *tukre hota hai jigar ji hi pe ban jaati hai*
> *mustafa khan ki mulaqaat jo yaad aati hai*

The fear and frenzy that hits me every day drive me towards the desert.
I've got my head, a surge of craziness, a stone, and my chest to beat.
My heart breaks into pieces, and I can't control myself
when I remember my meetings with Mustafa Khan (Shefta).

On May 22, 1853, a Delhi newspaper published Ghalib's ghazal *baaziicha-e atfaal hai duniya mere aage*[5] with its tone that is decidedly prophetic and brimming with pathos and sadness.[6]

> *baaziicha-e atfaal hai duniya mere aage*
> *hota hai shab o roz tamaasha mere aage*
> *ik khel hai aurang-e sulaimaan mere nazdiik*
> *ik baat hai e'jaaz-e masiiha mere aage*
> *juz naam nahien suurat-e aa'lam mujhe manzuur*
> *juz vahm nahien hasti-e ashiya mere aage*
> *hota hai nihaan gard mein sahra mere hote*
> *ghista hai jabiin khaak p dariya mere aage*
> *phir dekhiye andaaz-e gul afshaani-e guftaar*
> *rakh de koi paimaana-e sahba mere aage*
> *iimaan mujhe roke hai to khiinche hai mujhe kufr*
> *kaa'ba mere piichhe hai kaliisa mere aage*
> *hai maujzan ik qulzum-e khoon kaash yahi ho*
> *aata hai abhi dekhiye kya kya mere aage*

The world is a kid's playground
in front of me.
Many acts are played out
in front of my eyes.
Each day when the sun rises and
each night when it sets.
The throne of Solomon
is a source of amusement for me.
I have heard them talk
about Jesus raising the dead.
Things do exist, but just in the name,
the reality of things is no more
than an illusion.
By going into the desert raises
such dust that it conceals
its very existence.
But the river is humble.
It rubs its forehead on the ground.
Just watch the flowering of
my creativity
if someone only takes the trouble
of putting a goblet of wine
in front of me!
Although faith pulls me backward,
the force of disbelief tears me apart.
What a predicament!
Kaba behind me and the Chapel facing me!
An ocean of blood
is rising like a high tide.
Maybe this is it.
Let us see what comes next
in front of my eyes.

In 1857, Ghalib had to live through one too many dangerous situations. He would not have survived the ordeal if he had not used his wit-laced persuasive skills. One day, some English troopers intruded into his home, and he was asked to appear before Col. Burn, who was camping in Qutubuddin Saudagar's haveli. Hali writes:

> Mirza appeared before Col. Burn in a typical Turkish Muslim outfit with his high fur cap. The officer looked at him with suspicion and asked, 'Are you a Muslim?' Mirza replied, 'Half!.' The officer gave a confused look and asked, 'What do you mean by half?' Mirza said, 'I drink wine, but I do not eat pork.' Hearing this, the officer couldn't control his laughter. Then Mirza showed him the letters of acknowledgment he had received from the

Queen in response to the qasida he had sent to London. The officer had a follow-up question, 'Why didn't you show up at the Hill where the British army was camping after the rebel forces were defeated?' Mirza answered, 'My status required me to be carried in a palanquin shouldered by four people. They all deserted me. How could I have come to the Hill?' Col. Burn was amused with the answers. He smiled and let Mirza go.[7]

Mirza writes in his Persian diary, *Dastambu,* about this incident:

> Free people don't hide anything. As a half-Muslim, I'm free from the hardship of a prison house in the same way as my vagrancy saves me from the fear of infamy and ill-repute. For a very long time, I have been consuming French wine at night without any other food. I couldn't sleep if I were deprived of this. If Mahesh Das, whom I consider a brave man, a blessed being, and a man with a big heart, had not sent me the Indian wine, which had the same color as that of French but a better aroma, then I would not have survived.[8]

After this, Ghalib paid tribute to Mahesh Das in a ruba'i saying that in such days of suffering, the most generous Mahesh Das provided me with *aab-e hayat* elixir, which was denied to Alexander, the great, who had died looking for it.

During the uprising, Ghalib continued to visit the Royal Court, though he was not close to the regime. He keenly watched the situation. After the British took over on January 14, 1858, he wrote a letter to the Nawab of Rampur in words typical of his dialectical orientation.

> In this time of great turbulence, I kept myself away from the Court, but with this fear that if I stopped visiting, then my home would be deprived of the royal privileges, and even my life could be in danger. In my deeper self, I was unconcerned, but in my appearance, I maintained a friendly demeanor.[9]

The fact is that Ghalib's close friend and associate, Maulana Fazl-e Haq Khairabadi was one of the leading Ulemas, Muslim theologians. They had signed the Fatwa (religious commandment of Rebellion). There were many friends and disciples of Ghalib who had taken part in the uprising. Ghalib had even written a couplet *(Sikka-e she'r),* a chronogram of royal coronation that is usually stuck on the ceremonial gold coins, supporting coronation of the Crown that was announced and read out in the Court. Gauri Shankar and Jeevan Lal, the two British spies, had recorded an eye-witness account of Mirza's court appearances, and his chronogrammatic coronation couplet was included in their confidential reports. These testimonies formed the basis of suspension of his pension, his high position in the Court, and thereby he was cut off from receiving any privileges from the new rulers. This story is complex and tragic. Ghalib wrote to Yusuf

Mirza—a letter that is an example of his enigmatic saying both 'yes' and 'no,' 'I confess' and 'I deny' in the same breath, in an inventive poetic manner.

> I didn't compose any coronation couplet. Even if I did, the purpose was to save my life and my honor. This is no crime. Even if it is, it is not so serious that Queen's declaration of general amnesty is unable to erase it. God is great! Isn't it strange that manufacture of explosives, guns and cannons and lootings of magazines can be forgiven but not the two lines written by a poor, destitute poet?[10]

The coronation couplet ascribed by Gauri Shankar was written by Hafiz Ghulam Rasool Veeran, a disciple of Zauq, but what Jeevan Lal said as the couplet written by 'Mirza Naosha' was the work of Ghalib. Both these couplets have been identified. Naosha was Mirza's title. The couplet by Ghalib reads as under:

bar zar-e aaftaab-o nuqra-e maah
sikka zad dar jahaan Bahaadur Shaah

On the gold of the sun
and silver of the moon,
coins are struck everywhere
in the name of Bahadur Shah.

The resumption of the Court position and the restoration of pension took quite some time. By then, Ghalib had lost his zeal and his enthusiasm. At a time when most of the lanes and neighboring homes were deserted and enveloped in darkness, Ghalib wrote in a letter:

> I live in a city named Delhi and the street named Ballimaran. But I can't find a single friend whom I knew and loved living here. Make no mistake. Both rich and poor, high and low, have left this place. Those who have remained are being asked to leave, home after home is found wrapped in darkness.[11]

(via Mir Mehdi Majrooh)

There were places around Chandni Chowk where people's bodies were hanging from the trees with a noose around their necks. Ghalib shared his pain in the following verse in a private letter addressed to Alauddin Khan Alai:

bas k fa'aal-e ma yureed hai aaj
har silahshor inglistaan ka
ghar se bazaar mein nikalte huye
zahra hota hai aab insaan ka
chowk jis ko kahein vo maqtal hai
ghar bana hai namuuna zindaan ka
shehr-e dehli ka zarra zarra khaak

tishna-e khuun hai har musalmaan ka
koi vaan se na aa sake yaan tak
aadmi vaan na ja sake yaan ka
is tarah ke visaal se yaarab
kya mite dil se daagh hijraan ka

Every British Tommy has become bloodthirsty.
Fear and danger stalk those who walk out of their home.
Chandni Chowk has become an open hanging place.
Every house has been turned into a prison cell.
Every particle of the great city of Delhi, it seems,
is thirsty for the blood of Muslims.
When it is not safe to go from anywhere to anywhere,
what fun is meeting or not meeting the loved ones!
Everywhere, the specter of death looms large.

Let no one get this idea that I am dying because of my destruction. Although orders to kill these people were given by the British, the deed was done by dark-skinned faces of our own. Among those who were killed, there were those in whom I had reposed my hopes and aspirations, and there were those who were recipients of my affection. There were my friends, and there were my disciples, my lovers, my beloveds. All of them are now reduced to a pile of dust. It is excruciating to bear the loss of one friend but think of the one who is mourning the loss of so many friends. Why shouldn't he be miserable in his life? Alas! I have lost so many friends. Now when I die, there would be no one to mourn for me.[12]

(via Tafta)

Tafta's book *Sumbulistaan* was poorly printed. Looking at it, Ghalib, a lover of Mughal sense of beauty and aesthetics, was deeply saddened. Painfully he reacts thus: 'Ah! I was shocked to see the lousy printing of the book and the ruined contents. It reminded me of the wandering Begums of the Royal Fort, moon-like beauties, but in rags, soiled, dirty clothes, torn down slippers ...'

Lastly, we have Mirza's letter to Alauddin Ahmed Khan:

O the partner of my breath! This is not the Delhi where you were born. This is not the Delhi where you used to come to take lessons from me in Shaban Beg's haveli. This is not the Delhi that I have known from the age of seven. It is a camp, an army camp! The servants of the king are now paid five rupees a month. Of the ladies of the royal house, who are old, have become pimps, and the young ones are prostitutes.

Shefta had acquired his hatred of the British from his patron and teacher, Momin. His estate was confiscated, and he was sentenced to serve a prison term of seven years. Released after an appeal, he wrote a 13-couplet elegy on the 'Death of Delhi' (*Dehli Marhuum*), which was not included in his published divan. Here are two couplets from this soulful elegy.

vohi jalva nazar aata hai tasavvur mein hamein
mit gaye phir bhi ye baaqi hai nishaan-e dehli
gar n kahvein k ye dilli hai to hargiz n pare
dilli vaalon ko bhi dilli p gumaan-e dehli

In my imagination, I see the same old spectacle.
Everything is destroyed, but even then, there is a mark of Delhi.
I can't restrain myself from uttering the word Dilli with a sigh.
Even people who live here doubt whether this is Delhi.

Mir Mehdi Majrooh and Qurban Ali Beg Salik were forced to leave the city. It is not clear whether Salik was able to return, but he did write a ghazal and a qat'a about Delhi's wrecking. Majrooh roamed around and then finally settled in Panipat, but his heart was still in Delhi. He requested Ghalib to write him letters giving an account of what was happening. It is clear from one of Ghalib's letters, written in September 1862, that Majrooh returned briefly to participate in a mushaira where participating poets were asked to write about the ruination and devastation of Delhi. In the anthology *Fariyaad-e-dehli*, we find a seven-couplet ghazal written by Majrooh. Here are two couplets from that ghazal.

ye kahaan jalva-e jaan bakhsh butaan-e dehli
kionke jannat p kiya jaaye gumaan-e dehli
in ka be-vaj-h nahien loot ke hona barbaad
dhuundhen hain apne makiinon ko makaan-e dehli

What a spectacle of the idols of Delhi!
Because paradise looks like a copy of Delhi.
There is a reason why it was looted and ruined.
Homes of Delhi are searching for their residents.

Dagh was inside the Fort when the attack happened. According to Sheikh Mohammad Ismail of Panipat, he left the Fort along with others who ran to save themselves. In this state of bewilderment, he left behind verses that he wrote in his younger age. He regretted this loss all his life. He penned a *Shahr Aashoob* that was included in the excellent anthology *Fughan-e Dehli*. Here are some couplets from that composition.

ye shahr vo hai k har uns o jaan ka dil tha
ye shahr vo hai k har qadrdaan ka dil tha
ye shahr vo hai k hindostaan ka dil tha
ye shahr vo hai k saare jahaan ka dil tha
rahi n aadhi yahaan sang o khisht ki suurat
bani hui thi jo saari bahisht ki suurat
ba-rang-e buu-e gul ahl-e chaman chaman se chale

ghariib chhor ke apna vatan vatan se chale
n puuchho zindon ko be-chaare kis chalan se chale
qiyaamat aaii k murde nikal kafan se chale
muqaam-e amn jo dhuundha to raah bhi n mili
ye qahr tha k khudaa ki panaah bhi n mili

The heart of every living being was this city.
The heart of every enlightened person was this city.
The heart of Hindostan was this city.
The heart of the whole world was this city.
It was reduced to a pile of broken pieces of stones and bricks.
Nothing less than the replica of paradise was this city.
Just as the fragrance leaves the rose, guardians of the garden had to go.
Even the poor were forced to leave their hearth and their homes.
Don't ask the helpless prisoners how they were ordered to depart.
Faced with an apocalypse, the dead walked out of their coffins and ran.
If they were in a peaceful place, they didn't find a path.
It was nothing but resurrection; even God didn't come to the rescue.

Like many other Urdu poets, Mohammad Husain Azad carried personal wounds inflicted by the British. His father, Maulvi Mohammad Baqir Ali, founded the famous 'Urdu Akhbar,' the first Urdu daily newspaper of Dehli, which supported and carried the news of the Rebellion all through the struggle, was shot dead by the British soldiers for the crime of assisting the Rebellion. It was alleged that he had aided the rebels in the murder of Principal Taylor. A warrant for the arrest of Mohammad Husain Azad was also issued, but he had fled before he could be caught. He spent many years hiding around cities in South India before he finally surfaced and settled in Lahore. According to Azad's grandson, Agha Mohammad Baqir, he was a great critic of the activities of the East India Company. All print copies of the newspaper were confiscated after the Rebellion. Some copies are preserved in the National Archives of India. The print edition of May 24, 1857 carried a war-like poem titled *Fateh Afvaaj-e Sharq,* (Victory of the Indian Forces), which is a living testament to Azad's love of his country. The poem was confiscated, and Azad, after the occupation, was charged by the British. Still, to avoid being hanged, he escaped to Nilgiri hills in South India and remained untraceable for years. This newspaper is preserved in the National Archives of India, New Delhi.[13] Five couplets of this chronogram poem are given below. The last couplet states the date of the Rebellion as 1273 H. (1857).

Fateh Afvaaj-e Sharq
(The Victory of the Indian Forces)

hai kal ka abhi zikr k jo qaum-e nasaara
thi sahib-e iqbal o jahaan bakhsh o jahaan daar

It is a matter of recent past that
we talked about the British people.

They were people of the grandeur
and rulers of the world.

sab jauhar-e a'ql un ke rahe taaq p rakkhe
sab naakhun-e tadbiir o khirad ho gaye bekaar

The pearls of wisdom
stayed unused in a niche.
The toolbox of tricks and
learning proved of no use.

kaam aaye n i'lm o hunar o hikmat o yahiin
puurab ke talangon ne liya sab ko yahiin maar

The knowledge of craftsmanship,
and strategies and schemes were of no avail.
The soldiers who came from the East killed
everyone on the spot.

ye saaniha vo hai k n dekha n suna tha
hai gardish-e garduun bhi a'jab gardish-e davvaar

This tragic incident was such
that we had not seen it or heard about it.
The cycle of time is indeed
a baffling and mystifying cycle.

is vaaq'ae ki chaahi jo azad ne taariikh
dil ne kaha, qul fatabiroo yaa ulil absaar[14]

When Azad tried to look up
the chronogram of this incident,
a sound came from the heart:
'For those who have eyes,
this is a moment of retribution.'

Even Hali was not spared ordeals of the conflict. He reached Panipat, his place
of birth, after being a victim of the dacoits, suffering much distress and personal
injuries in the travel. The uprising put an end to a traditional way of life. It was
the culmination of the Mughal Empire and a glorious civilization that lasted
several centuries. Hali touched upon some of the painful aspects of this forced
transformation in a stanza poem that had a memorable line.

tazkirah-e dehli-e marhuum ka ae dost n chher
n suna jaaye ga mujh se ye fasaanah hargiz

O, Friend, don't tell me the story of the death of Delhi.
I will not be able to listen to these desolate tales of horror.

Due to his age and temperament, Bahadur Shah Zafar was not a forceful companion for the rebels. He supported them reluctantly while at the same time

listening to the peddlers bribed by the British, who always hammered him with detrimental accounts of the revolutionaries. But we must give him credit for standing up to the British, though he and his entire family paid a hefty price for doing that. General Hudson brutally killed the three princes; their heads placed on a platter were callously presented to the king. Later, these heads were displayed on the entrance to the Dilli Gate for the people of Delhi to see the excruciating end of the Mughal rule. Zafar's poetry is a tragic guide to his miserable and helpless state of mind. According to Munshi Jivan Lal, the king had recited a few couplets[15] in support of the rebels in a Court meeting on August 2, 1857, with Azurdah and other leading intellectuals in attendance. Since the British spies recorded these accounts, they are somewhat broken, missing some words. The translation is given as paraphrasing.

> khuda kare k diin ke dushman tabaah o barbaad ho jaayein
> khuda kare k firangi niist o nabuud ho jaayein
> qurbaaniyaan de ke e'id qurbaan ke tahvaar ko manaao
> aur dushman ko teh tegh karo k koi bachne n paaye

> May God help us in destroying our enemies!
> May God help us in wrecking the power of the British!
> Make sacrifices and celebrate the festival of Eid in gay abandon.
> Kill the enemy with your shining swords and spare no one.

Vinayak Damodar Savarkar (1883–1966), the Hindu nationalist leader, had mentioned[16] that when rebel forces were facing defeat, someone satirically said:

> damdame mein dam nahien khair mango jaan ki
> ae zafar thandi hui shamshiir hindustaan ki

> There is not much life left
> in your drumbeats. Run for your life.
> O Zafar, the sword of Hindostan
> has become blunt.

Bahadur Shah Zafar spontaneously had retorted in the following couplet.

> ghaaziyon mein buu rahe gi jab talak iimaan ki
> tab to london tak chale gi tegh hindustaan ki

> If warriors are fighting to sacrifice
> in defense of their faith and love for country,
> the sword of Hindostan will take the fight
> right up to the doorways of London.

Zafar's poetry written during this period has been lost. The responsibility for the safe keeping of the king's verse rested with Hakim Ehsan Ullah Khan. It is generally believed as a confidante and physician of the king, he might have double-crossed and destroyed it, or this treasure was lost during the conflict. Only some pieces have surfaced here and there. The exceptional quality of

Zafar's compositions is that it offered an accurate description of the situation in a soulful language filled with great pathos. Let us look at the following ghazal published posthumously in the collected works of Bahadur Shah Zafar.[17] As per practice of compiling divans, the ghazal was included under the letter *Nuun*.

jin galliyan mein pehle dekhien logan ki rang ralliyaan thien
phir dekha to un logaan bin suuni pari voh galliyaan thien
aisi ankhiyaan miiche pare hain karvat bhi nahien le sakte
jin ki chaalen albeli aur chalne mein chal- balliyaan thien
khaak ka un ka bistar hai aur sar ke niche pathar hai
haae voh shaklein pyaari pyaari kis kis chaao se palliyaan thien
talkhi uthaai maut bhi chakhhi khaak sab un ko chaat gai
jin ki baatein miithi miithi misri ki si dalliyaan thien
roz bahaaraan luut-te the voh ja ja kar jin baagaan mein
'shauq rang' ab jo dekha vaan phool hain aur n kalliyaan thien

In the alleys, where we saw people having rollicking celebrations,
when I looked again, there were only empty streets, but no people.
Lying on the bed with closed eyes, I can't even take a side.
Those who strolled in style, rambling, chattering, and babbling,
sleep on a bed made of dirt and had a stone as a pillow.
Alas, those ravishing faces, how dear, raised with lots of love,
they suffered, they died, and even dust didn't leave any trace of them.
Those who spoke sweetly, and their words were like cubes of sugar;
spring was their companion when they visited their gardens,
alas Shauq Rang![18] when I looked now, there were no flowers, no buds.

The following couplet became a quotable quote:

kitna hai badnasiib zafar baa'd-e marg bhi
do gaz zamiin bhi n mili kuu-e yaar mein

How unfortunate is Zafar even after his demise!
He couldn't get two yards of the burial ground
in the beloved's alley.

The devastation of Delhi was unexpected and total in every respect. Every resident went through great personal torment, with loss of homes and deaths of friends and relatives. Many poets expressed their sorrow in their *Shahr Aashobs* (poems were written about the death and destruction of a city). Here is a selection of couplets out of score upon scores that encapsulate the sad story of the city's fall in tragic yet rhythmical compositions.[19]

Ghulam Dastgir Mubeen

pasand-e khaatir har khaas o aa'm thi dehli
talism-e dilkash o jannat muqaam thi dehli

tarab fazaaye jahaan sub-h o shaam thi dehli
gul-e khushi se mu'attar tamaam thi dehli
ujaara aisa chaman jis ke gham se dil hai khuun
mite khizaan ki hava khaak mein mile garduun

Delhi was the city of choice for the highly sophisticated
as well the ordinary folks.
Its magic stole one's heart, and it was just like paradise.
There was an ambiance of cheerfulness in Delhi,
each morning and evening.
The rose of happiness perfumed the entire city of Delhi.
Seeing this garden devastated,
my heart is reduced to a receptacle of blood.
The autumn breeze is damned, and Heavens hit the dust.

Hakim Mohammad Taqi Sozaan

vo naazniin k nazaakat bhi dekh ghabraave
k jis ki bistar-e gul par se niind ur jaave
gumaan mein bi jo n ho kya khayal mein aave
likha azal ka jo taqdiir saamne laave
pakar ke zulf kiya un ko qatl nange sar
saba ke chhuye se hote the jo parishaan tar
barhana pa koi nikla koi garebaan chaak
kisi ki chashm thi giriyaan kisi ke sar par khaak
har ek bed sa larzaan tha badal-e gham-naak
thi dushmanon ki bhi har samt se in pe taak
qadam n uth-ta tha jo voh qadam uthaate the
hazaaron thokrein khaate the girte jaate the

Those beauties whose elegance
was a concern for the taste itself.
Those who slept on the beds of roses
to get their sleep.
How would it enter one's imagination
if something could not be expected?
What was written in the beginning,
fate brought it forward.
Caught by their curls, they were murdered
with their heads uncovered.
These were the people who were bothered
by the breeze rubbing off them.
Someone ran out barefoot,
someone with a torn collar.

Someone had a tear in their eyes;
someone had dust in their hair.
Everyone trembling like the soft reeds,
sorrowful like a cloud.
The enemy was chasing them
from every angle.
The feet could not be lifted
when they tried to raise them.
They were getting hit, and
they were hurt, falling around.

Hakim Mohammad Mohsin Khan Mohsin

vo log bistar-e sanjaab par jo sote the
sahar gulaab se jo munh ko apne dhote the
tamaam u'mr ko lahv o laa'b mein khote the
vo baal baal mein moti sada pirote the
ab un ka haal tabaahi se aisa abtar hai
bichhona khaak hai aur khisht baalish-e sar hai
rakha tha dehli ka logon ne naam i'shq-aabaad
basaan-e khaana-e aa'shiq vo ho gaaii barbaad

Those who slept on beds covered with silken sheets.
Those who washed their faces in the morning in rose water.
Those who spent their lives in pursuit of pleasures
Those who were discriminating and demanding.
Now their condition has deteriorated with destruction.
Dirt and grime in their bed, and a stone is a pillow.
People called Delhi, a city where love would forever flourish.
But like the plummeting shack of a lover, Delhi also is ruined.

Hussami

Hussami was a folk poet, a street singer. He used to sing the following ghazal,
which some writers have ascribed to Bahadur Shah Zafar. But Qazi Abdul
Wadud, a great scholar, says that it belongs to Hussami.

n dabaaya zer-e zamiin unhein n diya kisi ne kafan unhein
n hua nasiib vatan unhein n kahien nishaan-e mazaar hai
n tha shahr dehli ye tha ik chaman kahuun kis tarah ka tha yaan aman [this is repeat]
jo khitaab tha voh mita diya faqat ab to ujra dayaar hai
gaaii yak-bayak jo hava palat nahien dil ko mere qaraar hai
karuun is sitam ka main kya byaan mera gham se siina figaar hai
ye ri'yaa-e hind tabaah hui kaho kya kya in pe jafa hui
jise dekha haakim-e vaqt ne kaha ye to qaabil-e daar hai

n tha shahr dehli ye tha ik chaman kahuun kis tarah ka tha yaan aman
jo khitaab tha vo mita diya faqat ab to ujra dyaar hai
sabhi jaa voh maatam-e sakht hai kaho kaisi ye gardish-e bakht hai
n vo taaj hai n vo takht hai n vo shah hai n dyaar hai[20]

They didn't get a burial;
they didn't get a coffin.
They didn't get the land,
and there was no sign of a grave.
Delhi was not just a city;
it was a garden with peace all around.
The city's name has been erased;
it's nothing but a ruined place.
The wind suddenly changed direction,
and my heart had no calm.
How can you describe this terrible event?
My heart is afflicted with distress.
The people of India suffered gravely,
and they were targets of aggression.
The ruler watched all this
and said that this was deserved.
It was not a city of Delhi, it was a garden,
and it had total peace.
The title was erased, and now it is nothing
more than a ruined place.
There is mourning all around,
and what can we say about our fate now.
Not the same Crown, not the same throne,
not the same king, not the same Court.

Several poets expressed their sorrow in their ghazal couplets.

Mumtaz Husain Ahqar

kaun sa ghuncha-e dil tha k n pazhmurdah hua
hind mein aisi chali baad-e khizaan-e dehli

Name a flower of the heart that was not withered.
Delhi came in the grip of the autumn breeze
that moved around the land of India.

Qadir Bakhsh Sabir

baske gulzaar hai zakhmon se tan ik aa'lam ka
ban gaaii mausam-e gul fasl-e khizaan-e dehli

The wounds of the world are blooming and flowering.
The spring has turned itself into autumn for Delhi.

Mohammad Mohsin Khan Mohsin

ab jo dilli hui aabaad to kya khaak hui
jin se ziinat thi kahaan hain vo javaan-e dehli

The coming back of Delhi is not worth anything.
Where are the young ones who made Delhi a paradise?

Qurban Ali Beg Saalik captured the prevailing mood in his Foreword that he wrote for *Fughan-e Dehli*:

> Such a revolution that the tongue has no control except to talk about what is happening. You can't stop your heart from filling up with sadness, and you can express your feelings only in your verse. Who is so powerful to listen to these heart-pulling stories and not cry? When I hear a couplet about these events, my ears can't take it. I want to cry, but I can't.

There was a discernible tendency among the Urdu poets to blame their rulers and even themselves for the destruction that was caused by the British. Look at these couplets.

Hussami

jaise jaise ham ne gunaah kiye
ye unhien gunaahon ka baar hai

All the sins that we committed.
It is the outcome of those sins.

Mubeen

zulm goron ne kiya aur n kaalon ne
ham ko barbaad kiya apne hi aa'maalon ne

The tyranny was unleashed neither by the whites nor by the blacks.
Our doings and predicaments ruined us.

Zahir

koi zaahir mein n tha is ki kharaabi ka sabab
apne aa'maal hue aafat-e jaan-e dehli

You can't find a reason for this catastrophe.
Our actions proved to be a calamity for the soul of Delhi.

Several poets found death a desirable state than living and facing reality. Look at these lines.

Aazurdah

kaash ho jaaye zamiin shaq to sama jaayein ham

Wish this ground opens up
so that we lose ourselves and vanish.

Farhat

tujhe chhor gaaii hai ajal kahaan
jahaan saans lena bhi baar hai

O my death, where have you left me?
I can't even breathe.

Dagh

pukaarte hain ajal ko ajal nahien aati
I 'm calling for death to come. It doesn't.

The events of 1857 constitute a significant shift in Urdu literature that divides the old (classical) from the modern. We can say that the post-1857 period marked the start of the contemporary era in literature and fine arts. People learned to live with the excesses of British rule and think and plan about the political and nationalistic implications for the country. For the next quarter-century, India was like a country that had lost its soul. Except for some religious reformers and the traditionalists, people, by and large, carried on with their lives. They learned to live with their defeat as a historic shift on which they had no control. As the old social norms died, they paved the way for the emergence of a new social environment that was supported by the laws imposed by a new ruling class. More opportunities opened up for education. Within the Muslim and Hindu communities, a new type of leader advocated education as a solution for many social and economic ills. Between 1857 and 1887, new universities were established in Bombay, Calcutta, Madras, Punjab, and Allahabad. By the end of the century, Bombay and Calcutta universities offered courses and degrees in science and technology. The English language increasingly became the language of commerce and government and thus helped unify the country. Indian entrepreneurs started to learn manufacturing techniques that substituted the workforce with machines, thereby facilitating the birth of modern factories manufacturing textiles and other goods of daily use. The founding of the Indian National Congress in 1885, with help from both Indian and English intellectuals, was an event of great political importance. With time, it became the pivot for the struggle for India's independence. We shall examine the impact of these developments in the following chapters.

Notes

1 Ali Jawad Zaidi, *Naghma-e Azadi* (Lucknow: Publications Bureau, Department of Information, 1957), p. 5. Translation by Surinder Deol.
2 The tragic fall of the Oudh was beautifully depicted in Prem Chand's masterpiece — a short story titled *Shatranj Ke Khilaari,* which was later adapted for a classic movie of the same title by the celebrated filmmaker, Satyajit Roy which won many awards.
3 Tafazzul Husain Kaokab, ed. *Fughaan-e Delhi,* Vol. I (Delhi, 1863).
4 Charles Metcalf, ed. *Ghadar Ki Sub-h o Shaam, Daily Dialy Diary of Moenuldeen Hasan Khan and Jivan Lal,* pp. 188 and 197.
5 Kalidas Gupta Raza, ed. *Divan-e Ghalib Kamil, Nuskha-e Raza* (Mumbai: Saakaar Publications Pvt. Ltd., 1995), p. 443. Also for Ghalib's life during 1857, refer to Gopi Chand Narang (Surinder Deol, trans.) *Ghalib: Innovative Meaning and the Ingenious Mind* (New Delhi: Oxford University Press, 2017), pp. 426–432.
6 Natalia Prigarina (Osama Faruqi, trans.) *Mirza Ghalib* (Hyderabad, 1997), p. 292.
7 Altaf Husain Hali, *Yaadgaar-e Ghalib* (Lahore: Sheikh Mubarak Ali Tajir-e Kutb, 1897), p. 36.
8 Hali, p. 37.
9 Imtiaz Ali Arshi, *Divan-e Ghalib, Nuskha-e Arshi* (Aligarh, 1958), p. 437.
10 Hasrat Mohani, ed. *Intikhaab Urdu-e Mualla,* 1903–1908 (Aligarh), p. 249.
11 Hasrat Mohani, ed. *Intikhaab Urdu-e Mualla,* 1903–1908 (Aligarh), p. 58.
12 Hasrat Mohani, ed. *Intikhaab Urdu-e Mualla,* 1903–1908 (Aligarh), pp. 91, 318. All quotes on this page are drawn from *Urdu-e Mualla.*
13 Ali Jawad Zaidi, *Naghma-e Azadi* (Lucknow: Publications Bureau, Department of Information, 1957), p. 12.
14 Holy Quran, Surat-ul Hashr, Aayat 2. Hijri 1273 is 1857 in Gregorian Calendar.
15 Charles Metcalf, ed. *Ghadar ki Sub-ho Shaam,* p. 197.
16 Veer Savarkar, *The Indian War of Independence 1857* (New Delhi: Abhishek Publications, 2019).
17 Bahadur Shah Zafar, *Kulliyaat-e Zafar,* Divan I. (Kanpur: Munshi Nawal Kishore, 1876), p. 195.
18 *Zafar's* penname for Hindi verse.
19 These materials are drawn from the historic and basic anthology *Fughaan-e Dehli.* The first edition of this manuscript was published in 1863. The second edition came out a few years later. The third edition was published in 1913 with a new title *Fariyaad-e Dehli.* The fourth edition with the original title was published in 1954 in Lahore. The original hand-written manuscript of 1862 is preserved in the Litton Library of Aligarh Muslim University from where these compositions were recorded in the course of author's research.
20 Zaidi, *Naghma-e Azadi,* p. 10. Many scholars have researched this ghazal, but the decisive word is that of Qazi Abdul Wudood in his series of essays, *Aawaara-gard Ash'aar,* 1995. Published by Khuda Bakhsh Oriental Public Library, Patna. Pages 37–38. See also Quarterly *Nuquush,* Lahore, Editor, Mohammad Tufail. Ghazal Number, 41,42, May June1954, Page 397.

3

UNEASY CALM BEFORE THE STORM
1857–1914

Muslim suspicions of the Indian National Congress were not allayed by the fact that its control had passed from the hands of the liberals and moderate elements into those of the Maratha leader Tilak, whose anti-Muslim opinions and activities were well-known. The partition of Bengal (1905) gave the Muslims of East Bengal a majority in the newly constituted province of East Bengal and Assam, where they could develop the resources of a Muslim majority area to their advantage. Vehement Hindu opposition to the partition seemed to Muslims additional evidence that the Hindus were reluctant to part with their own power and influence. The Muslims had also been alarmed by the growing hostility shown by Hindu revivalist movements like the Ārya Samāj and the Mārātha glorification of Shivaji's rebellion against the Mughal empire. All these factors led them to establish the All-India Muslim League in 1906. Despite Muslim opposition to the introduction of representative institutions, it was already clear that the British could not resist Hindu pressure in this direction indefinitely ... Acceptance of the principle of separate electorates was the first official recognition on the part of the British that the Muslims and the Hindus were not a single people.[1]

De Bary, Hay, Weiler, and Yarrow

Mohammad Husain Azad (1827–1910) and Maulana Altaf Hussain Hali (1837–1914) ushered in what we consider as the era of modern Urdu poetry. Azad's contribution was more historical than literary. Hali was like the high priest of Urdu *nazm,* who started a silent revolution in poetry and literature. He explored and invented new modes of poetic expression and widened the boundaries of how poetry was written. He gave it an ideal and made the poets conscious that poetry had a function to perform, which was to spread awareness of social and political issues of the time. To better appreciate Hali's silent revolution, we need

DOI: 10.4324/9781003360841-4

to map and know about the social and political movements that arose toward the end of the nineteenth century.

After the 1857 uprising, India's social structure that was stable for over a century degenerated and broke into pieces. That fundamental change shook the foundations of the old order. The need for change, which was felt for a long time, acquired great urgency. The community leaders and the intellectual elites had become aware that radical social transformation was necessary. Brahmo Samaj and Wahabi movement, acting separately, brought the reality that the cultural degeneration was profound and had become a disabling factor for any positive action. They raised their voice in favor of equality, economic fairness, and social justice. The steps that they undertook were, in a way, progressive, but both the organizations were unfortunately caught up in restrictive religious revivalism. Deoband madrassa was established in 1867. Shah Waliullah admonished his followers to adopt puritanical religious practices to face the future challenges. There was a grand spiritual revival and renewal among the Hindus, kindled by the words and writings of great spiritual saints and leaders like Swami Ramakrishna Paramahamsa, Swami Vivekananda, and Maharishi Dayanand. There is no doubt that these Muslim and Hindu leaders did excellent service in their respective social orbits. But on the negative side, it must be noted that instead of reform, these organizations and these leaders commanded followers to lead a spiritual life that satisfied the traditional definition of purity, avoiding everything that modern life or modernity had to offer. The fight for political freedom from the British thus evolved into urgency for religious resurrection and freedom.

This tendency to return to a glorified past and find satisfaction with the achievements of the days gone by also entered the literature. The British rule was the new reality after the failure of the uprising. Psychologically, people found it hard to accept that they had lost their freedom and country. Therefore, they sought solace in the past that had ceased to exist. Hali's preface to his *Yaadgar-e Ghalib* and the entire text of his resurgent *Musaddas Maddo Jazr-e Islam* reads like an elegy of the past. Muslims were reminded of the time of their greatness. Mohammad Husain Azad had a similar objective when he wrote his book *Aab-e Hayaat*. Azad focused his attention on creating biographical portraits of great Muslim poets and literary figures to secure a place for them in the hearts and minds of his readers. Nazir Ahmed made a similar effort in the novels that he wrote.

The outcome of this rush to the glorification of the past, and that too, with a high dose of religious fervor, was unintended religious fanaticism and fundamentalism. A feeling arose among Muslims that their political downfall resulted from their spiritual debasement. Religion was, therefore, the medicine for all their ills. This revivalism, which could have taken many other forms, became simply religious revivalism. Everything was now seen through the fundamentalist lens. Attaining political freedom became a religious goal. In the long run, this created a problem in the struggle for independence because the tension between political and religious purposes was challenging. Even when they demanded political freedom from colonialism, these religious movements looked upon political and economic challenges faced by the masses as their deviation from the religious path and going back to the old religious order was thus presented as the only solution. As we move into the twentieth century, this idea of my-religion-before-everything-else became the ground for separatism.

The first showdown between these two communities appeared on the question of language. As Hindus had rediscovered the glories of their past and the role that Sanskrit and Devanagari script had played in it, they petitioned that Hindi written in Devanagari script be given the status of a second court language, with Urdu remaining a working language for all practical purposes. Sir Syed and other Muslim leaders vehemently opposed this move because they considered Urdu their cultural language after Arabic and Persian. This fight occurred in Uttar Pradesh, home to both these languages. As Muslims refused to accommodate Hindus in this demand, the first seed of political dissension and division between the two communities was sown. It suited the British since they had pursued this political strategy since the beginning.

It is interesting to note that Syed Ahmad Khan (1817–1898), popularly known as Sir Syed, was up to this point a great supporter of Hindu–Muslim unity, and he used to describe them as two eyes of the same face, changed his views. The educational institutions that he had created, a Persian madrassa in Ghazipur, an English teaching center, and the Scientific Society, though open to all communities, became centers for the education of Muslims primarily. The Muhammadan Anglo-Oriental College (later known as Aligarh Muslim University) was established to serve the same purpose. The Anjuman Taraqqi Urdu was designed under the patronage of Sir Syed and his associate Mohsin-ul-Mulk in 1886, soon after Hindu leaders founded Kashi Nagari Pracharini Sabha Benares in 1893. Over the years, Sir Syed started using the word *qaum,* meaning 'the nation' solely for the Muslims. Within a short period, he assumed the mantle of being a leader of India's Muslims. Sir Syed was given the honor of 'Star of India' in 1869. Later, he was given the title of 'Khan Bahadur' and knighted by the British Government (KCSI) in 1888 for his' loyalty to the British Crown.

Sir Syed Movement and Arya Samaj had their beginnings in the same time-frame. Both aimed at educational, social, and cultural reform. Their spheres of influence had boundaries, and their points of view were communal at their core. Both organizations raised their voice for promoting and protecting their respective religions. Sir Syed provided a new interpretation of some Islamic principles, especially those that conflicted with the newly emerging scientific worldview while giving a forceful defense of the core of the Islamic belief system. Arya Samaj beckoned Hindus to revert to the Vedic past and the teachings of scriptures that had once made India great. Both the movements provided support to some progressive ideas. They implored followers to overcome inferiority complex, receive an English education, and cultivate a desire to move forward to a new socio-political reality. Despite these positive aspects, both these movements were conflicted. Without understanding the complexity of further economic and social complications, Arya Samaj advocated a move to the past. It was against all non-Vedic influences – Islamic, Bhakti, Sufi. It created a reaction in the Muslim community, and thus new impediments in forming a joint forum for the struggle for freedom. The negative interpretation of the idea of a *nation* was a crucial setback.

Sir Syed led this, along with everyone else. It strengthened the position of the new British administration, especially his instructions to the Muslims to stay away from politics. This was direct support to the British. He went a step further and advised the British to reorganize the Indian Army along religious lines. All these steps, taken together, created a chasm that widened with time. There is an excellent zigzag of love and hate relationship in the political graph of coming decades as the nationalist leaders try to bring the two communities near each other, but time and again, the bonds are broken, followed by communal riots and bloodshed. The ideology of separatism triumphed when the country was divided based on religious differences. The partition tore the subcontinent apart, followed by the unprecedented bloodbath that killed and uprooted millions.

There is no doubt that Sir Syed's efforts were based on fairness and a sincere desire to bring the two communities together in the beginning. His patriotism was unquestionable. He wanted to create a fusion of the East and the West. He thought that English education could work as an effective tool of cultural transformation. But some of his religious and cultural views followed by his associates led to irreversible positions that strengthened separatism. A friendship with the British became pursuit of patronage. Instead of working for the economic uplift of the Muslim masses, Sir Syed's associates adopted sycophancy and slavish admiration of the British as their ideal goal. The long-term effect of this development was that Muslims were no longer participating in the struggle for freedom. In the words of Maulana Abul Kalam Azad, this proved to be 'a big stone in the path of national progress … and gave the British government a rock to shatter national aspirations.' The direct and indirect influence of the Sir Syed Movement thus strengthened colonial power. Although leaders like Shibli, Syed Sulaiman Nadvi, Maulana Mohammad Ali, Maulana Shaukat Ali, Dr. Ansari, Hakim Ajmal Khan, and Maulana Abul Kalam Azad made great efforts to maintain Hindu–Muslim unity, the damage was already done. We shall see the after-effects of this in the poetry of Hali, Akbar Allahabadi, and Allama Iqbal.

All this ebb and flow of the national graph threw challenges for the creativity of different poets in different ways because poetry too had a crucial role in the freedom struggle since it addressed and moved the masses. Hali was younger than Sir Syed by 21 years. By the time he attained consciousness as an adult, Sir Syed had already formulated a Muslim framework. The religion-based ideas of Sir Syed impacted Hali, and it cast a shadow on his mental development. Firaq Gorakhpuri has mentioned that Hali was born with a flair for writing both love poetry and poetry in support of the land and faith. Yet, Sir Syed's influence at one stage limited the scope of his poetry.

The young Hali had watched the painful disintegration of the Mughal empire. He accepted British rule as an unavoidable reality. He thought that Muslims had reached the bottom of their economic, moral, and spiritual downfall. They had lost the ability to govern a vast country. British had power on its side. Therefore, any fight against them was futile, and following in the footsteps of Sir Syed; he also accepted working with the British as the only choice. According to Ehtisham Husain,

> Hali supported the adoption of Western ideas as a means for future progress. He did not have a clear political vision. Sometimes he dreamt of independence and believed that with the advent of mass public education and scientific progress, India would find a path to be free in the future.[2]

Hali was the first Urdu poet who was influenced by Indian politics. He shed tears about India's enslavement. Although he followed Sir Syed about keeping peace with the British, his poetry sparked the country's social progress and patriotism. There is a deep shadow of sadness in his verse, and a feeling of utter disgust for ignorance, suffering, and helplessness of the people. About Hali's masnavi *Hubb-e Watan,* Professor Ale Ahmad Suroor, wrote: 'This masnavi is not only about the country's natural beauty or its glorious past; it sheds light on an aspect of patriotism that could be attained only by selfless service.'[3]

Hali's work *Masaddas* is a masterpiece. We can call it Urdu's first important long poem. This was written solely for Muslim readers, and it is a religious work. Nonetheless, it has the air and a touch of India's natural and social ecology. According to Sardar Jafri, 'Hali described the downfall of Muslim social structure with such emotional intensity that *Masaddas* could be taken as a complete picture of the undoing of India's exploitative landlord system.'[4] This poem is the foundation of our nationalistic poetry.

There is no doubt that the British rule was exploitative, cruel, and despicable in many respects. It introduced India to the capitalistic market economy. An unintended consequence struck deep into the ancient economic modes of production, distribution, and profiteering. Slowly and gradually, India was transformed into an industrialized economy that brought new avenues for public education, free press, new means of transportation (especially railways), a postal system, and higher political consciousness. The middle class significantly benefitted from its access to higher education in India and abroad, and as a result, liberal ideas found greater acceptance. Muslim community that was a victim of extreme poverty, corrupt organizations, and out-of-date ideas showed a willingness to accept new ideas though somewhat less than the Hindu community. Hali saw this change, and in his poetry, he stated that the internal peace and freedom that we had gained from the British was something new; at no time in past India had this kind of openness and breathing space. In one place, Hali describes law and order as a distinctive blessing of the British government. At the time of

Queen Victoria's jubilee celebration, he penned a qasida. Here is a line from that composition.

sat jug se hai ye hind ke haqq mein kahien behtar
This situation is better for India than the ancient idea of a true age.

Satya yuga, an ideal state of governance in which Truth alone is the final arbiter, is part of the Hindu belief system, a common usage in public parlance. He also wrote a *marsia,* an elegy, at the demise of Queen Victoria.

qaisar ke gharaane par rahe saya-e yazdaan
aur hind ki naslon p rahe saaya-e qaisar

May God bless the Crown, the House of Hanover,
and let the Crown protect generations of Indians!

The logical consequence of these thoughts was that Hali opposed the Indian National Congress. Yet, unlike Sir Syed, he never relinquished his strong support for Hindu–Muslim unity, which he considered an ethical issue rather than a political posture. Hali also felt that the British presence was a blessing for Muslims. Therefore, he often preached peace with the British while urging his followers to take advantage of new avenues for material progress. This is seen in his poems *Falsafa-e Taraqqi* (The Philosophy of Progress) and *Li Hai Karvat Ek Muddat Se Zamaane Ne Badal* (The Changing Times).

Later in his life, Hali had a change of heart about Sir Syed's ideology. It was clear that the latter was yielding too much to the pressure of the British. Therefore, he was losing the support of more enlightened elements in the Muslim community. Jamaluddin Afghani, a leader in the Pan-Islamic movement, didn't have kind words for Sir Syed. He said that he was not ready to 'pour even a handful of dust on Sir Syed's doings.' Hali joined Viqar-ul-Mulk and Mohsin-ul-Mulk, two of Sir Syed's close companions, in compiling a statement denouncing some of Sir Syed's pro-British actions, but that statement was not issued because of Sir Syed's death. Hali finally gave in to pressure and wrote a biography of the departed leader.

We find a discernable change in Hali's thinking after Sir Syed's death. He became a supporter of the Swadeshi Movement. He wrote:

This movement will benefit the country. The positive outcome is already coming to the forefront, slowly and gradually. People have found the tunnel that is being used to transfer India's wealth to foreign countries. But it will not be an easy job to close this channel. In the short run, it is like fighting against the force of nature. Rome was not built in a day. Even if it takes one hundred years, India will finally come out victorious.[5]

Hali sought moderation, both in life and politics, and his actions rarely crossed the boundaries of peace with all. Compared with Hali, Shibli Nomani (1857–1914) was against any accommodation with the British. By the time Shibli grew up and gained political consciousness, the path chosen by Sir Syed had served its utility. Sir Syed movement had become an instrument of colonialism. Shibli raised his voice to inform the Muslim masses about reality. Shibli had fundamental differences with Sir Syed. He had grown up in an atmosphere where opposition to the British rule was commonly shared position. Seeking British patronage was against Shibli's grain. In his masnavi, *Sub-he Watan* (Dawn of the Land), Shibli obliquely said few words of praise for Sir Syed, but he refused to write his biography. Shibli was connected with Deoband School which, at that time, supported freedom and political struggle. Sir Syed movement, on the other hand, was all about political expediency and instructed its followers about how best they could serve the new rulers. There is a qat'a penned by Shibli about Sir Syed's political life.

> *koi puuchhe to main kah duun ga hazaaron mein ye baat*
> *ravish-e syed-e marhuum khushaamand to n thi*
> *haan magar ye hai k tahriiq-e syaasi ke khilaaf*
> *un ki jo baat thi 'aavurd' thi 'aamad' to n thi*

> If anyone asked me,
> I would say this among thousands.
> The path shown to us by deceased Syed
> was not simply adulation,
> but it is true that his opposition
> to the political movement was expediency,
> there was nothing spontaneous
> or natural about it.

Shibli was younger than Sir Syed by 40 years and Hali by 20 years, and thus he was able to see the future better than them. He was the product of traditional religious upbringing coupled with the new western-style education. Therefore, some form of mental conflict and a generation gap was inevitable. By 1880, India was in the grip of an economic crisis. Farmers were being crushed. The traditional industries were closing down due to their inability to compete against the goods being imported from Britain. There were signs of an impending famine. This was happening in 1877 when Queen Victoria was ceremoniously holding her court in Delhi. The façade of the British government being 'justice-loving' was unraveling. An Indo-European poet writing in Urdu captured the tragic irony in the following couplet.

> *gulistaan-e jahaan mein kya khizaan ne gul khilaaya hai*
> *k har barg-e shajar ko zaa'fraani kar dikhaaya hai*

> What cruel deed autumn
> has wrought in the land's garden!
> Each leaf of trees and plants
> is wearing a dry and dying look.

The English education provided an unintended benefit. Indians were now able to read about the French Revolution (1789), America's declaration of independence (1776), national movements in Italy and Ireland. Now, they had easy access to the ideas of Thomas Pain (1837–1809), a political activist; Herbert Spencer (1820–1903), a biologist who was the originator of the concept of 'survival of the fittest,' Edmund Burke (1729–1797), a member of British Parliament, who supported the impeachment of Warren Hastings for the crimes he committed in India; John Stuart Mill (1806–1873), a leading proponent of liberty who helped women's right to vote as member of the British Parliament; Voltaire (1694–1778), French philosopher who advocated freedom of speech, freedom of religion, and separation of church and state, Martin Luther (1483–1546), a seminal figure in the Reformation, Giuseppe Garibaldi (1807–1882), who attained fame for his ideas of national independence, and Mazzini (1807–1872), who defined the role of popular democracy within a republic. The writings of these thinkers and various other lovers of liberty inspired Indian intelligentsia to dream about the time when India will attain its freedom.

There was another issue that created a good deal of commotion. British had given a justice system to India, but it was lopsided. No Britisher or European could be tried in a court presided over by an Indian judge. Albert, who was a council member, introduced a bill that aimed to correct this anomaly. Everyone should be equal in the eyes of the law. But this idea received bitter opposition from the resident Britishers, and therefore Albert's bill was defeated in the assembly. This was a moment of a rude awakening for Indians. They came to realize that nothing would be given them on a platter. Freedom required effort and continuous struggle. This sentiment was well-expressed in a poem published in a newspaper from Lahore.

> *ae saakinaan-e khitta-e hindostan barhho*
> *aage nikal gaye hain bahut kaarvaan barhho*
> *ham log tum mein hain k jaras kaarvaan mein hai*
> *chilla raha hai tuuti-e hindostaan barhho*

> Residents of India, march ahead.
> The other caravans have advanced,
> You should move too.
> Are the people self-inspired,
> or are they waiting for the caravan bell to ring?
> The poet of India is crying and pleading
> that all should move.

The Indian National Congress had come into being as a result of the effort of several enlightened Indians and Britishers that included Allan Octavian Hume, a political reformer; William Wedderburn, a member of the British Parliament; and several leading Indian thinkers such as Surendranath Banerjee, Badruddin Tyabji, M. G. Ranade, Dadabhai Naoroji, Dinshaw Vacha, and Pherozeshah

Mehta. The goals of this organization were moderate; to improve the representation of Indians in the provincial assemblies and councils. Initially, it was nothing more than a debating society. Followers of Sir Syed were afraid of joining the Congress Party, and their attitude could be best described as nonpolitical. In the words of a commentator, these people carrying the 'dead body of education' close to their chest. Under these circumstances, it is not a small feat of Shibli that he implored Muslim masses to join politics and to participate in political activities. His message was 'get the maximum benefit that the West has to offer,' but do not shy away from India's struggle for complete independence.

Shibli was an exceptional Muslim scholar who had mastery over four languages –Arabic, Persian, Turkish, and Urdu. He undertook a major project to write a biography of the Prophet titled *Siirat-un Nabi* in seven volumes (Shibli completed only two volumes in his life, and the remaining five were completed by his disciple, Syed Sulaiman Nadvi). Shibli is described as a historian, a literary critic, and a biographer; besides he was a poet too. Hali's poetry is filled with aspirational sentiments, an aggregation of molten lava, but in Shibli's case, poetry was a call to action in which molten lava flows like a river. He favored Western education, but unlike Sir Syed it was not an end, an excuse to get a government job. He wanted educated men and women to be enlightened and use their love of freedom and openness to lay the foundation of an independent India. An analysis of his poems shows that he did not look at issues of the time with a religious or theological lens. For him, the patriotic and the national angle superseded everything else. He brought Urdu poetry closer to the problems of the day-to-day life. He wrote against defeatist mentality, monarchical dictatorships, and looting of native lands by the colonial powers. He tried to persuade *ulema* (clergies and theologians) to join the national freedom movement. He counseled Muslim masses to seek the path of liberation and to shed the mentality of enslavement.

The struggle for freedom at the start of the twentieth century was subjected to new challenges. Not only India but the entire Asiatic region faced a new reality. The Russo-Japanese War of 1904–1905 between two empires resulted in a victory for Japan. This was a significant event because it was the first time an Asian country had defeated a European power. The 1913 coup in Turkey put the country under the control of three pashas, and after the defeat of the Ottoman Empire at the end of the First World War, the empire was partitioned into several states. The Turkish War of Independence, initiated by Mustafa Kemal Ataturk, gave birth to a new Turkey in 1922. In 1912, the Republic of China was established under the leadership of Sun Yat-sen. All these developments had an impact on India's political landscape. The Congress Party that had functioned as nothing more than a forum for the exchanging ideas for the first 20 years of its life became politically active. The new crop of Congress leaders like Bal Gangadhar Tilak, Bipin Chander Pal, Aurobindo Ghosh, Lala Lajpat Rai, among others, emphasized the need for direct action. Once again, there was a famine in the country. Lord Curzon, who wanted to improve matters, sadly made some decisions that created high levels of political resentment. He divided Bengal into two parts based on religious lines. Bengalis, both Muslims and Hindus, who were at the forefront of the freedom movement, vehemently opposed this move, and because of their unity it got cancelled. The cumulative result of all these developments was strengthening of freedom movement – a high point not reached before.

Daily newspapers and magazines were increasingly becoming a source of news and information to the general public. There were some new entrants in the field of Urdu journalism that made a substantial difference. It included *Al-Hilal*, a magazine edited by Maulana Abul Kalam Azad. Professor Ale Ahmad Suroor was right when he mentioned that Azad transformed religious sensibility into political consciousness with a literary flavoring. Wahiduddin Saleem edited the *Muslim Gazette*. This newspaper was the result of Shibli's efforts, and his landmark article titled *Musalmanon Ki Political Karvat* (Political Awakening of Muslims) was published in it. However, he used *Al-Hilal* for publishing his poetical work that often-contained attacks on the Muslim League. The other liberal Urdu papers that were politically active included *Oudh Punch, Hamdard, Hamdam* and *Madina*; all major writers of the time wrote in these publications.

The All-India Muslim League was established in 1906. Its ideology was strongly based on the idea of two-nation theory, meaning Hindus and Muslims constitute two nations, and thus they could not exist within one sovereign country. The idea of a separate state abetted by the British, which matured into a concrete idea several decades later, was the outcome of ideology whose seeds were sown earlier. Shibli correctly saw the League as an impediment in the path of the struggle for freedom. He strongly opposed the ideas propagated by the League and dubbed them as friendly to the British rulers. They saw a strategic advantage in creating a rift between Hindu and Muslim communities. The people dubbed the policy as 'Divide and Rule,' pursued by the British. The League, which was not ready to make any sacrifice for the country's freedom, became the party of rich Muslim landowners and merchants trying to extract favors from the foreign rulers.

Shibli saw the activities of the League as an unwelcome development and did not shy away from criticizing them in his writings. His mind was fixed on the goal of India's independence from the British, and he was not ready for any compromise. Two years before his death, developments in Turkey caught the attention of Indian Muslims. The intervention in the domestic affairs of what was known as the mighty Ottoman Empire was seen as a conspiracy by the western powers to subdue and destroy a major Muslim country. Shibli wrote a remarkable poem titled *Shahr Aashob-e Islam* (An Elegy for Islam) and read it in a public meeting in Lucknow. According to his disciple, Syed Sulaiman Nadvi, Shibli touched hearts while reciting his poem and deeply moved the masses. Shibli was the first among the ulema, says Nadvi, to take an active interest in political matters and openly support the Congress Party. He was a great believer in Hindu–Muslim unity. Because he was aligned with the progressive elements, according to Professor Ale Ahmad Suroor, Shibli had a greater influence on the following generation of Muslims than any other Muslim leader. His opposition to the politics of extracting benefits from the British rulers and currying favors for small concessions struck a chord. His opposition to the Aligarh movement was based on his inner passion for freedom. Shibli profoundly influenced the next generation of Muslim leaders like Abul Kalam Azad, Abdus Salam Nadvi, Zafar Ali Khan, and Mohammad Ali.

Akbar Allahabadi (1846–1921) was an interesting literary personality whose light vein and sarcastic poetry gained wide popularity after both Hali and Shibli passed away. His point of view was essentially negative; he sided neither with Sir Syed followers nor the progressives within the Congress Party. He was neither a typical conservative nor a religious reformer. He opposed Gandhi and made fun of him while dubbing the struggle for freedom as a futile effort. Although he achieved success in his life because of western education, deep in his heart he was critical of western culture and English education. He urged Muslim women to observe purdah and avoid English education.

> *Hamida chamki n thi English se jab begaana thi*
> *ab hai sham'e anjuman pahle chirag-e khaana thi*

> Hamida was not so sparkling and affable
> when she had not received English education.
> Now she is the glittering light of the assembly.
> Before she was a dim earthen lamp of the household.

Akbar's poetry, though amusing in some respects, was in fact a negative event for Urdu literature. For Akbar, the best option for Indians was to do nothing and be indifferent to the national struggle or any form of modernization.

> *akbar ki jo maano beth raho kuchh bhi ho lekin sabr karo*

> If you listen to Akbar, just sit there,
> whatever happens, be indifferent and patient.

While people focused on the satirical elements of his poetry, he was promoting his do-nothing approach that was highly damaging. Look at the following couplet.

> *hargiz n mustaqil samajh is inqilaab ko*
> *rakh raah-e raast bhonkne de in kalaab ko*

> Do not consider this talk of revolution
> as something permanent.
> Just stay on your path and
> let these *dogs* bark.

He considered Hindus and Muslims as two nations and did not believe in the concept of separation between Church and State. As a light streak poet, he could afford to blow hot and cold simultaneously while supporting the idea of Muslims as a separate nation. He opposed Sir Syed for promoting English education, while he himself had received legal education in English and was holding the position of a magistrate. He might be hilarious, but he was negative and antinational influence.

The clear vision of nationalism, especially India as an independent nation, is seen in the poetry of Durga Sahai Suroor and Chakbast. We shall have more to say about Suroor later. At this point, let us talk about Brij Narayan Chakbast (1882–1926) who hailed from a family of Kashmiri pandits, and was born in Faizabad. As a trained lawyer, he spent most of his life in Lucknow. He wrote ghazals, poems, and masnavis, and we can easily find the influence of Anis and Atish in his poetry. Chakbast was a political activist, and he openly supported leaders like Gandhi, Annie Besant, Gokhale, and Ranade. His book *Sub-he Watan* published posthumously in 1926 contained patriotic, nationalistic, reformative, and political poems. Here are some of his couplets.

> *vatan ki khaak se mar kar bhi ham ko uns baaqi hai*
> *maza daamaan-e maadar ka hai is mitti ke daaman mein*
> *naya bismil huun main vaaqif nahien rasm-e shahaadat se*
> *bata de tu hi ae zaalim tarapne ki ada kya hai*
> *zabaan-e haal se ye lucknow ki khaak kahti hai*
> *mitaaya gardish-e aflaak ne jaah o hasham mera*
> *aziizaan-e vatan ko ghuncha o barg o samar jaana*
> *khuda ko baaghbaan aur qaum ko ham ne shajar jaana*
> *charaagh qaum ka raushan hai arsh par dil ke*
> *use hava ke farishte bujha nahien sakte*

Even after death, I have not lost
Affection for the soil of my land.
I get the love of my mother's hem
in the lap of this soil.
I am newly wounded, and I am unfamiliar
with the ritual of martyrdom.
I leave it to you, my tyrant,
how to crush my pain and anguish?
Each particle of Lucknow is expressing herself
in today's idiom.
The imperialists destroyed me and
stole my rank and riches.
I looked at my compatriots as a bud,
leaf of a tree, and fruit.
And God as the gardener
of my country as a tree.
The lamp of the nation
burns brightly
on the sky of my heart.

> The agents of imperialists
> cannot douse the lamp,
> how hard they might try.

Allama Iqbal (1877–1938) started writing patriotic poetry in his early years. He joined Muslim League during his stay in London. But he was unhappy with the Muslim political leaders for their factional conflicts that lasted the whole of 1920s. This was a period of great turmoil, rising high hopes and great disappointments as Congress and League came close to an agreement and then drifted apart. Mohammad Iqbal was elected president of the Muslim League in 1930 and this is what he said in his presidential address at its Allahabad session on December 29, 1930:

> I would like to see the Punjab, North-West Frontier Province, Sindh and Baluchistan amalgamated into a single state. Self-government within the British Empire, or without the British Empire, the formation of a consolidated Northwest Indian Muslim state appears to me to be the final destiny of the Muslims, at least of Northwest India.

This statement should not obfuscate the fact that Iqbal always took pride in calling himself an Indian, as seen in the following two couplets.[6]

> *main asl ka khaas somnaati*
> *aaba mere laati o manaati*
> *hai falasfa mere aab o gil mein*
> *poshiida hai raaz haae dil mein*

> In truth, I belong to Somnath tradition.
> My ancestors were idol worshippers.
> This philosophy is deeply a part of my being.
> This is the secret that resides in my heart.

He expresses a similar sentiment in a Persian couplet.

> *mra biini k dar-hindostaan diigar nami biini*
> *brahman zaada o ramz aashnaaye ruum o tabriz ast*

> Look at me, there is no one in India like me.
> Although I'm of a Brahmanic descent,
> my love for Ruum and Tabriz is unbounded.

About his proposal for four Muslim majority provinces (stated above), Iqbal clarified the misunderstanding that a letter by a commentator named Dr. Edward Thomson had created. In a letter addressed to Raghib Husain of Calcutta, Iqbal stated in March 1934:

> Please pay attention. Edward Thomson is confusing my scheme with the proposal of Pakistan. I support the creation of a Muslim province within an

Indian Federation. The Pakistan point of view envisages a Federation that would have an independent relationship with England.

This distinction was further clarified in a book authored by K. K. Aziz. He wrote:

> We should remember that Iqbal did not support the founding of an independent Muslim state. On the other hand, he supported an entity which was to remain a part of India. He also did not discuss the future of Bengal (which later became Bangladesh) … In view of this, it is wrong to call Iqbal the founder of Pakistan or to say that as a poet he saw the dream of country's partition. Such an interpretation would be highly misleading.

In Allama Iqbal's poetry, we find many flavors; he has Ghalib's lyricism, Hali and Shibli's social zeal, vision of resurgence of Islam and profound love of the country. Notwithstanding his slowly developing liking for ideas of separatism, especially in the later phase of his career, his patriotism for the land was uncompromising. He was born in Sialkot and he belonged to a migrant Kashmiri family of Sapru Brahmins who had embraced Islam. The poetry written by him before his visits to England and during the early decades is the finest example of great nationalist poetry. Although, he reached the pinnacle of his fame as a Pan-Islamist poet, writing mostly on resurgent and self-fortifying Islamic themes and supporting the idea of 'self-determination for Muslim majority states.' Yet, it must be said that he retained all his patriotic and nationalist poems without deletion of a single word in his landmark Urdu collection *Baang-e-Dara* (The Call of the Marching Bell), published 1924. It started with a beautiful couplet ascribed to the ancient Sanskrit poet philosopher Bhartari Hari.

phuul ki patti se kat sakta hai hiire ka jigar
mard-e nadaan par kalaam-e narm o naazuk be-asar

A delicate petal of a flower
can pierce the heart of a diamond
but the best of poetry is of no avail
to a person who is not responsive.

Baang-e-Dara contains some of the most beautiful poems ever written about the natural beauty and the richness of India's cultural heritage. The milestone collection begins with a beautiful long poem on the Himalayas. It contains tributes to India's religious leaders such as Hindu deity Rama, Guru Nanak, Swami Rama Tirtha, and several references to Gautama Buddha. There is a short poem on the Vedic *Gayatri Mantra,* entitled *Aaftaab.* He was an anti-imperialist to the core and shunned western culture. We will talk about Iqbal's anti-West and freedom poetry in the next chapter. He wrote some of his inspirational Pan-Islamist poetry in Persian to reach wider audiences outside the country, but like Ghalib, despite love for Persian, he never gave up on Urdu. Here are some of his milestone Urdu poems as a patriot and champion of Indian nationalism. They are unsurpassed in their beauty and charm; hardly any other poet of Urdu has created verse with such spontaneous and immaculate perfection and heart-warming zeal and love that Iqbal possessed. These poems, *Tarana-e-Hindi, Naya Shiwala,* and *Hindustani Bacchon ka Qaumi Geet* are unparalleled. Despite subsequent changes in his ideology, there are parts of Iqbal's oeuvre that are immortal. Here are some selected verses.

Tarana-e-Hindi

saare jahaan se achha hindostaan hamaara
ham bulbulein hain is ki ye gulsitaan hamaara
parbat vo sab se uuncha hamsaaya aasmaan ka
vo santri hamaara vo paasbaan hamaara
godi mein khelti hain jis ki hazaaron nadiyaan
gulshan hai jin ke dam se rashk-e jinaan hamaara
ae aab-e ruud-e ganga vo din hain yaad tujh ko
utra tere kinaare jab kaarvaan hamaara
mazhab nahien sikhaata aapas mein bair rakhna
hindi hain ham vatan hai hindostaan hamaara
yuunaan o misr o roma sab mit gaye jahaan se
ab tak magar hai baaqi naam o nishaan hamaara
kuchh baat hai k hasti mit-ti nahien hamaari
sadiyon raha hai dushman daur-e zamaan hamaara
Iqbal koi mahram apna nahien jahaan mein
maa'luum kya kisi ko dard-e nihaan hamaara

India's Anthem
Ours —
India is the finest
and the greatest in the world.
We are nightingales
and this is our garden.
Our highest mountain
is the sky's neighbor,
it is our sentry
and our watchman.
Thousands of rivers
rise and fall in its lap.
Because of this,
even Heavens are envious.
O river Ganges!
Do you remember the day
when our caravan stopped

by your shore?
Religion does not teach
hatred towards anyone.
We are Indians, compatriots,
and India is our land.
Greece, Egypt, and Rome –
there is no trace
of their ancient culture.
We are still there
with our culture and our name.
There is a reason
that we have survived
wars and ordeals,
though time and tide
have been unkind to us.
There is continuity
of culture over centuries.
Iqbal, you can't share
with anyone
what's in your heart.
Alas, no one knows anything
about your deep distress
and consummate love.

Naya Shivaala

sach kah duun ae brahman gar tu bura n maane
tere sanam kadon ke but ho gaye puraane
apnon se bair rakhna tu ne buton se siikha
jang o jadal sikhaaya vaa'iz ko bhi khuda ne
tang aa ke main ne aakhir dair o haram ko chhora
vaa'iz ka vaa'z chhora chhore tere fasaane
patthar ki muuraton mein samjha hai tu khuda hai
khaak-e vatan ka mujh ko har zarra devta hai
aa ghairiyat ke parde ik baar phir utha dein
bichhron ko phir mila dein naqsh-e duii mita dein
suuni pari hui hai muddat se dil ki basti
aa ik naya shivaala is des mein bana dein
duniya ke tiirthon se uuncha ho apna tiirath
daamaan-e aasmaan se is ka kalas mila dein
har sub-h uth ke gaaein mantar voh miithe miithe
saare pujaariyon ko mai piit ki pila dein
shakti bhi shanti bhi bhaghton ke giit mein hai
dharti ke baasiyon ki mukti priit mein hai

A New Temple

Dear Brahman —
Please do not feel bad
if I say something.
Idols in your idol-house
have passed their usefulness.
Enmity with other folks,
you have learned from the idols.
Theologians have received
the same teaching
from the preachers of my faith.
But feeling restless,
I have put the temple
and the mosque aside.
I have given up on teachings
that I received
and I'm also giving up
on your traditional stories.
God resides in stone idols —
this is what you believe.
But every particle
of the soil of this land
is sacred to me.
Let us remove the veils
that separate us.
Let us unite those
who were separated, and
remove the mark of duality
forever from our lives.
The hearth of the heart
has been barren for a long time.
Let us build a new temple
in this land of ours.
In all the places of pilgrimage,
ours should be the highest.
Its domes and spires
should touch the edges
of the sky.
Rising early in the morning,
we should chant sacred mantars,
and we should offer
the wine of love
to all our devotees.
Strength and peace are found

in spiritual recitations.
Salvation of people
who live on this earth
is found in love.

Hindostani Bachchon Ka Qaomi Giit

chishti ne jis zamiin mein paighaam-e haq sunaaya
nanak ne jis chaman mein vahdat ka giit gaaya
taataariyon ne jis ko apna vatan banaaya
jis ne hijaaziyon se dasht-e arab chhuraaya
mera vatan vohi hai mera vatan vohi hai
yunaaniyon ko jis ne hairaan kar diya tha
saare jahaan ko jis ne ilm-o hunar diya tha
mitti ko jis ki haq ne zar ka asar diya tha
turkon ka jis ne daaman hiiron se bhar diya tha
mera vatan vohi hai mera vatan vohi hai
tuute the jo sitaare faaris ke aasmaan se
phir taab de ke jis ne chamkaaye kahkashaan se
vahdat ki le suni thi duniya ne jis makaan se
miir-e arab ko aaii thandi hava jahaan se
mera vatan vohi hai mera vatan vohi hai
bande kaliim jis ke parbat jahaan ke siina
noah-e nabi ka aa kar thahra jahaan safiina
rifat hai jis zamiin ki baam-e falak ka ziina
jannat ki zindagi hai jis ki faza mein jiina
mera vatan vohi hai mera vatan vohi hai

A National Anthem for Indian Children

Where Chishti recited the Word of Almighty
Where Nanak sang the song of the oneness of all beings
That which Mongols invaded and then embraced
That which Arabs made their home after leaving their own
That is my land, that is my land!
The originator of wisdom that puzzled the Greeks
The source of knowledge and skill to the whole world
Its soil was endowed by God to be a wellspring of wealth
Its riches filled pockets of Turks with precious diamonds
That is my land, that is my land!
The stars that had once fallen from the sky of Persia —
The wisdom of India put them together to brighten the Milky Way
The home and hearth from where the melody of oneness originated
The spring from where the cool breeze blew to touch the Prophet
That is my land, that is my land!
The birthplace of great seers and the land of mountains like Sinai's

The places where Noah's boat had landed after the great deluge
The land whose elegance is nothing but a stairway to the sky
The nation whose air makes people feel they are living in paradise
That is my land, that is my land!

At the start of the twentieth century, Urdu poetry had become a significant part of the broader struggle for India's independence. We saw the evidence of this in the works of Iqbal and Chakbast. Many other poets who joined the nationalist struggle in this period include Ismail Meeruthi, Wahiduddin Saleem, Shauq Qidwai, Azmat Ullah Khan, and Brij Mohan Dattatreya Kaifi.

Another shining star joined the galaxy of Urdu poets. He was Syed Fazl-ul-Hasan Hasrat Mohani (1875–1851), an activist, a freedom fighter, and a highly appealing poet. He learned from past masters like Mir and Ghalib about how feminine beauty is captured in verse. The famous slogan *Inqilaab Zindabaad* is strongly associated with his name. He used it in 1921 and it gained a lot of popularity. That was the time when the enthusiasm of the nationalistic movement was also catching up. Under Gandhi's influence, Hasrat opened a shop selling khadi (hand-spun coarse cloth). He was a mercurial personality; for some time he was associated with the Muslim League, but after partition, he refused to go to Pakistan and spent the last years of his life in India. Here are some milestone couplets from a memorable ghazal.

rasm-e jafa kaamyaab dekhiye kab tak rahe
hubb-e vatan mast-e khwaab dekhiye kab tak rahe
ta b kuja huun daraaz silsila haae fareb
zabt ki logon mein taab dekhiye kab tak rahe
naam se qaanuun ke hote hain kya kya sitam
jabr b zere niqaab dekhiye kab tak rahe
daulat-e hindustaan qabza-e aghiyaar mein
be a'ddad o be-hisaab dekhiye kab tak rahe

How long will this oppression
continue to succeed? Let us see.
How long will patriots keep
dreaming of freedom? Let us see.
How long will this cruelty
of oppression last? Let us see.
How long will people's patience
last? Let us see.
How long will this persecution last
under the garb of law? Let us see.
How long will this tyranny stay hidden
under the cover of law? Let us see.
How long will the treasures of India
remain under foreign rule? Let us see.

Treasures with no limits or counts?
Let us see.

Since Hasrat spent time repeatedly in jail for his nationalistic views, he wrote some of his best ghazals within the four walls of prison. Here he is reflecting on the paradoxical situation of doing hard labor while dealing with his urge to write lyrical verse.

> hai mashq-e sukhan jaari chakki ki mushaqqat bhi
> kya turfa tamaasha hai Hasrat ki tabii'yat bhi

> Laboring hard in prison, grinding flour
> and composing ghazal couplets –
> what a playful combination
> for a strange poet called Hasrat.

Hasrat is part of the continuing struggle, and his fervor increased as the nationalist movement intensified. We shall say more about this as we move on. There is hardly any closure in the march of nationalist poetry, except the demise of a senior poet and when someone else takes up the baton. The crusade goes on. It was at the start of the twentieth century that Urdu poetry was deprived of the voices of Durga Sahai Suroor (died 1911), Hali (died 1914), and Shibli (died 1914). But their places were soon occupied by other great poets like Allama Iqbal, Chakbast, and Hasrat Mohani. The start of The First World War in 1914 had a lasting impact on the freedom movement, with the entry of leaders like Gandhi, Jinnah, and Nehru. As we move into the 1930s, we also witness the birth of the Progressive Writers Movement that produced poets of exceptional caliber who added an element of romance to their yearning for a free India.

Notes

1 Theodore De Bary, Stephen N. Hay, Royal Weiler, and Andrew Yarrow, *Sources of Indian Tradition* (New York: Columbia University Press, 1958), p. 748.
2 Ehtisham Husain, *Adab aur Samaaj* (Bombay: Kutab Publishers, 1948).
3 Ale Ahmad Suroor, *Naye aur Purane Chiragh* (Lucknow: Lucknow University, 1946).
4 Sardar Jafri, *Taraqqi Pasand Adab* (Aligarh: Anjuman Taraqqi-e Urdu).
5 Ehtisham Husain, *Rivayat aur Baghavat* (Lucknow: Idara-e Ishaa'at-e Urdu, 1947).
6 Ram Parkash Kapur, *Rashtariya Sahara Daily* (New Delhi, August 30, 2003).

4

THE FIRST WORLD WAR AND ITS AFTERMATH

The question of a 'national language' on its own was a problematic one. The claims of linguistic surveyors that India was a country of a few hundred languages had been ridiculed by Nehru in his *Discovery of India* as academic quibbling: he claimed that 'Hindustani' was intelligible across much of North India, and that the 'few hundred' idea was the invention of a colonial imagination intent on describing India as a fragmented society. Nehru regarded 'Hindustani' as a potential national language for India: 'it must not be too Sanskritised or too Persianised which would divorce it from large masses of people.' Although Hindi and Urdu had 'developed separate literary forms', he believed that 'no great language can grow up if it is based on literary coteries'. Earlier, Nehru had argued that Hindi and Urdu were not mutually conflictual and should come closer together to 'develop into one language, with two scripts, for India', to form 'our great national language', while at the same time the 'present literary forms' of Hindi and Urdu 'represent a certain individual genius and background' and should therefore 'be allowed to develop without interference from the other'.[1]

Benjamin Zachariah

The First World War started in 1914. Turkey joined Germany in opposition to Britain. Because Indian Muslims sympathized with Turkey, the British government took immediate action to put Muslim political leaders in jail. Many leading Urdu newspapers, such as *Al-Hilal* and *Hamdard,* were asked to cease publication. Commenting on this situation, Maulana Shibli Nomani wrote a satirical poem tagging Ghalib's famous sarcastic couplet as a rhythmic punch line that deepened the undercurrent of irony and turned it into a gem of a poem.

ek germany ne mujh se kaha iz rah-e ghuruur
aasaan nahien hai fat-h to dushvaar bhi nahien

DOI: 10.4324/9781003360841-5

bartaania ki fauj hai das laakh se bhi kam
aur is pe lutf ye hai k tayyaar bhi nahien
baaqi raha france to vo rind-e lam-yazal
aayien shanaas-e sheva-e paikaar bhi nahien
main ne kaha ghalat hai tera daava-e ghuruur
diivaana tu nahien tu hushiyaar bhi nahien
ham log ahl-e hind hain german se das gune
tujh ko tamiiz-e andak o bisyaar bhi nahien
sunta raha vo ghaur se mera kalaam aur
phir vo kaha jo laaiq-e izhaar bhi nahien
'is saadgi pe kaon n mar jaaye ae khuda
larte hain aur haath mein talwaar bhi nahien'

A German spoke to me with pride and vanity,
winning is not easy, but it is not difficult either.
British forces number even less than a million.
And the exciting part is that they are not even ready.
That leaves France, which is a known drunk from the beginning.
Brainy, but they don't know how to fight a war.
I said that your claim to vanity is false.
Not completely mad, but not smart either.
We Indians are ten times the size of Germany.
You have no sense of what is less and what is more.
He listened to my poetic recitation with great attention,
and making me speechless, he said:
'Who would not be baffled, O God,
on watching this recklessness.
The beauty is engaging in a fierce fight
but not knowing how to wield a sword.' [Ghalib]

The authorities were offended by Shibli's poem, and a warrant was issued for his arrest. But due to a strange coincidence, he was released from the prison of life before he could be arrested by the British. The poem was banned.

The colonial regime tried to win the support of Indian masses for the war by giving them petty concessions, such as – import duty on cotton was raised, and a promise was made to have greater Indian representation in the administration. The Congress Party welcomed these measures in good faith, stopped its anti-establishment agitation, and started cooperating with the government in the war effort. The extreme wing of the Congress Party was not pleased with the so-called promises of the Raj. Bal Gangadhar Tilak (1856–1920), who was released from the prison in 1914, took no time in restarting his political activities, and he established the Home Rule League. The League became a movement by 1916, and because of the efforts of Annie Besant (1847–1933), it reached all parts of the country. Muslims supported Turkey in this fight, and they joined those elements of Congress, who also opposed the British. This cooperation resulted in the Lucknow Pact of 1916, whereby Congress and the Muslim League formed a joint front in their opposition to the war. Annie Besant was, however, arrested in 1917. It led to strong condemnation by the masses, and it worked like adding fuel to the fire. There were voices in support of the Home Rule that arose from all parts of the country. Some memorable poems by Chakbast belong to this period. Here are few lines from 'The Song of My Land' (*Vatan ka Raag*).[2]

> *zamiin-e hind k rutbe mein sab se aa'la hai*
> *ye Home Rule ki ummiid ka ujaala hai*
> *talab fuzuul hai kaante ki phuul ke badle*
> *n lein bahisht bhi ham Home Rule ke badle*
> *vatan parast shahiidon ki khaak laaein ge*
> *ham apni aankh ka surma use banaaein ge*
> *ghariib maan ke liye dard dukh uthaaein ge*
> *yahi payaam-e vafa qaum ko sunaaein ge*
> *talab fuzuul hai kaante ki phuul ke badle*
> *n lein bahisht bhi ham Home Rule ke badle*

The land of India is best of all in its stature.
It is the luminescence of the hope of Home Rule.
We should not desire thorns in place of flowers.
We would not accept paradise in place of Home Rule.
We would bring ashes of the patriotic martyrs.
We would turn that into kohl for our eyes.
Knowing that we are poor,
we would carry the burden of good and bad.
It is the pledge of loyalty to the nation
that we would broadcast.
We should not desire thorns in place of flowers.
We would not accept paradise in place of Home Rule.

The combined efforts of Congress and the Muslim League greatly influenced the policymakers. Edwin Samuel Montagu (1879–1924), who served as Secretary of State for India between 1917 and 1922, came to India. The result was the Montagu-Chelmsford Reforms that introduced greater representation for Indians, and it became the basis of the Government of India Act 1919. Consequently, the Imperial Legislative Council was divided into two parts – the Central Legislative Assembly and the Council of States, and provincial governments were given a more significant say in matters relating to public health, education, agriculture, etc. But these reforms failed to satisfy the demands of Congress and the Muslim League. The British tried to repress the opposition and passed the Rowlatt Act in 1919 that curtailed press freedom and the movement of people. Several members of the Council, including Mohammad Ali Jinnah (1876–1948) resigned in protest. Mahatma Gandhi (1869–1948) launched a nationwide protest against the Rowlatt Act. The reaction in Punjab was the strongest. In April 1919, hundreds of people gathered at the Baisakhi Day festival in Jallianwala Bagh for a peaceful protest but acting Brig. Gen. Dyer ordered his troops to open fire, resulting in 379 deaths. The Amritsar massacre created great turbulence and inflamed anti-British feelings throughout the country.

It was a turning point in the history of the freedom movement. Punjab was put under Martial Law for two months. The censorship of news was so extreme that the report of this ruthless massacre reached London after eight months. The following extempore qat'a by Allama Iqbal captures the people's mood on this tragic event.

> *har zaa'ir chaman se ye kahti hai khaak-e baagh*
> *ghaafil n rah jahaan mein tuu gardon ki chaal se*
> *siincha gaya hai khuun-e shahiidaan se is ka tukhm*
> *tu aansuuon ka bukhl n kar is nihaal se*

> The dust of this garden
> is telling every visitor to this place
> where roses bloom.
> Don't be too complacent
> about the tricks of times.
> The blood of the martyrs
> has nurtured every seed.
> Do pay your tribute, don't save tears!

Iqbal's qat'a traveled orally from one person to another. Because of the Martial Law, newspapers were shut down. Yet, in some areas of the country, a lot was written and published about this brutal tragedy, but little record has survived.

It was quite clear, wrote Dr. Abid Husain, that there was a vast chasm between promises made by the British government and their implementation. There was no straight path between the two. Everything was wrapped in the twisted ways of colonialism and the unpredictable character of the government.

The sanctions imposed upon the Caliph and the Ottoman Empire at the end of the First World War were why the Indian Muslims were greatly perturbed about the British policies, and this disillusionment gave birth to the Khilafat Movement that created quite a commotion and lasted from 1919 to 1924. The leaders of this movement included prominent Muslim leaders like Ali Brothers (Shaukat Ali and Mohammad Ali Jauhar), Hakim Ajmal Khan, and Maulana Abul Kalam Azad. The result was an alliance between the Congress Party and the Khilafat leaders in 1920 to work together to achieve the objective of Khilafat and Swaraj. This movement also helped Mahatma Gandhi to ensure Hindu–Muslim unity and put into practice the principles of civil disobedience for the first time. Another good outcome was the founding of Jamia Millia Islamia by the nationalist leaders in 1920 to promote national values in education. The Jamia Millia Islamia was headed by Hakim Ajmal Khan with Dr. Zakir Husain as the vice chancellor, two devout disciples of Gandhi. The Jamia was one of the three institutions established under Gandhi's leadership as a nursery for ideas of independent nationalist education or Basic Education – free from British control and financial support. Dr. Abid Husain correctly summed up the impact of these developments when he wrote

> The civil disobedience initiative and independent education were responsible in helping people to overcome defeatism and helplessness and gave rise to a hope that a nation under foreign rule could still aspire to have confidence in their ability to govern themselves.[3]

These developments influenced Urdu literature as well. All significant poets of the day wrote poems supporting the continuing struggle for freedom. These included some well-known names like Hasrat Mohani, Zafar Ali Khan, Niyaz Fatehpuri, and Tilok Chand Mehroom. Notice the sentiments expressed by Mrs. Zahida Khatun Shirvania in her short poem.

> *jannat ki diid se hai dil shaadmaan hamaara*
> *shukr-e khuda vatan hai hindostaan hamaara*
> *kahte hain ham ko hindi hubb-e vatan hai iimaan*
> *kya puuchhte ho diin o naam o nishaan hamaara*
> *ho jaaye kaash saabit ruuhon ki kuucha gardi*
> *ban jaaye kaash gaandhi har nau-javaan hamaara*
> *jaan se badan se khuun se hindostaan ke hain ham*
> *hairat k kyon nahien hai hindostaan hamaara*

When we look at paradise, our heart is delighted.
Thank God that India is our land!
We are called Indians, and the love of the country is our faith.
Why are you asking what we believe in? What is our identity?
We wish that the principle of reincarnation is proved right!
We wish that every young man should become someone like Gandhi!
We are Indians from our bodies and our blood.
We are sad that India is not ours because it is still not free.

The period between the two World Wars was when the freedom struggle reached its peak. Poet Hasrat Mohani, known for his extreme views, proposed at the Congress session in Ahmedabad in 1921 that the word Swaraj should be defined as complete freedom. Mahatma Gandhi, because he believed in a gradual approach to attaining freedom, did not accept the suggestion, leaving Hasrat quite unhappy and disappointed. Several proposals consistent with Gandhi's belief in nonviolent agitation were adopted at the All-Parties Conference in January 1922, but the Viceroy rejected all of them. It forced Gandhi to start his civil disobedience movement once again. He was sentenced to six years of imprisonment. As the Khilafat Movement had ended, the British went back to their old playbook – divide and rule – giving rise once again to Hindu–Muslim riots.

The Nehru Report presented at the Congress session in Calcutta in 1928 demanded dominion status for India. It contained a warning that if this demand was not met within a year, Congress Party would be forced to demand total freedom. Since the British did not accept the dominion status demand, the Congress Party announced on January 26, 1930, that it wanted complete independence from the British rule, the same as Hasrat Mohani had demanded in 1921. There was great jubilation with this announcement, and the echoes of *Inqilaab Zindabaad* were heard all over the land. Poet Anand Narain Mulla captured this new mood in the following words.

shauq hua be-hijaab
khatm hua daur-e khwaab
aa gaya roz-e hisaab
qaum ka chamka shabaab
zindabaad inqilaab
zindabaad inqilaab

Our desire has been unveiled.
The period of dreaming is over.
The day of reckoning has arrived.
The beauty of the nation has brightened.
Long live the revolution!
Long live the revolution!

Mahatma Gandhi launched his Salt Satyagraha, also known as the Dandi March of 1930 (it lasted for about one month). It was a civil disobedience movement against the British monopoly in the salt trade. But very soon, it became the movement for India's independence. Over 24 days, the march covered 240 miles, and each day thousands of people joined the protest. More than 60,000 were jailed. In the struggle for India's freedom, this was a significant landmark, and after this, there was no going back to anything less than total freedom. A critical facet of this movement was the participation of working farmers from the North-West frontier to the fields of Gujarat; the farmers spoke with one voice. Lord Irwin called for the Second Roundtable Conference in London, which flopped. As a result, civil disobedience movement started once again in which more than a million Indians were jailed. Ramsay MacDonald, the British prime minister, announced in August 1932 his decision regarding separate electorates, known as the Communal Award, in which minorities, mainly Muslims, were given the right to elect their representatives based on a principle of weightage that undermined the Hindu majority. It was yet another attempt by the Empire to divide India based on caste and religion. As a reaction to this development, the All-India Congress Committee once again in 1934, ratified the concept of Swaraj, meaning complete freedom from the British Raj. The feelings of patriotic Indians were captured by poet Tilok Chand Mehroom (1887–1966) in his short poem.

bharki hai is se firqa-parasti ki aag aur
har firqa apni dafli pe gaata hai raag aur
dheli hui kamand a'daavat ki baag aur

phunkaarta hai aaj ta'aasub ka naag aur
hai is ke muunh mein zehr communal award ka
hindi hain aur qahr communal award ka

Once again, the flame of fanaticism has risen.
Every religious group is singing a different song.
The threads that bind us as one nation have been loosened.
The serpent of fanaticism is once again making its hissing sound.
In its mouth, it carries the poison of the Communal Award.
Indians are suffering the calamity of the Communal Award.

The poetry of Brij Narain Chakbast (1882–1926) represented the most exquisite sentiment of patriotism. He was not a poet who was obsessed with the rose and the nightingale. He was a poet of India – the India of Akbar and Pratap. His tone was measured, not too extreme, not too mellow. He wrote on different subjects, but the expression of his love for his country took precedence. His first love and commitment were a bright and shining vision of the country. Look at the following couplet.

vatan ke ishq ka but be-niqaab nikla hai
naye ufaq p naya aaftaab nikla hai

The idol of my love for my country
has been unveiled.
In the new horizon,
a shining sun has appeared.

Here are a few lines from his famous poem titled 'The Voice of the Nation' (*Aavaaza-e Qaum.*) [4]

ye khaak-e hind se paida hain josh ke aasaar
himaaliya se uthe jaise abr-e gauhar-baar
lahu ragon mein dikhaata hai barq ki raftaar
hui hain khaak ke parde mein haddiyaan bedaar
zamiin se arsh talak shor Home Rule ka hai
shabaab qaum ka hai zor Home Rule ka hai
vatan ke ishq ka but be-niqaab nikla hai
naye ufaq se naya aaftaab nikla hai
ye josh-e paak zamaana daba nahien sakta
ragon mein khuun ki haraarat mita nahien sakta
ye aag vo hai jo paani bujha nahien sakta
dilon mein aa ke ye armaan ja nahien sakta.

From the soil of India have appeared
signs of great zeal and passion.
From the Himalayas have arisen
clouds of gems and pearls.

The blood in our veins
is showing the speed of lightning.
In the veil of dust,
our bones have gained awareness.
From the land to the sky,
there is a tumult of Home Rule.
The youth belongs to the nation,
while force is freedom for the land.
The idol of love for the nation
has been unveiled.
A new sun has risen from the new horizon.
Nothing can subdue this passion
and this enthusiasm.
It cannot diminish the circulation
of blood in our veins.
It is a fire that can't be put down
by any means.
Once this zest has taken hold in our hearts,
it has to stay forever.

On the death of Tilak, Chakbast wrote in his eulogy.

shor-e maatam n ho jhankaar ho zanjiiron ki
chaahiye qaum ke bhiisham ko chita tiiron ki

Don't cry over the dead;
listen to the sound of chains
of those who are imprisoned.
The nation's Bhishma[5] has died.
He needs a pyre of arrows.

Akbar Allahabadi (1846–1921) was not a supporter of the freedom movement. But after the Rowlatt Act and the massacre of Amritsar in 1919, even he was compelled to raise his voice. He wrote a poem tagging the famous lines of Bahadur Shah Zafar.

nigaraani-e maraahil kabhi aisi to n thi
tund mauj-e lab-e saahil kabhi aisi to n thi
badguumaani teri qaatil kabhi aisi to n thi
"baat karni mujhe mushkil kabhi aisi to n thi
jaisi ab hai teri mehfil kabhi aisi to n thi"

Circumstances were not as unfortunate before.
The arc of the high tide was never so close to the shore.
O murderer, I never saw you so indifferent before.
It was not so difficult to express myself before.
Your assembly, the way it is, was nothing like this before.

Akbar was known for his double-edged sense of humor and satire in his poetry. He wrote a long poem titled *Jalwa-e Darbar-e Delhi* on the celebration of the coronation of George the Fifth in Delhi in 1911, which the Emperor attended. On the surface, it is a descriptive poem capturing different facets of activities, but underneath it was a satire on the excesses of the rulers while the people whom they ruled were suffering in poverty and slavery.

Here are some of his defining couplets from this period.

> *u'mr zindaan mein kati shauq-e rihaaii rukhsat*
> *ho gaya uns mere paaon ko zanjir ke saath*
> *ye tarz ehsaan karne ka tumhien ko zeb deta hai*
> *maraz mein mubtila kar ke mariizon ko dava dena*
> *goliyon ke zor se karte hain vo duniya ko hazm*
> *is se behtar is ghiza ke vaaste chuuran nahien*
> *dast-e gulchiin phir raha hai shaakh-e gul par be-daregh*
> *kaun sunta hai chaman mein andaliib-e zaar ki*

After spending life in prison,
my desire fulfilled,
I do not need a release order.
As my feet refuse to free themselves,
it seems they had fallen in love
with the chains.
It is a style of doing favors
that suits you very well.
First, you give the malady
and make them patients
Then you give them
the medicine.
It is your way of treating
your sufferers.
With the help of bullets
they swallow the world.
For this kind of diet,
there is no better condiment
that would help digestion.
The flower picker is walking around
near the branches of flowers
without any regret or hesitation.
Who listens to the laments of the afflicted
nightingale in this garden?

Akbar's poetry constitutes a dilemma for the critics because he writes couplets for and against the same issue. He was neither for the British nor against them. He was neither for the independence movement nor totally against it. He spent most of his time as a civil servant, and therefore he could not write against his superiors. He was opposed to Western education, but he received an English education and sent his son for higher studies to London. Although he criticized Gandhi's ideology several times, he confessed his admiration for Gandhi in his verses.

> *madkhuulah-e government Akbar agar n hota*
> *us ko bhi aap paate Gandhi ki gopiyon mein*

> If Akbar were not a concubine
> of the government
> you would have found him
> among the *gopis* of Gandhi.

It was only during his retirement that he started expressing his views without any constraint. But he remained ambivalent. During his early life, he wrote verses in which he made several sarcastic and denigrating comments about Mahatma Gandhi's leadership and the freedom movement in general. This collection, titled *Gandhi Nama,* was posthumously published in 1948 while he had died in 1921. Here are some interesting verses.

> *bhai Gandhi ki ravish mein bahut ummiid nahien*
> *hai voh dilchasp magar vusa'at-e taqliid nahien*
> *hamaare mulk mein sar-sabz iqbaal-e farangi hai*
> *k nun-cooperation mein bhi shaakh-e khaana-jangi hai*
> *faqat zid hai jo kahti hai k 'jab apni zabaan kholo*
> *hamaare peshwaaye mulk gandhiji ki jai bolo'*
> *jai ki bhi sada uththe gi charkhe bhi chalein ge*
> *lekin y samajh lijiye sahib n taalein ge*

> There is no hope in Gandhi's style
> It might be interesting
> but he cannot be followed.
> It is the British whose star is bright
> Even the idea of non-cooperation
> is based on separation.
> Unnecessarily they insist
> that whenever you open your mouth
> everyone must raise the slogan –
> 'Gandhiji ki Jay!'
> There will be shouts of Jai – Jai
> The spinning wheels
> will do its run.
> But take it from me
> the Sahib is not going
> to leave this country.

Akbar's main problem was that he could not resist looking at politics from the lens of religion. Notice his focus on the sacred Zamzam water in the context of the Ganges, or bringing in cows in the context of camels, or alluding to traditional Islamic practice of animal sacrifice of Gandhi's *Ahimsa*, nonviolence.

> aab-e zamzam se kaha mein ne 'mila ganga se kyon
> kyon teri tiinat mein aisii naa-tavaani aa gaii'
> ab sheikh ji muqiim brahman ke paas hain
> gaayein ucchal rahi hain qasaayii udaas hain
> isi mel ka aajkal hai zahuur
> khuda jaane zulmat hai is mein k nuur

> I told the sacred Zamzam water
> why did you mix with Ganges water.
> How come in your essence,
> you have become so weak.
> Now the Sheikh is with the Brahman —
> the cows are happy
> but the butchers are unhappy
> and out of their business.
> It is the coming together
> at present.
> Who knows whether it is
> desirable or undesirable.

Therefore, Akbar's wise advice was:

> politiiki jhagre chhoro
> in baaton se ab munh moro

> Leave aside this trick
> and treat of politics
> Better turn your face away
> and sit quietly.

This negative attitude had repercussions since Akbar, used religion to advise Muslims against their participation in the freedom struggle. Although he couched his criticism in satirical poetry, the ideas that he advocated were quite retrograde. Furthermore, his attacks on the Ali brothers for supporting Gandhi and creating political awareness among Muslim masses and making them participate in India's fight for freedom cannot be treated as humor, and it is unadulterated negative politics.

Maulana Mohammad Ali and Maulana Abul Kalam Azad were suns and moons of the same sky. But Azad was an intellectual, and his voice was looked upon as the voice of wisdom. Ale Ahmad Suroor is correct when he said that Abul Kalam Azad freed the minds of people and Mohammad Ali their hearts. Mohammad Ali was a mujahid (fighter), but he had the eye of a poet. He spoke the language of the heart and wrote powerful prose, but if anyone wanted to look into his soul, he had to read his verse. He wrote ghazals, using Jauhar as his *takhallus,* reaching back to some of the themes and metaphors from classical poetry, but he enthused them with new meaning. He took out the old goblet for pouring in the new wine. Look at the following couplet where he addressed Indian farmers.

> *vaae naadaani k tu muhtaaj saaqi ho gaya*
> *mai bhi tu mina bhi tu saaqi bhi tu mehfil bhi tu*

Due to your innocence and naiveté,
you have become a helpless wine pourer.
You are the wine, and you are the goblet,
you are the wine pourer,
and you are also the meeting place.

Mohammad Ali Jauhar was a path-breaking leader who was razor-focused on achieving political goal. He used verse with the commitment of a poet and did not degrade its quality to promote his politics. His poetry contains heartbeats of lover and the strivings of a soldier in his fight for freedom. Here is a selection of some of his most memorable verses.

[1]

> *daur-e hayaat aa-ye ga qaatil qaza ke baa'd*
> *hai ibtida hamaari teri intiha ke baa'd*
> *jiina vo kya k dil mein n ho teri aarzu*
> *baaqi hai maut hi dil-e muddu'aa ke baa'd*
> *qatl-e husain asl mein marg-e yaziid hai*
> *islaam zinda hota hai har karbala ke baa'd*

The time of my life will come
after the cruel death.
My commencement will follow
your culmination.
What is the purpose of life
if my heart has no desire for you?
There is only death
after the heart that has lost its intent.
The martyrdom of Husain in reality
is the death of Yazid.
Islam reinvigorates itself
after every Karbala.[6]

[2]

> *khaak jiina hai agar maut se darna hai yahi*
> *havas-e ziist ho is darja to marna hai yahi*
> *had hai pasti ki k pasti ko bulandi jaana*

ab bhi ehsaas ho is ka to ubharna hai yahi
naqd-e jaan nazr karo sochte kya ho jauhar
kaam karne ka yahi hai tumhein karna hai yahi

If one lives with the fear of death,
life is meaningless like dust.
If you are passionate about life,
then it subsumes death.
There is a limit to degradation
that we consider low to be high.
If you have this insight,
then it is a way for you
to emerge from lowliness.
Be ready to sacrifice.
No reluctance, no fear.
What are you thinking, Jauhar?
This work is worth doing
and you have to do it.

[3]

tashna lab huun muddaton se dekhiye
kab dar-e maikhaana-e kausar khule
taaqat-e parvaaz hi jab kho chuke
phir hua kya gar hava mein par khule
faiz se tere hi ai qaid-e farang
baal o par nikle qafas ke dar khule

You can see my lips
are parched for ages.
I am waiting for the door
to the tavern of Kausar to open.[7]
When the power to fly was lost,
then what does it matter
that the wings opened in the air.
Thanks to the prison of the colonialists
that I gained my wings to fly
and the doors to freedom opened.

[4]

n namaaz aati hai mujh ko n vuzu aata hai
sajda kar leta huun jab saamne tu aata hai

I do not know how to pray
or to purify me.
But I know how to bow
when I see you in front of me.

[5]

ye bhi kya pairavi-e haq hai k khaamosh hain sab
haan 'an-al haq' bhi ho mansuur bhi ho daar bhi ho

What kind of defense of the Divine is this
Why is everyone silent?
Yes, there should be a declaration, 'I'm the Truth!'
We should have Mansur himself, and
we should not mind the hanging post.

Despite the score of dedicated and inspiring poets mentioned above, the post-First World War period belongs to Allama Iqbal. He committed all his energy to being a poet-philosopher. He was a remarkable Islamic thinker and not an activist politician. Although his poetry runs parallel to the track of political events, he never aspired to be a political leader. As a poet, his heart was in those issues that touch human beings in general and passionate individual freedom. In his younger years, he showed a strong streak of patriotic fervor, which was secular and a devout patriot, as we have already seen. He wrote articles showing how colonial exploitation was the root cause of India's poverty and industrial backwardness. He did not hold back his anti- imperialist feelings, as we can see from most of his verse. Here is a lancet-like four-liner.

dayaar-e maghrib mein rahne vaalo khuda ki basti dukaan nahien hai
khara jise tum samajh rahe ho vo ab zar- kam a'yyaar ho ga
tumhaari tahziib apne khanjar se aap hi khudkushi kare gi
jo shaakh-e naazuk p aashiyaana bane ga naa-paayedaar ho ga

People of the West, please remember
that God's creation is not a trading shop.
What you think as the reality
will prove to be fake and deceptive.
Your civilization will self-destruct
and commit suicide with its carver.
The nest you have built,
is on a fragile and brittle branch
would never be firm and stable.

It is generally believed that Iqbal's thinking underwent a radical shift after his travel to Europe and being a disciple of Professor R.A. Nicholson. He embraced Islamic theology and philosophy as a central theme of his poetry, emphasizing self-identity and self-assertion as the mark of a resurgent Islam. He wrote profusely in Persian. It is not commonly known that out of his almost 12,000 verses, more than 7,000 were written in Persian. They consist of seven collections, whereas there are mainly three collections in Urdu. One of them, titled *Bang-e Dara* is unquestionably his magnum opus. The Persian verse has three masnavis, of which *Asrar-e Khudi* and *Javed Nama* are considered to be the most accomplished. While *Baang-e Dara*, alluded to above, has quite a few alluring and heart-touching patriotic poems such as *Himalaya, Tarana-e Hindi, Naya Shivala, Tasveer-e Dard*, Swami Rama Tirtha, Ram, Nanak, and *Aftaab* based on *Gaayatri Mantra* – famous mantra from the Vedas. The book also contains excellent poems on Islamic resurgence such as *Khizr-e Rah, Masjid-e Qurtaba*, and *Zauq o Shauq*. *Ibliis ki Majlis-e Shura*. Even when the subject was the glory or fortification of Islam, Iqbal continued to reflect upon nationalist issues of the day. He did not hesitate to share his feelings of sadness about the atmosphere of defeatism in the country, especially the sufferings of the poor and the attitude of indifference of the ruling imperialists. Here are two signature selections, 'A Portrait of Despondency' from *Baang-e Dara* and 'A Ray of Hope' from *Zarb-e Kaliim*.

Tasveer-e Dard

nahien minnat kash-e taab-e shuniidan dastaan meri
khamoshi guftagu hai be-zabaani hai zabaan meri
ye dastuur-e zabaan bandi hai kaisa teri mehfil mein
yahaan to baat karne ko tarasti hai zabaan meri
rulaata hai tera nazzaara ae hindostaan mujh ko
k i'brat khez hai tera fasaana sab fasaanon mein
diya rona mujhe aisa k sab kuchh de diya goya
likha kilk-e azal ne mujh ko tere nauha khwaanon mein
vatan ki fiqr kar naadaan musiibat aane vaali hai
teri barbaadiyon ke mashvare hain aasmaanon mein
zara dekh us ko jo kuchh ho raha hai hone vaala hai
dhara kya hai bhala a'hd-e kuhan ki daastaanon mein
ye khaamoshi kahaan tak lazzat-e fariyaad paida kar
zamiin par tu ho aur teri sada ho aasmaanon mein
n samjho ge to mit jaao ge ae hindostaan vaalo
tumhaari daastaan tak bhi n ho gi daastaaanon mein
jalaana hai mujhe har sham'a-e dil ko soz-e pinhaan se
teri taariik raaton mein charaaghaan kar ke chhoruun ga
pirona ek hi tasbiih mein in bikhre daanon ko
jo mushkil hai to is mushkil ko aasaan kar ke chhoduun ga

A Portrait of Despondency

It is grim to gain patience to listen to my excruciating story.
Silence is like a conversation, and silence is my speech.
What is this situation of forced silence in your meeting place?
Here I yearn to say something, but I am forced to stay quiet.
This panorama, this view, O my India, makes me shed tears.
Your story is worth learning in all the stories out there.
When you gave me tears, you had given me all that I wished for.
The barge of eternity has placed me among your mourners.

O ignorant one!
Take care of your country as calamity is going to strike.
How to ruin you is the subject of conspiracies in the skies.
I implore you to think about what is happening and
what is about to happen.
What is there in the stories of the times gone by?
How long will this silence last?
Make your aspirations loud and clear.
You are on this earth, but your voice
should be heard in the skies.
If you don't understand the gravity of the situation,
O people of India,
you will run the risk of extinction.
Your story will not be found in the book of stories.
My companion, please spare me and let me deal with
the affairs of the heart because I will not rest
until the scar of love is made apparent.
It is my job to brighten every candle-like heart
with a hidden fire of mine.
I determined that I would illuminate all your nights.
The separate particles must be arranged in one rosary.
If this is difficult, I will make this difficult task easy for you.

Shua-e Ummiid[8]

suuraj ne diya apni shuaaon ko y paighaam
dunya hai ajab chiiz kabhi sub-h kabhi shaam
ik shokh kiran shokh misaal-e nig-h-e huur
aaraam se faarigh sifat-e jauhar-e siimaab
boli k mujhe rukhsat-e tanviir ata ho
jab tak n ho mashriq ka har ik zarra jahaan taab
chhoruun gi n main hind ki taariik faza ko
jab tak n uthein khwaab se mardaan-e garaan khwaab
khaavar ki ummiidon ka yahi khaak hai markaz
Iqbal ke ashkon se yahi khaak hai sairaab
is khaak se uthe hai voh ghawwaas-e ma 'ani
jin ke liye har bahr-e puraashob hai paayaab
but-khaane ke darvaaze p sota hai brahman
taqdiir ko rota hai musalmaan tah-e mahraab
mashriq se ho bezaar n maghrib se hazar kar
fitrat ka taqaaza hai k har shab ko sahar kar.

A Ray of Hope

The sun gave a message to its far-reaching rays.
This world is a strange place.

Sometimes morning, sometimes evening.
An audacious ray that was bright, bright like a houri's glance
not caring about rest, agitative like mercury.
imploring the sun to give her such power to brighten
until every particle of the orient starts to shine and sparkle.
I shall not forsake the darkness that has fallen upon India, and
the sons of the soil are sunk in slumber.
I must wake them up.
Hopes of the Orient depend on them.
Iqbal is imploring with his tears to saturate this land.
The Moon and the Pleiades derive their light from this land.
It has produced men of great thought and intuition
who could cross all hurdles that befell them.
But now the Brahman sleeps at the threshold of his temple, and
the Muslim inside the mosque bewails his fate!
Do not get entangled in this or that.
The call of the hour is to drive away from the darkness of night
and usher in a truly bright sunrise!

These poems are heart-rending, and they show the deeply nationalistic spirit of the poet. Nevertheless, Iqbal's mind was like the restive ray, truly mercurial, and it kept thinking and evolving. Maybe during his visits to Europe, he saw the resurgence of fascist governments and the cult of power at close quarters. These conditions might have influenced Iqbal as it suited his ideology of fortification of *self* and thoughts of pan-Islamism, so much so that a poet who at one stage said with heart-rending conviction.

> *pathar ki muuraton mein samjha hai tu khuda hai*
> *khaak-e vatan ka mujh ko har zarra devta hai*

> God resides in stone idols,
> it is what you believe.
> But every particle
> of the soil of this land
> is sacred to me.

Later declared in a poem called *Wataniyat* in *Baang-e Dara*:

> *in taazaa khudaaon mein bara sab se vatan hai*
> *jo pairaahan is ka hai voh mazhab ka kafan hai*

> Among the new gods that have lately arisen,
> the biggest is the *country*.
> Beware the mantle it wears.
> It is the death shroud of the religion!

Iqbal rejected the idea of separation of Church and State and insisted that the two should not be separated because it was against the spirit of Islam. Furthermore, due to the twists and turns of the British when they pitched one religion against the other, religion became the reason for the failure of the Round Table Conference in London. The British Government unilaterally declared the Communal Award in 1932. The Congress rejected it right away while the Muslim League hailed it. But the Award was declared law, and it was implemented right away. Iqbal welcomed it. The Award opened the door for division of the country. This was when Iqbal was in correspondence with Mohammad Ali Jinnah and was trying to convince him to accept the idea of the 'self-determination of the Muslim majority states' as outlined by him in his Allahabad Address.

Before moving to other contemporary poets, let's not forget to note and commend Iqbal's unforgettable short poems on Swami Rama Tirtha, Sri Ram, and Guru Nanak. Iqbal was an admirer of Swami Rama Tirtha. In 1904, one year before departing for London, Iqbal discovered the depths of Rumi's *Masnavi,* and he shared it with the Swami, while the latter introduced Iqbal to Vedanta. There was such a close relationship between the two that Iqbal wrote a heartfelt tribute to Swami Rama Tirtha.

Here are selected lines from beautiful short poems by Iqbal on Sri Ram and Guru Nanak:

> *hai ram ke vujuud par hindostaan ko naaz*
> *ahl-e nazar samajhte hain is ko imaam-e hind*

India is proud of Ram's existence.
Perceptive thinkers consider him
to be the splendid Spiritual Guide.

The extraordinary thing about Iqbal's poem about Guru Nanak is that he compares him with Buddha. He highlights the core theme of their teachings, namely, unity of existence and equality of humanity. Both had condemned the caste system of Brahmans, which was the bane of Hinduism. Iqbal succinctly alludes to ancient India not caring for the message of Buddha while it was hailed and accepted by far-off countries of the Far East. But after centuries, the same message was brought back by enlightened and blessed saints such as Guru Nanak. The belief in the absolute truth and the unity of mankind was rekindled, and it re-awakened the whole of India. The poet's words touch one's inner being with artistic subtleness and an undercurrent of unity of existence and the oneness of humankind.

> *qaum ne paighaam-e gautam ki zara parva n ki*
> *qadr pahchaani n apne gauhar-e yak dana ki*
> *barhaman sarshaar hai ab tak maye pindaar mein*
> *sham'e gautam jal rahi hai mehfil-e aghiyaar mein*
> *butkada phir baa'd muddat ke magar raushan huua*
> *nuur-e abraahiim se aazar ka ghar raushan hua*
> *phir uthii aakhir sadaa tauhiid ki panjaab se*
> *hind ko ik mard-e kaamil ne jagaaya khwaab se*

The nation did not care for the significance of Gautam's message.
They did not realize the true value of their own unique jewel.
The Brahman is intoxicated by the wine of power and stature.
The candle of Gautum's enlightenment is lighting others' gatherings.
The light of Ibrahim brightened the house of Azar.
The voice of unity of mankind was once again heard in the land of Punjab.
India was awakened from its slumber by an Exemplary Being.

It is remarkable how perceptive and inclusive Iqbal's creativity had been. Although Hasrat Mohani is the first communist poet of Urdu, we can see traces of socialist thought in Iqbal even before Hasrat and before the appearance of progressives. He is said to have written the following couplet in 1921.[9]

aashna apni haqiiqat se ho dehqaan zara
dana tu kheti bhi tu baraan bhi tu haasil bhi tu

Dear Farmer, get to know your reality.
You are the grain; you are the harvest,
you are the produce.

In his poem *Sarmaaya o Mehnat,* Iqbal explicitly addresses a laborer.

uth k ab bazm-e jahaan ka aur hi andaaz hai
mashriq o maghrib me tere daur ka aaghaaz hai

Rise and meet the new World Order!
Both in the East and the West
it is the beginning of a new era.

In one of longer poems, 'Ibliis Ki Majlis-e Shura,' that was included in his last collection, *Armaghan-e Hijaz* (1938), Iqbal refers to Marx as '*niist paighambar, valekin dar baghal daarad kitab,*' meaning he is not a prophet, but he holds a Book under his arm. In Islam, the sacred Quran is The Book, and Muslims are generally called *ahle Kitab*. In this context, the way Marx is alluded to is quite a tribute.

Let's now briefly take up some other poets in this period. Zafar Ali Khan (1873–1956) was born in Sialkot, and he received his bachelor's degree from Aligarh College. He was the owner and an editor of *Zamindar,* a famous Urdu daily newspaper from Lahore, and he was a staunch follower of Maulana Shibli for his views about social justice and love of the land. Here are some verses from his patriotic poetry.

naquus se gharaz hai n matlab azaan se hai
mujh ko agar hai i'shq to hindostaan se hai
tahziib-e hind ka nahien chashma agar azal
ye mauj-e rang rang phir aaii kahaan se hai
zarre mein gar tarap hai to is khaak-e paak se
suuraj mein raushni hai to is aasmaan se hai

It has nothing to do with the sound
of a gong or a call to the prayer.
If I'm in love, that love is reserved for India.
If the fountain of India's culture
was not found at the beginning of the cosmos,
then from where have these
waves of color come.
If there is a perturbation in a particle,
it comes from this sacred soil.
If there is shine in the sun,
it is derived from this sky.

About Hindu–Muslim unity, he wrote.

hindu jo shiir hon to musalmaan hon shakar
dono mein ittifaaq ka rishta barhaaye jaa

If Hindus are like milk,
Muslims should be the raw sugar.
The bonds of amity should be strengthened
between the two.

Hasrat Mohani (1875–1951) was an outstanding poet and activist. As mentioned earlier, he is given credit for coining the slogan *Inqilaab Zindabaad*, demanding complete independence at the Ahmedabad session of the Congress Party in 1921. In terms of his politics, Hasrat was not as straightforward as he should have been. He joined the Congress Party at an early age in 1904, but there were times when he broke ranks with Congress and supported the Muslim League. At the 1926 communist conference held in Kanpur, he read his presidential address, and as a result, he is treated as one of the founders of the Communist Party of India. He is known to have said.

n sarmaayadaaron ki nakhvat rahe gi
n hukkaam ka jor-e bejaa rahe ga
zamaana voh jald aane waala hai jis mein
kisi ka n mehnat p daava rahe ga

Neither the pride of capitalists will last long,
nor the oppression of the rulers will continue.
The time is coming very soon
when no one shall benefit
from another's labor.

He was a staunch supporter of the production of khadi (home-spun coarse cloth) and its use, and at one time, he ran a store in Kanpur selling khadi clothing. He was arrested several times for his anti-British activities. After the partition, he decided to stay in India. He was a member of the Constituent Assembly of India that drafted the Indian Constitution, but he did not sign it.

Hasrat's ghazal poetry, mostly written during his imprisonment, is highly romantic and a favorite of musicians. There are several ghazals where he also expressed his feelings for the freedom struggle and the ordeals of life inside the prison. Notice the *chakki ki mushaqqat* metaphor in the following couplet.

hai mashq-e sukhan jaari chakki ki mushaqqat bhi
kya turfa tamaasha hai Hasrat ki tabii'yat bhi

Laboring hard in prison, grinding flour
and composing ghazal couplets –
what a playful combination
for a strange poet called Hasrat.

And these two couplets.

apna sa shauq auron mein laayein kahaan se ham
ghabra gaaye hain be-dili-e ham-rahaan se ham
kuchh aisi duur bhi to nahien manzil-e muraad
lekin ye jab k chhuut chalein kaarvaan se ham

How can I fill others
with the same zeal that I have?
I am surprised by the delay
of fellow lazy travelers.
The destination that we seek
is within our reach.
But for us to succeed,
we have to break
ahead of the slow travelers.

And lastly, there is an excellent message for the freedom fighters.

ai k nijaat-e hind ki dil se hai tujh ko aarzu
himmat-e sar buland se yaas ka insidaad kar
qaul ko zaid o umar ke had se siva aham n jaan
raushani-e zamiir mein aql se ijtihaad kar
gair ki jid o jahd par takiya n kar k hai gunaah
koshish-e zaat-e khaas par naaz kar e'timaad kar

If India's freedom is your heart's desire,
you have to keep your spirit high,
and avoid the feeling of despair.
Do not take seriously what others say.
Let the light of your inner self
show you the way.
Do not rely too much on
what others do.
Keep the torch burning
and be proud of yourself!

The period during and after the First World War (1914–1924) saw the emergence of many new Urdu poets who became powerful voices of the protest. It included Josh Malihabadi (1898–1982), who was described by Ale Ahmad Suroor as a poet with great power of articulation and command over the language, though his verse mostly lacks depth. The rolling thunder of his anti-British agitational poetry is, however, representative of the politically turbulent tenor of the time. We shall examine Josh's work in detail in Chapter 10 of the book. The other poets from this era who deserve mention include Syed Sulaiman Nadvi (1884–1953), Waheeduddin Saleem (1869–1927), Niyaz Fatehpuri (1884–1966), Iqbal Suhail (1884–1955), Afsar Meeruthi (1895–1958), Ahmaq Phaphoondvi (1895–1957), Jigar Moradabadi (1890–1960), Hafeez Jalandhari (1900–1982), Anand Narayan Mulla (1901–1997), and Ravish Siddiqi (1909–1971). To this list, we can also add Shad Azimabadi (1846–1927), and Seemab Akbarabadi (1880–1951).

While the mainstream Congress Party was committed to the ideal of nonviolence in its freedom struggle, some nationalists used extremist methods. One name that stands out in this context is Ram Prasad Bismil (1897–1927), who was part of the aggressive revolutionary movement. He participated in Mainpuri and the Kakori conspiracies of 1918 and 1925, respectively, with his friend Ashfaq Ullah Khan (1900–1927). Both of them were hanged in Faizabad Jail in 1927. Ram Prasad Bismil wrote the following ghazal before his death, which became the critical verse to come out of the freedom struggle.

> sarfroshi ki tamanna ab hamaare dil mein hai
> dekhna hai zor kitna baazu-e qaatil mein hai
> vaqt aane par bata dein ge tujhe ai aasmaan
> ham abhi se kya bataayein kya hamaare dil mein hai
> khench kar laaii hai sab ko qatl hone ki ummiid
> aa'shqon ka aaj jamghat kuuch-a e qaatil mein hai
> main khara maqtal mein qaatil kah raha hai baar baar
> kya tamanna-e shahaadat bhi kisi ke dil mein hai
> ae shahiid-e mulk o miiat tere jazbon ke nisaar
> teri qurbaani ka charcha ghair ki mahfil mein hai[10]

The desire to sacrifice my life for my land
is supreme in my heart.
We must see how much force
is there in the arms of the murderer?
When the time comes,
we shall speak to you, Oppressor.
How can we tell you now
what is in our hearts.
I am standing at the gallows
and the murderer is saying
time and again:
Is there anyone ready
to be martyred?

> Those who are willing to die for the country
> I admire their courage and conviction.
> The talk of your valor and sacrifice
> is heard in the assembly of the oppressor.

The 1930s saw the rise of the Progressive Writers Movement. Urdu poetry witnessed the emergence of many talented poets, including Josh Malihabadi, Faiz Ahmed Faiz, Makhdoom Mohiuddin, Sahir Ludhianvi, Majaz, Ali Sardar Jafri, Jan Nisar Akhtar, Kaifi Azmi, Majrooh Sultanpuri, and many others who joined the ranks of nationalist poets. These national and progressive poets supported the freedom movement, but they also presented a dream of a new, postindependence India free of poverty, disease, caste discrimination, and maltreatment of women. That was when the whole country was echoing with the poetry of freedom and revolution. We shall examine their creative zeal and contribution in the next chapter.

Notes

1 Benjamin Zachariah, *Nehru* (New York: Routledge, 2004), p. 208.
2 Ali Jawad Zaidi, *Naghma-e Azadi* (Lucknow: Publications Bureau, 1957), p. 21.
3 Ehtisham Husain, *Tanqiid aur Amli Tanqiid* (Delhi: 1952), p. 280.
4 Abdur Razzaq Qureshi, ed., *Nawaa-e Aazaadi* (Bombay: Adabi Publishers, 1957), p. 161.
5 Bhishma, also known as Bhishma Pitamaha and Gangaputra Bhishma, is a character in the *Mahabharata*. He was blessed with a boon from his father that he could choose the time of his death. He died in the Kurukshetra War and while he was lying on his deathbed of arrows, he gave instructions to Yudhishitra.
6 This is considered to be one of the signature couplets of the poet.
7 A reference to Quranic Surah (108) Al-Kawther, a stream in paradise. The narration says that the water of the stream is whiter than milk and sweeter than honey.
8 Zaidi, p. 24.
9 Quraishi, p. 249.
10 This couplet is sourced from *Daily Bande Matram*, Lahore, 1929.

5

THE PROGRESSIVE AND NATIONALIST POETRY

The Urdu–Hindi controversy was uncalled for. All recognized the Urdu language's richness: it was a matter of pride for most people in UP, including Hindus, to be well-versed in Urdu. Love of Urdu poetry transcended class and religious boundaries in UP. Everybody enjoyed the pulsating ambiance of a *mushaira* (poets' gathering) when Hindu and Muslim poets well-versed in Urdu recited their compositions, poems, and *ghazals*, enthralling the audience. Urdu had become the language of culture and sophistication, and Urdu spoken in the Lakhnavi style uplifted one and all. No doubt emotionally, Urdu tended to strengthen Muslim solidarity, but Hindus shared the cultural ethos of the literature and philosophy expressed in Urdu over the generations. However, with the growth of separatism, especially with the Aligarh movement's surge, the Muslim intelligentsia sought to promote an Islamic political identity, creating antipathy towards the Hindu community. Hindu enthusiasts also, many of them well-known leaders of the Congress, were responsible for injecting bitterness into the controversy.[1]

D. N. Panigrahi

Starting with 1935 and up to when India gained independence is the period associated with the birth and growth of the progressive writers' movement. This movement widened and enriched the boundaries of Urdu literature and shook its roots with new creative contributions. The progressives put their faith in socialistic principles that found strength in the success of the revolution in Russia in 1917 and the birth of the Soviet Union, a state dedicated to implementing these principles. By the third decade of the twentieth century, organizations devoted to promoting laborers and farmers' interests had gained strength. They were instrumental in creating a new awareness in these groups about their sufferings and denying their rights by the colonial regime.

DOI: 10.4324/9781003360841-6

Allama Iqbal (1877–1938) was the first Urdu poet who felt the miseries of the working classes. He wrote a classic poem *Khizr-e Rah* which, according to Professor Ale Ahmad Suroor, deserves the same regard that is accorded *New Testament* as the beginning of the New Age. In a section of the poem titled 'A Song of the Angels,' Iqbal directly addresses the labor class and gives them the message of positive action and empowerment.

> *utho meri duniya ke ghariibon ko jaga do*
> *kaakh-e umaraa ke dar o diivaar hila do*
> *jis khet se dahqaan ko muyassar n ho rozi*
> *us khet ke har khosha-e gandum ko jala do*

Poor of the World, wake up!
Shake the doors and windows of the rich and powerful.
The field that doesn't provide a living wage to the farmer,
burn every sheaf of wheat of that field.

Hasrat Mohani (1875–1951) was the first Urdu poet who had accepted the socialistic worldview even before the progressive movement. During the first conference of the Communist Party of India held in Kanpur in 1926, Hasrat chaired the reception committee. In his address, he presented a detailed enunciation of the principles of communism. But most of his life, he used poetry as a shield to promote his sympathy for the working classes. For instance, in one of his couplets, he prophesied the coming age when only wealth producers will fully claim wealth rewards.

> *zamaana vo jald aane vaala hai jis mein*
> *kisi ka n mehnat p daa'va rahe ga*

The progressive movement formally came into being in 1936. Its declaration included leading writers such as Munshi Premchand, Moulvi Abdul Haq, Dr. Abid Husain, Firaq Gorakhpuri, Ali Abbas Husaini, Qazi Abdul Ghaffar, Ahmed Ali, Mahmooduz Zafar, Rasheed Jahan, and Majnun Gorakhpuri. The movement's message spread quickly, and writers and poets, both new and old, became its members. Despite some hiccups and problems, the movement influenced much beyond its known boundaries in the beginning.

Since its inception, love of humanity, patriotism, anti-colonial bias, and the love of freedom had been abiding values associated with Urdu literature. During the mid and late thirties, the upcoming War's danger became apparent, and Fascism had raised its ugly head in Europe. Progressives felt that it was a time that democratic aspirations and yearning for India's freedom needed greater focus. These writers were ready to enter the fight for freedom, and they were prepared to make sacrifices that came with that determination. The new writing expressed support for the changes that were taking place in the lives of ordinary people. In essence, what they were saying could be paraphrased in the following words:

> We, the progressive writers, are the custodians of the country's best traditions. We accept those values because of the respect of our humanistic

and pluralistic traditions, and we own them fully. We shall support those endeavors to make our country a better place for all its citizens. We want that the fundamental problems faced by our country should become the main thrust of the new literature. We realize that our challenges are combating hunger, poverty, social backwardness, and enslavement by a colonial power.

The founders of the progressive movement were symbols of what was best in thought and creativity, and they showcased the best ideas for the country's future. They believed that we could end the division between rich and poor. If we are a free country, we can generate wealth with help from science and technology. We can build a society where all human beings can have equal opportunities for progress. The primary responsibility of literature is to create a climate for the emergence of order.

This new vision was best described in the address Munshi Premchand (1880–1936) delivered as president of the first conference of the progressive writers' movement held in Lucknow. He said:

> When we adopt the global point of view, we cannot accept an economic order that enslaves thousands for one entity's benefit. Then our self-worth and humanity would revolt against oppression and colonial exploitation. Then we would not be satisfied by simply putting our best ideas on a piece of paper. We would rather expend our effort to create and shape a new order that does not negate our love for beauty, happiness, self-worth, and humanitarianism. An artist does not live for his comfort, recreation, and for being the center of attraction in a circle of admirers. Let us not degrade him. He is the reality that walks behind forces such as freedom and politics; he is the torch symbol that brightens the face of reality and human values for everyone to see.[2]

Unfortunately, Munshi Premchand died soon after this conference. Encouraged by the participation of leading poets like Josh Malihabadi and Firaq Gorakhpuri in the movement, a whole new generation of younger poets was sucked into it. These included names like Makhdoom, Sahir Ludhianvi, Sardar Jafri, Jan Nisar Akhtar, Ali Jawad Zaidi, Majaz, Jazbi, Masood Akhtar Jamal, Akhtar Ansari, Kaifi Azmi, Majrooh, and Salam Machhli-Shahri. Later, Faiz Ahmad Faiz also joined the movement after he was influenced by the revolutionary ideas of Rasheed Jahan and Mahmooduz Zafar.

Because these poets were young, they were also romantic due to their vibrant youth. This is how Sardar Jafri described them:

> These were serious folks, who were fully aware of their social responsibilities, and that was why their poetic outcomes reflected a high level of thoughtfulness. They revealed different levels of personal maturity, life experiences, and patterns of thought. Some of them were followers of

Gandhi's non-violence approach. Some considered Nehru as their idol. Some were communists. Some had little interest in social affairs. But they were united in one thing: they were ashamed of the country's enslavement, and they were in search of a way to reach the beautiful destination of their dreams - freedom.[3]

It was the time of great unrest. Political freedom had become a call for economic freedom because of the greater participation of trade unions and farmers' organizations in the struggle. India was getting ready to go head-to-head against the bulwark of British imperialism. The Government of India Act 1935 increased provincial autonomy, and six provinces were given bicameral legislatures. Elections based on separate electorates were held in 1937 and 1946, but these measures did not create peace and stability. Zafar Ali Khan, Editor, *Daily Zamindar*, Lahore, dismissed these reforms as a paper tiger. Other poets, including Josh Malihabadi, expressed similar sentiments. The Indian National Congress succeeded in getting an absolute majority in five provinces, but there was strong pushback from the Muslim League with a heavy dose of communalism.

The Second World War started in 1939, and the Viceroy, without consulting the legislative assembly, announced India's participation in the War. This prompted Congress ministers to resign. The Congress Working Committee asked the government if it could assure Indians that the country would be freed after the end of the War, then Congress might support the war effort, but its plea was ignored, and no assurance was offered. On the War front, Nazis were having great success. This prompted Sardar Jafri (1913–2000) to declare the end of colonialism.

hil chuka hai takht-e shaahi gir chuka hai sar se taaj
har qadam par dagmagaya ja raha hai saamraaj

The Royal Throne has been shaken as also the Crown.
Imperialism is wobbling every step of the way.

The Congress Party had refused to support the war effort. The progressives followed the nationalist sentiment while boycotting the War, calling it the 'War of Imperialism.' But when the Nazis attacked the Soviet Union and the British supported the Soviets, the progressives reversed their stance, and overnight, the 'War of Imperialism' became the 'War of Independence.' This exposed the weakness of progressives as they were seen as more devoted to ideology than to India's national interest.

In another disturbing development, the Japanese forces from the East had reached Malaya and Burma, and they were knocking on India's door. The British Cabinet sent an official delegation, known as Cripps Mission (headed by Sir Stafford Cripps), to India to consult with the Muslim League and Congress leaders. Sir Cripps worked to keep India loyal to the British war effort in exchange for a promise of elections and full self-government once the War was over. He discussed the proposals after consultation with the Indian leaders and published them. Both the parties rejected his recommendations, and no middle way was found, and the mission failed. The Congress Party moved toward the Quit India movement, further intensifying its opposition to the war effort.

The British imprisoned the entire Congress Party leadership for the duration of the War. Jinnah and the Muslims, to whom Cripps had offered the right to opt-out of a future Union, supported the war effort, and thus, in the opinion of commentators, he gained in stature in the British eyes. The Indian masses were greatly disappointed, and the communal elements found another opportunity to spread their virus of hatred. But the country had awakened. The Indian people spoke with one voice in favor of total independence. The poets' imagination was also aflame, and they sang passionate songs of the love of the land and desire for freedom from the British.

The Urdu language showed its best side in coming up with poetry that was soon turned into songs for people during their marches. Josh Malihabadi (1898–1956), an influential senior progressive poet and a leading voice of the age, also regarded as Poet of the Revolution (*Shaa'yir-e Inqilaab*), was a prolific writer who belonged to a family that had produced many poets and writers. As an editor of the magazine *Kaleem*, he wrote articles advocating India's independence. Because of the richness, flow, and thunder of his voice, he gained great popularity and respectability. Prime Minister Nehru was among his admirers. Here are a few lines from his passionate address to the East India Company (*East India Company ke Farzandon ke Naam*).[4]

> *khair aie saudaagro ab hai to bas is baat mein*
> *vaqt ke farmaan ke aage jhuka do gardanein*
> *ik kahaani vaqt likkhe ga naye mazmuun ki*
> *jis ki surkhi ko zaruurat hai tumhaare khuun ki*
> *vaqt ka farmaan apna rukh badal sakta nahien*
> *maut tal sakti hai ab farmaan tal sakta nahien*

Ye merchants and traders! It boils down to only one thing.
You bow your heads in front of the time's declaration.
Time will write a story about your exploits.
The red lettering of the headline needs your blood.
Time's proclamation cannot change its direction.
You could escape death, but not the time's thrust.

Firaq Gorakhpuri (1896–1982) was another leading voice of the progressives. He was born in a family that valued cultural roots and Kayastha traditions. He was a high-achievement student who gained mastery over Sanskrit, Persian, and Urdu early. He earned his master's degree in English and spent nearly all his life as an English professor at Allahabad University. He was selected for the Indian Civil Service, but he gave it up to join the freedom movement. He was imprisoned along with Jawaharlal Nehru, which turned into a lifelong friendship between the two of them. One outstanding literary achievement of Firaq as a poet was his effort to bring Urdu and Hindi closer. He was inspired by Sanskrit *rasa* theory of aesthetics and India's spiritual heritage, and these influences are noticeable in his writing. Firaq received multiple honors, including Padma Bhushan (1968), Jnanpith Award (1969), and Sahitya Akademi Fellowship (1970). Here are excerpts from Firaq's poem *Aazaadi* in which he expresses strong emotional support for India's freedom.[5]

> *meri sada hai gul-e sham'a-e shaam-e aazaadi*
> *suna raha huun dilon ko payaam-e aazaadi*
> *lahu vatan ke shahiidon ka rang laaya hai*
> *uchhal raha hai zamaane mein naam-e aazaadi*
> *faza mein jalte dilon se dhuaan sa auth-ta hai*
> *are ye sub-he ghulaami! ye shaam-e aazaadi!*
> *faza-e shaam o sahar mein shafaq jhalakti hai*
> *k jaam mein hai mai-e laala faam-e aazaadi*

I lend my voice to the rose-like candle of freedom's evening.
I am presenting to the hearts of the listeners the message of freedom.
The blood of the martyrs has given us its reward.
The echo of freedom, its name, is being heard everywhere.
Our surroundings are filled with the smoke of burning hearts.
Bemoan this morning of slavery! Hail this evening of freedom!
In the environs of the morning and evening, we find twilight.
The spirit of freedom that has the color of tulips is in our wine glasses.

Asrar-ul-Haq Majaz Lakhnavi (1911–1955), known for his highly attractive voice delivery and charismatic personality, was quite forthright in his poem 'An Address to the Foreign Guest' telling the foreign occupiers bluntly to find their way and quit the country. Here are some excerpts.[6]

> *musaafir bhaag vaqt-e bekasi hai*
> *tere sar par ajal mandla rahi hai*
> *teri jebon mein hain sone ke tore*
> *yahaan har jeb khaali ho chuki hai*
> *ye aa'lam ho gaya hai muflisi ka*
> *k rasm-e mezbaani uth chuki hai*
> *n de zaalim fareb-e chaara saazi*
> *ye basti tujh se ab tang aa chuki hai*
> *munaasib hai k apna rasta le*
> *vo kashti dekh saahil se lagi hai*

Intruders, you better quit this land.
It is the time of your helplessness.
Death is hovering over your head.
In your pocket are gold bars, but

every pouch here has been emptied.
The state of our poverty has reached a stage
where we cannot oblige any outsider.
Oppressor, it is time you stop playing
your deceitful tricks and games.
The people of this land are now sick
and tired of your ploys and schemes.
It is proper that you find your way
as we have had enough of you.
Look there; your boat has already arrived.

Shamim Karhani (1913–1975)[7] earned fame for the lyrical quality of his poetry. Look at the following couplet.

tha zabanon par ye naa'ra 'aashiyaan ko chhor do.'
'chhor do aie ghaasibo! hindostaan ko chhor do'

All tongues had this slogan: 'Let our nest be free.'
'Leave it, oppressors! Leave India and go away.'

Shamim Karhani published a collection of poems called *Raushan Andhera* (Luminous Darkness) in the early forties. He had a special knack for conveying a powerful message in simple language. Let us look at selected verses from two of his poems.

Tuufaan

lo aaj vo tuufaan aa hi gaya
thi aas hamein jis tuufaan ki lo aaj vo tuufaan aa hi gaya
mazluum ki aahon ka baadal zaalim ke jahaan par chha hi gaya
parbat se raas kumaari tak khuunien parcham lahra hi gaya
lo aaj vo tuufaan aa hi gaya

Storm
Look, today, after all, that storm has come.
The storm we were waiting for.
The cloud of the sighs of the victims
has covered the world of the oppressor.
From the high mountains to the Cape of Comorin,
the bloodied banner has been unfurled.
Look, today, after all, the storm has come.

Here is a stanza from a second poem called 'A Portrait of the Mansion of Gold' (*Qasr-e Zar Nigaar*).

hayaat ko sharaar par tapa rahi hai zindagi
hari bhari javaaniyaan jala rahi hai zindagi
sitaare tor tor kar luta rahi hai zindagi

bane hue hain jashn-e qatl gaah ki bahaar
bana rahe hain zindagi ka qasr-e zar nigaar ham

Life is burning existence on hot coals.
Life is blazing young people who are at their prime.
Life is picking out stars and making them glow more and more.
The celebrations have been turned into a spring of the execution places.
Life has become a golden mansion of freedom lovers.

Makhdoom Mohiuddin (1908–1969), a Hyderabad poet who was also active in politics and was a Member Legislative Assembly of the State, on whose untimely death Faiz had lamented, wrote a lyrical poem called 'East' in which he not only talked about the desperate situation in the country, but he also included a message of regeneration and progress for the people. Here are a few couplets from that poem.[8]

jhar chuke hain dast o baazu jis ke us mashriq ko dekh
khelti hai saans siine mein mariiz-e diq ko dekh
ek qab-ristaan jis mein hon n haan kuchh bhi nahien
ik bhatakti ruuh hai jis ka makaan koi nahien
is zamiin-e maut pardarda ko dhaaya jaaye ga
ik naii duniya naya aa'dam banaya jaaye ga

Look at the East that has lost its hands and arms.
They are acutely suffering patients who can hardly breathe.
There is nothing there except a vast burial ground.
There is one wandering spirit that has no home.
We shall demolish this reign of death from this land.
We shall bring to life a new world and a new Adam.

Makhdoom is also known for his long poem titled 'Freedom of the Land' with a popular refrain *kaho hindostaan ki jai,* which talks about the inevitability of India's freedom. Here are selected lines from that often-sung poem.

kaho hindostaan ki jai
kaho hindostaan ki jai
kaho hindostaan ki jai
qasam hai khuun se seinche hue rangiin gulistaan ki
qasam hai khuun-e dahqaan ki qasam khuun-e shahidaan ki
ye mumkin hai k duniya ke samundar khushk ho jaaein
ye mumkin hai k darya bahte bahte thak ke so jaaein
zamiin-e paak ab na-paakiyon ko dho nahien sakti
vatan ki shama-e aazaadi kabhi gul ho nahien sakti
kaho hindostaan ki jai
kaho hindostaan ki jai

Hail India! Victory to India!
Hail India! Victory to India!

Hail India! Victory to India!
I take an oath in the name of this colorful garden,
nourished by the blood of martyrs.
An oath in the name of the blood of the peasants.
An oath in the name of the blood of martyrs.
It is possible that one-day oceans of the world would dry up.
The rivers may go to sleep, being too tired.
This land is now refusing to purify the impure anymore.
The flame of freedom of this land can never be doused.
Hail India! Victory to India!
Hail India! Victory to India!
Hail India! Victory to India!

Sikandar Ali Wajd (1914–1983) emphasized the importance of intense determination. He challenged people lost in worldly pursuits to sacrifice for the country and announced the onset of a new dawn of freedom. Wajd wrote poetry filled with a desire for independence while expressing people's sufferings under the control of an oppressive regime.

bazm-e taariik-e vatan ko raushni darkaar hai
shama' ki maanind jalne ka zamaana aa gaya
ho gaya hai aag tap tap kar ghariibon ka lahu
in salaasil ke pighilne ka zamaana aa gaya
ahl-e zindaan ko mubaarak ho faroghe sub-h-e nau
qaid-e zillat se nikalne ka zamaana aa gaya

The darkness of the country's meeting places needs light.
Time has come to burn like a candle.
The blood of the poor is sweltering like fire
after being exposed to the heat for a long time.
A time has come when these heavy chains must melt.
Felicitation to the prisoners for the new dawn!
A time has come to break open the prison of indignity!

Jigar Moradabadi (1890–1960) was well-known for the recitational musicality of his ghazal poetry. His work was mostly reflective of popular love themes. Yet, we see some couplets where he shared his agony about the political differences, disunity, and bloodshed in the country, but he did this in a lyrical (*taghazzul* laced) style.[9]

[1]

kabhi shaakh o sabza o barg par kabhi ghuncha o gul o khaar par
main chaman mein chaahe jahan rahuun mera haq hai fasl-e bahaar par

Sometimes on a branch, on the green, on a tree,
sometimes on a bud, on a rose, on a thorn –
I may live in any part of the garden,

it is my right to claim everything
that the spring has produced.

[2]

kaante kisi ke haq mein kisi ko gul o samar
kaya khuub ehtimaam-e gulistaan hai aaj kal
hai zakhm-e kaayenaat jo hindu hai in dinon
hai daagh-e zindagi jo musalmaan hai aaj kal

These days, there is nothing but thorns in one's life,
while another gets roses and garden produce.
What a way to arrange distribution in the garden!
The Hindu is a wound on the face of existence,
while the Muslim is a smudge on life's countenance.

[3]

koi ye chupke se un se puuchhe kahaan gaaye aap ke vaa'de
nichorta hai lahu ghariibon ka dast-e sarmaaya daar ab bhi
sifaarishein zaalimon ke haq mein payaam-e rahmat bani hui hain
nahien hai shaaista-e samaa'yat dukhi dilon ki pukaar ab bhi

Someone should ask them:
where have your promises gone?
The hand of a money lender is still
squeezing poor peoples' blood.
Commendations continue to be for oppressors
messages of merciful action.
No one treats cries of hearts filled with misery
gently and humanely.

Tilok Chand Mehroom (1887–1966) has a special place among freedom-loving
poets. He conveyed strong determination and a clear vision of an independent
India in his verse. Even in the most pessimistic moments of the freedom struggle,
he did not lose hope. He continued to present a bright candle of optimism, indi-
cating that the goal was within peoples' reach. Let us look at a few lines from his
poem 'The Flame of Hope.'

jalva-e sub-h yaqiini hai shab-e taar ke baa'd
daur-e iqbaal hai har qauom ko adbaar ke baa'd
jahd-e hasti se n ghabra k numaayaan ho ga
daura-e amn o amaan garmi-e paikaar ke baa'd

The beauty of dawn will indeed manifest
after the darkness of night.
Each nation gains prosperity after a period of adversity.
Don't be apprehensive about the daily struggles of life.
There shall be a period of peace when our battle is finished.

Ale Ahmad Suroor (1911–2002) made a significant impact by his scholarship, but he was also a poet who was convinced that the end of the freedom struggle was near. He presented a hopeful scenario in one of his couplets.

isi ummid pe baitha huun sar-e raah-guzaar
hijr ki raat hui hai to sahar bhi ho gi

I am sitting at the top of the way with this hope
that dawn always follows the night of suffering.

Ahmed Nadeem Qasmi (1916–2006) was a respected poet and a short story writer based in Lahore. He was known for encouraging new writers struggling in their younger years. Prefaces that he wrote for the two most influential books in modern Urdu literature, *Naqsh-e Faryadi* by Faiz Ahmed Faiz and *Talkhiyaan* by Sahir Ludhianvi, were considered powerful endorsements and brought great success to these poets after partition. Qasmi also supported Manto in his troubled years. He mentored Parveen Shakir and the talented Indian poet Gulzar, from Dina, Jhelum, the hometown of Qasmi. Here is a beautiful stanza about a country's leap to freedom from one of his poems.

muvarrikhon se kaho khuun mein daboein qalam
badal chuka hai iraade mein iztiraab apna
khizaan rahe k bahaar aaye har ch baadabaad
ab ik zaqand ka hai muntazir shabaab apna

Tell the historians
they should dip their fingers in blood.
Our restlessness has been transformed.
Either the autumn stays, or spring comes,
youth is looking for a single leap to reach the goal.

Jan Nisar Akhtar (1914–1976), a romantic ghazal poet who married Majaz's sister Safia and was the father of Javed Akhtar, one of today's significant progressive poets, brought his skills and sensibility to the songs of the liberation movement. He is known for his two-volume selection of Urdu patriotic poetry, *Hindustan Hamara*. Here are two stanzas from one of his popular lyrics.[10]

main un ke giit gaata huun
main un ke giit gaata huun
jo shaane par baghaavat ka a'lam le kar nikalte hain
kisi zaalim hakumat ke dharakte dil p chalte hain
main un ke giit gaata huun
main un ke giit gaata huun
jo aazaadi ki devi ko lahu ki bhent dete hain
sadaaqat ke liye jo haath mein talvaar lete hain
main un ke giit gaata huun
main un ke giit gaata huun

I sing songs of those
I sing songs of those
Who trample the hearts of the oppressors
carrying the banner of revolt on their shoulders
I sing songs of those
I sing songs of those
Who offer their blood to the goddess of freedom
Who carry swords in their hand in defense of what is true
I sing songs of those
I sing songs of those

Jan Nisar Akhtar showed his mastery over the ghazal genre in a composition that uses innovative metaphors to delineate a new role for the wine-house and the wine-server in the context of the freedom struggle.[11]

ye kis ne khatkhataaya aaj maikhaane ka darvaaza
har ik maikash yakayak be-piiye barham utha saaqi
ye kaise mai ke badle khuun chhalka tere shiishe se
ye kaise saaz se ik naghma-e maatam utha saaqi
baghaavat ki havaayein chal uthien shaayad gulistaan mein
ye paimaane ulat saaqi ye jaam-e jam utha saaqi
jo mumkin ho to tu bhi aaj rangiin jaam ke badle
lahu ke rang mein duuba hua parcham utha saaqi

Who knocked
at the door of the tavern?
Every drinker was vexed and left
without taking a sip, Saqi.
What kind of blood bounced
up and down in your goblet?
Why did a mournful melody arise
from your instrument, Saqi?
The winds of revolt arise and
are blowing in the garden.
Why not place the goblets upside down,
including those that Jamshed used.
If possible, even you should carry
in place of a drink —
a flag dipped in the color of blood, Saqi.

Ali Sardar Jafri (1913–2000) strengthened the tone and tenor of revolutionary poetry, and as a result, he added depth to the earlier attempts at this genre during the 1930s. He also showed courage in choosing topics that generated a strong reaction from the rulers. Let us look at a few lines from the poem that he called 'Freedom' (*Aazaadi*).[12]

puuchhta hai tu k kab aati huun main
god mein naakaamiyon ki parvarish paati huun main
raqs karti hain ishaaron par mere maut o hayaat
dekhti rehti huun main har vaqt nabz-e kaayenaat
jab kisaanon ki nigaahon se tapakta hai hiraas
phuutne lagti hai jab mazduur ke zakhmon se baas
tafriqqa parta hai jab duniya mein nasl o rang ka
le ke main aati huun parcham inqilaab o jang ka

You are asking me: when do I come?
I grow in the lap of failures and tumults.
Life and death both dance looking at my cues.
I continue to look at the pulse of the universe.
When peasants shed tears of sufferings from their eyes,
when wounds of laborers start to rot and bleed and
when fights break out over matters of caste and color,
then I come carrying the banner of revolution and War.

Majrooh Sultanpuri (1919–2000) was a significant poet of the progressive movement and a dominant voice among Bombay cinema's lyric poets. His father was
a police officer who decided to send him to a madrasa for traditional education
instead of a modern school. After completing his initial education, he was told to
be a *hakim* of indigenous medicine. He was not having much success as a *hakim*.
One evening he participated in a mushaira, and as a novice, he recited a ghazal
that he had composed. He presented it with a lilt, and that was a great success.
After that, there was no looking back. A prominent ghazal writer of the age, Jigar
Moradabadi, accepted him as a disciple and later introduced him to the film world.
He brought with him poetical creativity because he had a gift for musical sensibility. He was a perfectionist and sparse writer. His only collection of poetry, *Ghazal,*
was published from Anjuman Taraqqi-i Urdu, Aligarh in 1953. It was repub-
lished many times but with a few additions. Even after joining the progressives,
he never wrote in other genres except the ghazal. He received the highest honor
of the film world, the Dadasaheb Phalke Award, in 1993. Some of his couplets
became watchwords in the progressive and nationalist circles. Here are some:
[1]

main akela hi chala tha jaanib-e manzil magar
log saath aate gaye aur kaarvaan banta gaya

I started my voyage
towards the goal, all alone,
but people kept coming, and
it became a mighty caravan.
[2]

sutuun-e daar pe rakhte chalo saron ke charaagh
jahaan talak ye sitam ki siyaah raat chale

Keep offering your heads
on the hanging post
until this night of darkness
turns into dawn.

[3]

rok sakta hai hamein zindaan-e bala kya Majrooh
ham to aavaaz hain diivaar se chhan jaate hain

Majrooh, will the prison ramparts
dare to stop me?
I am the voice that filters
through the stone walls.

[4]

mujhe sehl ho gaien manzilein vo hava ke rukh bhi badal gaye
tera haath haath mein aa gayaa k charaagh raah mein jal gaye

The struggle for freedom and change
became easier for me
the moment you held my hand and
the lamps lighted up all the way.

Kaifi Azmi (1919–2002) was born in village Mizwaan, in Azamgarh district in Uttar Pradesh. He started writing ghazals at an early age, and as a result, he received many invitations to recite his ghazals at mushairas. He abandoned his studies to join the Quit India movement in 1942 and joined the Communist Party of India in 1943. Soon after, Kaifi was recognized as a significant poet in the Progressive Writers Movement. Kaifi also earned fame and admiration for his leadership in organizing workers' unions in the textile mills. He wrote lyrics for dozens of films, but he is most remembered for his song *'kar chale hum fida jan o tan sathiyo - ab tumhaare havaale watan saathiyo'* for *Haqiqat*, a 1964 movie about Indo-China War. He also wrote *Heer Ranjha*, a 1970 film, entirely in verse, which no other Urdu–Hindi poet has succeeded in doing. He received Padma Shri Award for his literary contributions and Sahitya Akademi Award for his collection *Awaara Sajde*. Kaifi wrote the following poem, *Makan* (Home), which contains a rich metaphoric message to India's people to arise and reclaim their homeland.[13]

aaj ki raat bahut garm hava chalti hai
aaj ki raat n footpaath p niind aaegi
sab utho main bhi uthuun tum bhi utho tum bhi utho
koi khirki isi divaar mein khul jaaegi
ye zamiin tab bhi nigalne pe aamaada thi
paanv jab tuuti shaakhon se utaare ham ne
haath dhalte gae sanche mein to thakte kaise
naqsh ke baa'd nae naqsh nikhaare ham ne
ki ye diivaar buland, aur buland, aur buland

baam o dar aur, zara aur sanvaare ham ne
aandhiyaan tor liyaa karti thiin sham'on ki lavein
jar diye is liye bijli ke sitaare ham ne
ban gaya qasr to pahre pe koi baith gaya
so rahe khaak pe ham shorish-e-taamiir liye
apni nas nas mein liye mehnat-e paiham ki thakan
band aankhon mein usi qasr ki tasviir liye
din pighalta hai usi tarah saron par ab tak
raat aankhon mein khatakti hai siyaah tiir liye
aaj ki raat bahut garm hava chalti hai
aaj ki raat na footpaath pe niind aaegi
sab utho main bhi uthuun tum bhi utho tum bhi utho
koi khirki isi diivaar mein khul jaaegi

The bellowing hot wind is streaming tonight.
Tonight, I shall not get any sleep on the footpath.
All arise, I will rise, you should rise too.
A window will open on this wall.
This land was determined to swallow us
when we brought down our feet from the broken branches.
How could our hands get tired while we were being molded?
We got new engravings after the old ones perished.
The walls got higher and higher.
We embellished our roofs and doors.
Whirlwinds used to break the flicker of our candles'
and that's why we set luminous stars for ornamentation.
When the mansion was ready, then someone came to occupy it.
In the tumult that followed, we went to sleep on the bare ground
keeping the hope alive for reclamation and reconstruction.
In every vein, we retained the weariness of constant hard work,
keeping the image of the same mansion in front of our closed eyes.
Days come and go on our heads in the same old manner,
and the night pinches our eyes with its black arrows.
The bellowing hot wind is streaming tonight.
Tonight, I shall not get any sleep on the footpath.
All arise, I will rise, you should rise too.
A window will open on this wall.

Sahir Ludhianvi (1921–1980) was born in a landlord family near Ludhiana town. His father had all the bad habits of wealthy landlords and had earned some notoriety marrying nearly a dozen times. Sahir's mother, Sardar Begum, who was frustrated about the family degeneration that did not value education for its only child, left her husband and came to live with her brother in Ludhiana. There was an extended custody battle amid severe financial constraints, but his mother stayed focused on her goal of letting her son attend a high school and college in Ludhiana.

Without completing his undergraduate degree, Sahir went to Lahore and published his first poetry collection *Talkhiyaan* in 1944. It shook the literary world, and Sahir soon earned a place among other leading poets of the Progressive Writers' Movement. *Talkhiyaan* remains, until today, one of the most popular collections of Urdu poetry. After partition, Sahir settled in Bombay and earned great fame as a film lyricist. Sahir's great appeal lies in his romantic poetry. Still, he also wrote several revolutionary poems in intent, which were addressed to Indian masses, inspiring them to join the freedom movement. Sahir was awarded Padma Shri in 1971, and a postage stamp in his memory was issued in 2013.[14]

Sahir wrote a short poem titled Blessed Moment (*Lamha-e Ghanimat*) that aimed to highlight a war that was taking place between imperialists and the fascist forces, leading to destruction on a vast scale on both sides. Also, within the imperialist camp, there were ideological divisions. 'Men are arguing in old gambling houses. Heavy cold chains are looking rusted. Breathe, it is a blessed moment.' The poet's message was simple: do not worry, oppressed masses, because oppressors are suffering in their way, and possibly this would be good news for you.

muskara ai zamiin-e tiira o taar
sar utha ai dabi hui makhluuq
dekh voh maghribi ufaq ke qariib
aandhiyaan pech o taab khaane lagiin
aur puraane qimaar khane mein
kohna shaatir baham ulajhne lage
koi teri taraf nahien nigraan
y giraanbaar sard zanjiirein
zang khurda hain aahani hi sahi
aaj mauq'a hai tuut sakti hain
fursat-e yak nafas ghanimat jaan
sar utha ai dabi makhluuq

Smile, my motherland covered in darkness and misery.
Raise your head, O oppressed masses.
Look near the horizon towards the West,
where winds look like a whirling vortex.
Men inside old gambling houses
are arguing like seasoned chess players,
and no one is caring for you.
These heavy old chains —
Maybe heavy, maybe of gritty metal
There is a chance that they can break today.
Breathe deeply; it is the opportune moment, dear friend!
Raise your head, my oppressed masses
You can get up and set yourself free!

The progressive writers and poets achieved distinction in widening the boundaries of patriotic feelings for the country. As an ideological departure, they encouraged their readers to think in a nonreligious manner about the day's significant social and political issues. With their opposition to religious fanaticism and sectarianism, they spoke against restrictions imposed on peoples' lives by the traditional caste system and inter-religious differences. Their great success came from building sustainable relationships with organizations supporting causes dear to farmers and peasants. Urdu poetry, as a result, gained new stature, and its popularity reached new heights. One facet of Urdu poetry that appealed to the masses was its effort to combine patriotism with romanticism. This new thematic approach touched both heads and hearts. On the one side, this poetry was a cry against injustice and a call for freedom; on the other, it was about love between men and women and between people belonging to different communities. The poets invented new metaphors and idioms. The talk about the dawn in the jailhouse or the chime and jingle of chains was poised by references to the beloved's cloud of tresses, intoxicated eyes, or her rose-like lips.

During the first five to seven years, the progress made had a significant impact. These writers achieved success, but they faced some hurdles too. Some inner tensions and jealousies were unhelpful. The movement passed through many beds of roses and numerous thorn-filled deserts. There were instances where someone like Sardar Jafri, who was associated with the movement since its inception, tried to tell other writers what they should or should not write. He also came up with an imposed poetics of false distinction between 'desire-based romanticism' and 'revolutionary-romanticism,' which was not productive or inspiring. In the poet's mind, these distinctions carried no weight. They wrote what their hearts dictated, and they did not like diktats or imposed agendas.

We should also mention that political poetry written by Josh, Chakbast, and Zafar Ali Khan was massive on patriotic sentiments. Its primary purpose was to shake up nation's conscience. That is why it had an 'impulsive tone' that was often filled with tumult and commotion. But the leading progressive poets, because of their innovative metaphors and inherent romanticism, softened the tone without lessening the impact that words had on peoples' psyche.

Before we close this saga of struggle for freedom and Urdu poetry's intricate and entwined involvement in it with the era's milestone poet, Faiz Ahmad Faiz (1911–1984), at the top of it, we must recall the dictum, 'every revolution ends up by devouring its own children' while mentioning, maybe, very briefly how deeply Urdu poets acclaimed and bewailed the great leader of the movement, Mahatma Gandhi, just a few months after winning the freedom. There is score upon scores of poems and there is hardly a poet who has not written about Gandhi's unique leadership; nonetheless, there are some that stand out among many, such as poems by Majaz, Anand Narain Mulla, Nushoor Wahidi, Sahir Hoshiarpuri, Ravish Siddiqi, Nazish Pratapgarhi, Iqbal Suhail, and Arsh Malsiani. Here are a few memorable lines by Majaz and a lesser-known woman poet Syeda Farhat.

Majaz

dard o gham-e hayaat ka darmaan chala gaya
voh khizr-e asr o iisa-e dauraan chala gaya
hindu chala gaya n musalmaan chala gaya
insaan ki justaju mein ik insaan chala gaya

The one who was a cure for the pain and misery
of life has gone away.
The one who was reminiscent of the era of
Khizr and Christ have gone away.
Neither a Hindu nor a Muslim has gone away.
The symbol of humanity's inspiration has gone away.

Syeda Farhat

sachhi baat hamesha kahna
sachhaayi ke raste chalna
baapu ne samjhaaya tha
baapu ne samjhaaya tha
ek khuda ne sab ko banaaya
us ka sab ke sar par saya
baapu ne samjhaaya tha
bapu ne samjhaaya tha
bharat maan hai maata sab ki
dharti maan an-daata sab ki
baapu ne samjhaaya tha
baapu ne samjhaaya tha
hindu muslim sikh 'iisaayi
aapas mein hain bhaayi bhaayi
baapu ne samjhaaya tha
baapu ne samjhaaya tha

Always speak the truth.
Never deviate from the path of truth.
Bapu made it clear to us.
Bapu made it clear to us.
There is one God for all humans.
He is the protector of us all.
Bapu made it clear to us.
Bapu made it clear to us.
Mother India is our mother.
This land is the mother and the provider.

Bapu made it clear to us.
Bapu made it clear to us.
Hindus, Muslims, Sikhs, and Christians –
the bond of brotherhood bounds them.
Bapu made it clear to us.
Bapu made it clear to us.

Faiz was the most creative and influential poet in the latter half of the twentieth century. There were other poets, but no one received as much accolade and touched hearts as Faiz. But fame is not the only measure of poetic greatness. The joy of poetry derives from many intangibles, but the poet's creative and distinctive golden touch plays a pivotal role and shakes up the literary canon. Faiz didn't get to the top in a day. He struggled and suffered a lot before he earned admiration and recognition. He started with *Naqsh-e Faryadi*, but with the second half of this collection and the following poetry collections, namely, *Dast-e Saba* and *Zindan Nama,* he gained the extraordinary stature of a poet with unique attributes. The reason for this success was neither biographical nor historical. If we look at the critical literary assessments among progressives of those early years, Faiz was ranked twelfth or fifteenth. But then we come to the day when Faiz's metaphorical structure and aesthetic sensibility and stylistic lyrical uniqueness coupled with his sweet-sounding poetic voice like that of *bulbul* and *rose* vanquished all contemporaries. The views of programmed critics lost their vigor and Faiz's importance improved by the day. Faiz was accepted as a distinctive creative and inventive voice of his age. Let us look at three of his poems.

Speak Up (*Bol*) is a short poem, and it is different from other Faiz poems in terms of its total, emotional directness. More than a poem, it is a declaration of free expression amid all kinds of challenges and constraints. Silence and silent suffering are not an option any longer. The poem makes its impact through its creative brevity, truth, and sincerity of the message. For people suffering under the imperial power's oppressive hand, there is only one thing one must do: speak up.

> *bol k lab aazaad hain tere*
> *bol zabaan ab tak teri hai*
> *tera sutvaan jism hai tera*
> *bol k jaan ab tak teri hai*
> *bol y thora vaqt bahut hai*
> *jism o zabaan ki maut se pehle*
> *bol k sach zinda hai ab tak*
> *bol jo kuchh kehna hai keh le*

Speak up – your lips are free now.
Speak up – you have a tongue
that is your possession.
This stout body belongs to you.

Speak up — you still control
your determination.
Speak up, and this little time is enough.
Before your body and tongue become extinct.
Speak up, that truth is still alive.
Speak up, whatever you have to say,
Now is the time.
Say it!

Faiz wrote the following poem a few days after the Second World War in 1939. He thought that the war would end British imperialism and pave the way for India's independence. The expression *chand roz* is significant because it highlights how close we were, in the poet's thinking, to attaining our goal of free India.

chand roz aur meri jaan faqat chand hi roz
zulm ki chhaaon mein dam lene p majbuur hain ham
aur kuchh der sitam sah lein tarap lein ro lein
apne ajdaad ki miiraas hai maa'zuur hain ham
jism par qaid hai jazbaat p zanjiirein hain
fikr mahbuus hai guftaar p taa'ziirein hain
apni himmat hai k ham phir bhi jiye jaate hain
lekin ab zulm ki mii'yaad ke din thore hain
ek zara sabr k faryaad ke din thore hain
a'rsa-e dahr ki jhulsi hui viiraani mein
ham ko rehna hai p yuun hi to nahien rehna hai
ajnabi haathon ka be-naam garaan baar sitam
aaj sehna hai hamesha to nahien sehna hai
chand roz aur meri jaan faqat chand hi roz

A few more days, my love,
just a few more days.
We are condemned to breathe
in the shadow of oppression
and we should suffer little more,
the aches and cries.
For what our forefathers endowed.
We are helpless, and our bodies are in prison,
our emotions are chained.
Our thoughts are held captive,
and our speech is being censored.
Bravo, we continue to live.
The days of tyranny
are now coming to an end.
Be patient.

The days of the captives
are coming to an end.
The nameless persecution
by the foreign hands
we must bear a few days,
but not for long.
A few more days, my love,
just a few more days!

The Dawn of Freedom (*Sub-h-e Aazaadi*) became the most talked-about freedom poem. At the time of freedom, Faiz was the Editor of *The Pakistan Times*, Lahore. The editorial he wrote that night could not hide his inner agony and distress. He might have written the first line of the poem the same night, but it was not finished right away. It took quite some time to be chiseled and done too artistically before it was published later.[15]

People on the right and the left were vexed as strangely it was not a poem of celebration but pain. They raised questions, especially about the opening lines beginning with *y daagh daagh ujaala, y shab-gaziida sahar* (This blemished sunrise, this daybreak of a night – mangled and mutilated). People on the right were upset that the poem did not celebrate Pakistan's creation, their golden dream. Those on the left felt that the poetry was too oblique and implicit. If you overlooked the poem's title, it did not read like a poem about the advent of independence. Why is freedom from colonialism not a *manzil* (destination)? Poet Ali Sardar Jafri, who strictly followed the party line, remarked that such a poem could have been written by a Muslim Leaguer or an RSS member. All these critics forgot that Faiz was a secularist and a humanist to the core. For him, the idea that Hindus and Muslims had to live in two countries, and there was so much tragic bloodshed and suffering because they worshipped different gods, was ludicrous. Secularism was a deeply held belief that he was not willing to compromise it. Faiz did not join the issue and simply said, 'As a poet, I will write what my inner self feels.' The partition was acceptable to many poets and politicians, but for Faiz, the last line best summed up his mental state: *chale chalo k voh manzil abhi nahien aaii* (Keep moving, we haven't reached the goal yet).

y daagh daagh ujaala y shab-gaziida sahar
voh intizaar tha jis ka y voh sahar to nahien
y voh sahar to nahien jis ki aarzu le kar
chale the yaar k mil jaaye gi kahien n kahien
falak ke dasht mein taaron ki aakhri manzil
kahien to ho ga shab-e sust mauj ka saahil
kahien to ja ke ruke ga safiina-e gham-e dil
abhi charaagh-e sar-e rah ko kuchh khabar hi nahien
abhi giraani-e shab mein kami nahien aaii

najaat-e diidaah o dil ki ghari nahien aaii
chale chalo k voh manzil abhi nahien aaii

This blemished sunrise, this daybreak of a night –
mangled and mutilated.
What we were waiting for, this is not the dawn.
This is not the dawn in whose expectation friends set out
in search of a journey's end, finding it somewhere –
in the wasteland of the sky where stars reach their goal.
I was hoping to find a shoreline somewhere of the night's slow-moving tide.
Somewhere it will find an anchor for this vessel of heart's grief.
The light on the streets knows nothing about it.
The night's affliction and the burden have not lessened.
The time when the eye and the heart find
some solace has not yet arrived.
Keep moving; we haven't reached the goal yet.

Faiz undoubtedly was the redeeming poet of the progressives and a significant poet of the age. His creative vision had a prophetic ring, and his ingenious deep structure was all his own. The above poem has lasting quality. What Faiz said at that moment was right then, but the struggle of the masses for a better life goes on. With this, we close a significant saga of our freedom struggle and the Urdu poetry's immeasurable involvement in it. The poetry gave us the slogan '*Inqilaab-Zindabaad*,' and revolution, of course, is a never-ending endeavor.

Notes

1 D. N. Panigrahi, *India's Partition: The Story of Imperialism in Retreat* (London: Routledge, 2004), p. 306. The quote has been edited for clarity.
2 A summary of the key ideas of the speech.
3 Sardar Jafri, *Taraqqi-Pasand Adab* (New Delhi: Anjuman Taraqqi Urdu Hind, 2013), p. 182.
4 Sabt-e Hasan, p. 133.
5 Zaidi, p. 27.
6 Sabte Hasan, p. 107.
7 Shamim Karhani called on Jawahar Lal Nehru in his open hour to present a copy of the book. After listening to his recitation, (February 1950) Nehru scribbled in Karhani's diary: 'A poet should make his life itself a poem. Shamim Karhani has sung of India's freedom. I hope he will continue to do so and enjoy this freedom.'
8 Sibte Hasan, *Aazaadi Ki Nazmein* (New Delhi: National Council for Promotion of Urdu Language, 2006), p. 95.
9 Sardar Jafri, *Tarraqqi Pasand Adab* (New Dehi: Anjuman Tarraqqi Urdu Hind, 2013). Jigar also wrote *Qaht-e Bengal,* a poem that was a powerful indictment of the imperialism.
10 Sibte Hasan, *Aazaadi Ki Nazmein* (New Delhi: National Council for Promotion of Urdu Language, 2006), p. 115.
11 Sibte Hasan, *Aazaadi Ki Nazmein* (New Delhi: National Council for Promotion of Urdu Language, 2006), pp. 116–117.

12 Sibte Hasan, *Aazaadi Ki Nazmein* (New Delhi: National Council for Promotion of Urdu Language, 2006), pp. 121–122.
13 The permission to reproduce this poem was received from the copyright holder.
14 For a detailed account of Sahir's life and poetic contribution, see Surinder Deol, *SAHIR: A Literary Portait* (New Delhi: Oxford University Press, 2019).
15 Faiz Ahmad Faiz, *Dast-e Saba* (Delhi: Azad Kitab Ghar, Delhi, 1953.)

6

THE BANNED AND WITNESS POETRY

It is my feeling that the twentieth-century human condition demands a poetry of witness. Czeslaw Milosz published his monograph, *The Witness of Poetry,* in 1983, and a phrase, 'poetry of witness,' entered the lexicon of literary terms, regarded skeptically by some as a euphemism for 'political poetry,' or as a poetry by other means. 'Witness' would come to refer, much of the time, to the person of the poet, much as it refers to a man or woman testifying under oath in a court of law. 'Poets of witness,' were considered by some to be engaged in writing documentary literature, or poetic reportage, and in the mode of political confessionalism.[1]

Carolyn Forché

The desire of the Colonial and Imperial power ruling India to perpetuate its domination was understandable. To fulfill this objective, many strategies were deployed, including the jailing of prominent leaders and protestors and ruthless methods to disperse peaceful crowds. The British rulers also understood the power of the written word, specifically its ability to energize young people's minds to join the freedom movement. As a result, they kept a careful watch over what was printed in newspapers and magazines. The District Collectors and Intelligence Agencies in all British provinces were given strict instructions to ban and confiscate all daily newspapers, monthly or weekly magazines, books, and posters that incited Indians to organize themselves seditiously against the Raj. The censorship was so strict that in some cases, even licenses of newspapers were canceled, and printing presses were sealed. Fortunately, copies of banned and confiscated materials were preserved in a cell of the National Archives of India (known by its earlier name) in New Delhi. Urdu is the most popular language of the freedom struggle, most of this material was written in it.

DOI: 10.4324/9781003360841-7

Several books, such as Munshi Premchand's first collection of short stories titled *Soz-e Watan* (Love of the Land), were put to the flames. Poet Ali Jawad Zaidi made a commendable effort of collecting some banned poems from the Archives. He entrusted the work of copying to two young coworkers, and the book *Zabt-Shuda Nazmein*,[2] which was presented to him on his superannuation, is a treasure of this poetic genre. In this chapter, we present carefully selected samples of these banned poems.

Some of these poems belong to poets we have already discussed in the preceding chapters, some to the patriot poets who sacrificed their lives for the motherland, and others to unknown poets or those who preferred to remain anonymous. An important point to remember is that these poems should not be read or assessed as works of literature, and they are expressions of fervent love for the country and its freedom. The sentiments expressed are more important than the literary worth of these verses. It is essential to keep this distinction in mind.

These poems also fall into the *witness poetry* genre because this is a record of what the poets were witnessing with their eyes, hearing with their ears, and how they were reacting first hand to the colonial empire's acts of tyranny and oppression. A poet does not carry a sword or a gun in his backpack, and his weapons are a pen and a piece of paper; he shames the oppressor with his words and creates a record for future generations to read and reflect.

Ram Prasad Bismil (1897–1927) was a poet and a revolutionary patriot who was hanged for his participation in Mainpuri and Kakori conspiracies. He gained great fame for his ghazal *sarfroshi ki tamanna ab hamaare dil mein hai /dekhna hai zor kitna baazu-e qaatil mein hai* (The desire to sacrifice my life for my land/is supreme in my heart. / We must see how much force/is there in the arms of the murderer?) that we read in Chapter 4. The following two ghazals written by Bismil are less known, presumably because these were banned by the British, and as a result, they were not available to the readers. In both these ghazals, we find the same revolutionary zeal that was found in *sarfroshi ki tamanna*.

Ghazal -1[3]

charcha apne qatal ka ab yaar ki mehfil mein hai
dekhna hai ye tamasha kaun si manzil mein hai

The stealthy gossip regarding my murder goes on
in the assembly of the oppressor.
Let us see how exactly does this spectacle
reach its cruel culmination.

desh par qurbaan hote jaao ab ae hindiyo
zindagi ka raaz muzmir khanjar-e qaatil mein hai

O, my dear compatriots,
this is the time for sacrifice!

Life's secret lies hidden
in the executioner's dagger.

saahil-e maqsuud par le chal khuda ra nakhuda
aaj hindostaan ki kashti bari mushkil mein hai

O boatman,
take me to the desired shore,
I pray, for God's sake.
Today, India's boat is rocking
in the troubled waters.

baam-e rifyat par charah do desh par ho kar fana
Bismil ab itni havas baaqi hamaare dil mein hai

By sacrificing your life,
take your country to the highest pedestal.
Bismil still has this much passion
left over in his heart.

Ghazal-2

asiiraan-e qafas se kaash ye saiyyaad kah deta
raho aazaad ho kar ham tumhein aazaad karte hain

If the keeper had said this much
to the prisoners in the cage. Stay free.
We give your freedom back to you.

raha karta hai ahl-e gham ko kya kya intizaar us ka
k dekhein vo dil-e naashaad to kab shaad karte hain

Sufferers of grief wait for that moment
in several ways —
when their unhappy hearts get
some happy tidings to see the scaffold.

ye kah kah kar basar ki u'mr ham ne qaid-e ulfat mein
vo ab aazaad karte hain vo ab aazaad karte hain

After repeatedly praying and wishing
We spent our lives in the prison of affliction.
We'll get our freedom at this moment.
We'll get our freedom at that moment.

sitam aisa nahien dekha jafa aisi nahien dekhi
vo chup rahne ko kahte hain jo ham fariyaad karte hai

I haven't seen such oppression.
I haven't seen such tyranny of the 'beloved'.
She asks me to stay quiet
Whenever I try to utter a word.

koi bismil banaata hai jo maqtal mein hamein Bismil
to ham dar kar dabi aavaaz se fariyaad karte hai

Someone makes the afflicted lover
look like a slaughtered animal in the killing field.
In a determined and deep voice then,
We make our last effort for freedom.

Ashfaq Ullah Khan Ashfaaq (1900–1927) was an associate of Ram Prasad Bismil
and was hanged along with him in 1927. He was a revolutionary poet whose
work was also banned by the British. We present below one of his couplets and
a short poem.

vatan hamaara rahe shad-kaam aur aazaad
hamaara kya hai agar ham rahe rahe n rahe

I want my country
to stay happy and free.
I'm insignificant.
Whether I live or die.

Shorish-e Junuun[4]

bahaar aaii hai shorish hai junuun-e fitna saamaan ki
ilaahi khair rakhna tu mere jeb o garibaan ki
bhala jazbaat-e ulfat bhi kahiin mitne se mit-te hain
a'bas hain dhamkiyaan daar o rasan ki aur zindaan ki
nahiin tum se shikaayat hamsafiiraan-e chaman mujh ko
meri taqdiir hi mein tha qafas aur qaid zindaan ki
zamiin dushman zamaan dushman jo apne the paraaye hain
suno ge daastaan kya tum mere haal-e pareshaan ki
ye jhagre aur bakhere bhol kar aapis mein mil jaao
a'bas tafriiq hai tum mein y hindu aur musalmaan ki

The Burning Passion
The spring has arrived,
bringing with it
some troubling madness.
O God, please take care
of my covering and my collar.
The lover's emotions can't be suppressed,
however hard you try.
The threats of the hanging post
and the jailhouse are futile.
I have no complaint against you,
fellow travelers of this garden.
I was destined to get a cage

in a prison house.
The earth under my feet
has become an enemy,
times are hard, and friends
have become strangers.
Where will you get the time
to hear the story of my suffering?
Forget these disputes and altercations
and, for God's sake, unite as one.
To call someone a Hindu or a Muslim
is exercise in futility.

Many people sacrificed their lives during the freedom struggle, but no one got as much reverence as Bhagat Singh (1907–1931), who was hanged at the age of 23 years for the killing of John Saunders, a British police officer. His death was mourned nationally, and the peoples' sentiments were best summed up by Subhas Chandra Bose, who said 'Bhagat Singh had become the symbol of the new awakening among the youth.' Kanwar Pratap Chand Azad, about whom we do not know much, wrote the following poem in which he highlights the fact that sacrificing one's life for the motherland is 'craziness,' but it is a craziness of a different sort. Martyrs who embrace a rope around their necks are in a frenzied 'intoxicated' state, which is a higher state of awakening where the cause of freedom becomes a much greater ideal than the life of an individual.

Diivaana Bhagat Singh[5]

aazaadi ka diivaana hai mastaana bhagat singh
bam kes mein pakra gaya diivaana bhagat singh
bhaarat ki ek shaan hai diivaana bhagat singh
har baaghi ka armaan hai diivaana bhagat singh
hoti thi meeting assembly mein jis dam k phenka bam
is kes mein pakra gaya diivaana bhagat singh
deta tha lal parcha vo lahore ke thaanon mein bhi
ho jaao hoshiyaar y kahta tha bhagat singh

Crazy Bhagat Singh
Crazy and intoxicated about freedom,
Bhagat Singh.
He was arrested in a case relating to a bomb,
Bhagat Singh.
He is the pride of India,
Bhagat Singh.
A role model for every revolutionary,
Bhagat Singh.
He threw a bomb in the Assembly session.

He was arrested in the bomb case,
crazy Bhagat Singh.
He was found distributing
proscribed posters of all places
in the police stations of Lahore.
Be aware and be ready,
that's what says, Bhagat Singh.

Poet Tika Ram Sukhan, an active member of Naujavaan Bharat Sabha, was greatly impressed by the following couplet of Maulana Zafar Ali Khan, editor of influential daily newspaper *Zamindar,* Lahore. He wrote in honor of Bhagat Singh on the day of his hanging.

tavaanaaon ke bas mein hai sar-e paaye hiqaarat se
karoroon na-tavaanon ki tamannaaon ko thukraana

The cruel oppressors have the power
to crush the aspirations
of millions of powerless and unarmed folks.
This is like rejecting the wishes and aspirations
of millions of people.

Tika Ram Sukhan used the same *qaafiya* and *radiif* to write the following ghazal,[6] of which two couplets are reproduced below.

koi kah de hakuumat se n uljhe nau-javaanon se
inhein sikhla diya hai zulm ne zaalim se takraana

Tell the rulers
not to mess with the young men.
As victims of oppression,
they have learned
how to face the oppressor.

yaqiinan inqilab-e hind ho ga ae sukhan ho ga
hamein zeba hai apne ghar p jhanda surkh lehraana

I'm sure that there will be
an Indian revolution.
Therefore, it is proper for us
to hoist a red flag at our homes.

Many poets wrote anonymously, or they used pseudo names for fear of arrest or punishment by the authorities. The following ghazal[7] has been attributed to a poet who identified himself as Usman, a typical Muslim name.

ilaahi hamein jald aazaad kar de
yahi aaj vird-e zabaan ho raha hai

O God, please grant us our freedom
This is the prayer on every lip today.
tumhaara tashaddud kahaan par nahien hai
yahaan ho raha hai vahana ho raha hai

Name the place
where your oppression is not seen.
It is happening here,
and it is happening there.
mazaar-e shahiidaan se aati sada hai
barho hindiyo imtihaan ho raha hai

There is a voice
that is coming
from the mausoleums
of the martyrs.
Indian people
move forward.
It's a challenging time.

Jallianwala Bagh massacre in Amritsar took place on April 13, 1919, in which hundreds died, and many more were injured. It was the most barbaric act of the British government. As the Martial Law was clamped and presses sealed, only rare pieces have survived. We have already quoted a landmark qat'a by Allama Iqbal on this tragedy. An unknown poet named Sarju captured the tragedy in the following poem.

Jallianwala Bagh

be-gunaahon par bamon ki be-khatar bau-chhaar ki
de rahe hain dhamkiyaan banduuq aur talvaar ki
baagh jalliaan mein ni-hatton par chalaaii goliyaan
pet ke bal bhi reingaaya zulm ki hadd paar ki
ham ghariibon par kiye jis ne sitam be intiha
yaad bhuule gi nahiin us daayar-e badkaar ki

Uninterrupted rain shower
of bullets
on the innocent people.
Threatening us
with guns and arms.
In Jallianwala garden,
unarmed people were ruthlessly shot,
and they were made to crawl on their bellies.
No limit to the oppression.
The one who committed
extreme acts of cruelty

with the innocent people,
we shall not forget
that bad bugger named
Dyer.[8]

During the struggle for freedom, newspapers were not the only means of mass communication. Pamphlets (one pagers) were used to convey revolutionary texts; be it notices for underground activities or poetical works that inspired people to fight for freedom. The following poem, written by Mahir, was distributed as a pamphlet by Dev Narain Pande of Kanpur.

Hindostaani Azaad Jamaa't Ka Pamphlet

hoti hain aazaad qoumein sar kata dene ke baa'd
khauf dil se ek dam bilkul hata dene ke baa'd
mil nahiin sakti hai aazaadi bila qiimat diye
rok sakta kon hai qiimat chuka dene ke baa'd
ved mein likha yahi ye hi likha hai quraan mein
hoti hain aazaad qomein sar kata dene ke baa'd

The Pamphlet of the Independent India Party

Nations get freedom
after making tremendous sacrifices.
By letting the fear
out of their minds.
We can't gain liberty
without paying its price.
But once the price is paid,
the way becomes clear.
This is written in the Vedas,
this is written in the Quran.
Nations get freedom
after making tremendous sacrifices.

Maharaj Bahadur Varma Barq (1884–1936) was a well-known poet from Delhi. He wrote several patriotic poems. The following poem is about *khaddar* (handspun coarse cloth) whose use was advocated by Mahatma Gandhi as a measure of self-reliance. *Khaddar* became the official garment of the freedom movement, worn by the national leaders and the ordinary freedom fighters.

Kamkhwaab Be-furogh Hai Khaddar Ke Saamne[9]

khaddar mein saadgi ki a'jab aan baan hai
qaayim isi se a'hd-e guzashta ki shaan hai
poshish amiir ki hai ghariboon ki jaan hai
kaisi a'jiib cheez ye gaarhe ka thaan hai

poshaak ahl-e hind ko zeba tariin hai ye
kamkharch aur saath mein baala nashiin hai ye
khaddar ka taar taar safaaii mein fard hai
is ki safa se makhmal-e ruumi bhi gard hai
bazaar is ke dam se badeshi ka sard hai
pahno ise vatan ka agar dil mein dard hai
atlas khajil hai gaarhe ki chaddar ke saamne
kamkhwaab befurogh hai khaddar ke saamne

The Silk is Without its Shine in Front of the Coarse Cloth

The hand-spun coarse cloth
has a strange display of simplicity.
Because of this, our handicraft tradition is revived,
and it appears glorious.
This is a garment
for the sophisticated and
heart's desire of the poor.
What an out of the ordinary thing
is this collection of coarse cloth.
For the people of India,
it is the best way to dress up,
and it costs less while at the same
it is a respectable wear.
Each thread of the coarse cloth
is unparalleled in neatness.
Compared to its smoothness,
even the velvet of Rome is like dust.
Because of its availability,
the foreigner's market is down.
You should wear it
if you feel within your heart
the sufferings of the land.
Silk is of no value
in comparison to this,
and the silk is without its shine
in front of the hand-spun cloth.

Many poems during the freedom movement were written about India as a country or India as a land of beauty. Here are two poems from the banned treasure. The first poem was written by a poet who identified himself as Anwar, a familiar name.

Hindostaan

aazaad ho ga ab to hindostaan hamaara
be-daar ho raha hai har nau-javaan hamaara

vo sakhtiyaan falak ki be aab o daana rahna
qaidi ka phir ye kahna hindostaan hamaara
bera utha liya hai aazaadiyon ka ham ne
jannat-nishaan bane ga hindostaan hamaara
soz-e sukhan se apne majnuun hamein bana de
bachchon ki ho zabaan par hindostaan hamaara
ik baar phir ye naghma anwar hamein suna de
hindi hain ham vatan hai hindostaan hamaara[10]

India
Our India
will become a free country.
Every young man
is experiencing a new awakening.
Those wounds inflicted by the rulers,
the days of want and hunger are over.
The prisoners are declaring:
India is ours.
We have come to undertake
this great challenge of gaining freedom.
Our dear India will become
a replica of paradise.
The sad melodies of sufferings
make us crazy like Majnuun.
The youth should sing together.
India is ours!
Anwar, sing this passionate song,
once again.
We are Indians.
India is ours!

The second poem was written by Maulana Zafar Ali Khan (1873–1956), an influential political commentator as editor of daily *Zamindar,* Lahore, and a famous patriotic poet.

Hindostaan

naquus se gharz hai n matlab azaan se hai
mujh ko agar hai ishq to hindostaan se hai
tahziib-e hind ka nahien chashma agar azal
ye mauj-e rang rang phir aaii kahaan se hai
zarre mein gar tarap hai to is khaak-e paak se
suraj mein raushni hai to is aasmaan se hai
hai is ke dam se garmi-e hangaama-e jahaan
maghrib ki saari raunaq is ik dukaan se hai

India

Not concerned with the voices
emanating from the temple or the mosque.
If I love something, that is India, my land.
If the source of India's civilization
is not a fountain that sprang
from the day of the creation of the universe,
then from where these colorful waves
are emanated.
If there is radiation and pull in the particles,
it must have come from this soil.
If the sun has the light,
it must have come from this sky.
Because of this ancient land,
there is the hustle and bustle in the world.
All the shine that the West is displaying
comes from this store of stores.

As an introduction to the following poem, written by Anwar, Narain Singh Musafir, editor of *Payaam-e Jang*, stated that Comrade Prem Dutt, a defendant in the Lahore conspiracy case, while in the court, used to recite this poem in his melodic voice from the witness box. He was often joined in this endeavor by other defendants.

Muqaddma Saazish-e Lahore Ke Asiiron Ki Aavaaz

bhaarat n rah sake ga hargiz ghulaam-khaana
aazaad ho ga ho ga aata hai vo zamaana
ab bher aur bakri mil kar n rah sakein ge
kar dein ge zaalimon ka ab band zulm dhaana
khuun khaulne lage ga hindostaaniyon ka
is past-himmati ka ho ga kahaan thikaana
bhaarat ke ham hain bachche bhaarat hamaari maata
hai is ke vaaste ab manzuur sar kataana
u'ruuj-e kaamyaabi par hindostaan ho ga
ho gi bahaar us din jab baaghbaan ho ga
chakhaayein ge maze barbaadi-e gulshan ke gulchiin ko
jab apni zamien ho gi aur aasmaan ho ga
shahiidon ki chitaaon par lagein ge har baras mele
vatan par marne vaalon ka yahi naam o nishaan ho ga

The Voice of the Defendants of the Lahore Conspiracy Case

India will not stay for long
a chamber of slavery.
Freedom is coming.

That time is coming.
The wolf and the sheep
shall no longer live together,
and we shall stop the cruelty
of the oppressors.
The blood of Indians
will seethe and simmer,
and the loss of effort
will not be seen anywhere.
We are children of Bharat.
Bharat is our mother.
For her honor, we shall offer
our heads as a sacrifice.
India will succeed
from one event to another.
Spring will come the day
we will own the garden.
The one who destroyed the garden
will face the consequences
for his actions.
When we own the sky
and we own the land.
The places
where the bodies of the martyrs
were reduced to ashes
are sacred to us.
People will assemble each year
for celebrations.
Those who sacrificed for the country,
this is how will always be remembered.[11]

Salam Machhli-Shahri (1921–1973) was a popular romantic poet, who also wrote patriotic poetry in his younger days. The following poem encapsulates the frustrations faced by the ordinary people as the British rule continued to suppress all dissent and criticism, and the cruelty they showed in the treatment of innocent people was unrestrained.

Majbuuriyaan

mujhe nafrat nahien hai i'shqiya ashaa'r se lekin
abhi un ko ghulaam aabaad mein main ga nahien sakta
mujhe nafrat nahiin hai husn-e jannat zaar se lekin
abhi dozakh mein us jannat se dil bahla nahien sakta
mujhe nafrat nahien paazeb ki jhankaar se lekin
abhi taab-e nishaat-e raqs-e mehfil la nahien sakta

abhi hindostaan ko aatshiin naghme sunaane do
abhi chingaariyon se barg-e gul rangiin banaane do

Suppressed Desires

I don't hate love couplets.
But I can't sing them
in the enslaved land.
I don't hate the paradise-like
the beauty of this land.
But living in hell,
I can't enjoy the pleasures
of the paradise.
I don't hate the melodious sound
of the ankle bells.
But I can't bring to my mind
the cheerfulness of the assembly
of the dancers.
Let India sing flaming melodies
for the time being.
Let the sparks shower color
to the branches holding roses.

When he was a student at the Government College in Ludhiana, Sahir Ludhianvi (1921–1980) wrote revolutionary poems and read them at student gatherings. He not only gained great popularity for his fearless activism among his fellow students but also received warnings from the district authorities. The following poem,[12] which appears to be the work of a youthful student, was probably written during the last days of Sahir's stay in the college. He moved to Lahore in 1940.

Shola Navaaii

hakuumat ki buniyaad dhaaye chala ja
javaanon ko baaghi banaaye chala ja
baras aag ban kar firangi ke sar par
takabbur ki duniya ko dhaaye chala ja
januun-e baghaavat n ho jin saron mein
unhein thokron se uraaye chala ja
ghariibon ke tuute charaaghon ki lao se
amiiron ke aivaan jalaaye chala ja
shahiidaan-e millat ki saugandh tujh ko
ye parcham yuun-hi lehlahaaye chala ja
parakhche ura daal arbaab-e zar ke
ghariibon ko baaghi banaaye chala ja
gira daal qasr-e shahanshaahiyat ko
amaarat ke khirman jalaaye chala ja

The Sparks of Fire

Go on demolishing
the foundation
of this oppressive
government.
Go on nurturing
the revolutionary impulses
of the motivated young men.
Become a ball of fire
for the heads of the foreigners,
the whites, and the British.
Go on demolishing
this world filled with arrogance
and haughtiness.
Those heads
that are not moved
by the spirit of revolt,
strike them hard and get them
out of the way.
With the help of the glow
of the broken lamps
of the poor,
set the mansions
of the rich on fire.
In the name of the martyrs
of the nation,
keep this revolutionary flag flying.
Tear apart masters
and lords of money.
Set the poor
on the revolutionary path.
Bring down
the grand citadels of rulers,
and set them on fire.

Notes

1 Carolyn Forché and Duncan Wu, eds. *Poetry of Witness* (New York: W.W. Norton & Company, 2013). Digital Edition.
2 Ali Jawad Zaidi, Khaliq Anjum and Mujtaba Husain, *Zabt Shuda Nazmein* (Delhi: Maktaba Jamia, 1975).
3 Both these ghazals were published in a newspaper, *Congress Pushpanjali*, in 1930.
4 This poem appeared in *Kirti Monthly*, Amritsar, 1930.
5 The poem was published in a book titled *Tarana-e Azad*.
6 The ghazal was published in a newspaper called *Mazdoor-Kisaan* in 1930.

 7 The ghazal was published in a newspaper or a magazine called *Dard-e Watan* in 1930.
 8 Acting Brigadier-General Reginald Dyer, who ordered the troops to fire at the inno-
    cent civilians.
 9 The poem was published in a book titled *Aah-e Bekas* in 1930.
10 This line is from *Tarana-e Hindi* of Allama Iqbal.
11 The last verse is tagged from public memory. It is a quotable-quote, and the original
    author is not known.
12 The poem was published in *Weekly Afghan* in 1939.

PART II

Leading Poets of the Freedom Struggle

7

DURGA SAHAI SUROOR JAHANABADI

I have read Suroor Jahanabadi's poetry from time to time. His words always touched my heart. He was a genuinely compassionate person. Urdu poetry that lacks quality and depth, but it is popular, was not something that attracted Suroor. Every poem that he wrote came from the depths of his heart. We can see a pulsating heart in every line in a poem written by him. It is correct to say that poets like Suroor are rare to find.[1]

Josh Malihabadi

Durga Sahai Suroor Jahanabadi (1873–1910) was born in a small town in district Pilibhit in Uttar Pradesh, and he was fortunate to find teachers who helped him learn both Persian and Urdu at an early age. He also possessed an inner yearning to be a *nazm* poet, which was something new at that time. His birth and death dates incidentally show significant coincidences. He was born almost during the same time (just a year later) when the new poetry or 'natural poetry' movement started from Lahore, Punjab. Allama Iqbal, one of the great poets of the twentieth century, was born four years later in 1877. Suroor departed almost four years earlier than Hali, who passed in 1914. This was an excellent period for the growth of the *nazm*, although the dominant genre of Urdu poetry was ghazal until then. Most Urdu poets wanted appreciation at customary mushairas, which required proficiency in ghazal writing, using established themes of classical poetry. There was hardly a forum or an audience for the recitation of *nazm* poetry. Nevertheless, in his unfortunately short span of life, the oeuvre of *nazm* Suroor left behind was astounding.

Finding a new direction proved challenging for Suroor, but he resolved this dilemma by focusing on nature and patriotic poetry. Maulana Hali and Mohammad Husain Azad, who had settled in Lahore after the 1857 Rebellion, had

DOI: 10.4324/9781003360841-9

already laid the foundation and had earned a good reputation in writing natural poetry under the aegis of the Anjuman-e Punjab set-up by the British Education Administrators. Yet, the art of writing a *nazm* was still in its infancy. Also, the struggle for freedom of the country had not yet gathered steam. Under these circumstances, Suroor's path was courageous because of the uncertainty surrounding his choice.

Suroor got early success because his compositions were published in major literary journals, *Adeeb* and *Makhzan,* both based in Punjab, which brought him fame and recognition. But other developments in his personal life pushed him to lose his peace of mind, which got the end of his life painfully early. He lost his wife, whom he loved passionately, and then his only son. This dual tragedy put him on a self-destructive course. He started to drink excessively, and he died at 37 – the age at which most poets start to gain maturity.

When we look at his body of work completed within a brief period, we are struck by a few things. First, he covered a vast array of subjects. There are patriotic poems that express his love for the motherland in words filled with great emotion while showing his distress at its occupation by an imperial power. His concept of the land is filled with sanctity. Therefore, he presents it as *Jagat Janani, Shakti, a* mother goddess, or the power of creativity, drawing images from ancient Indian mythology. He is the first Urdu poet who addresses India as a feminine entity, *Maadar-e Vatan,* Mother India, a centuries-old concept in India and comes from the roots implying *dharti* as the mother earth. All images associated with the country in Suroor's poetry are matriarchal. Every particle of the land was sacred to him, including its dust. We should remember that the concept of the land or the country in the Urdu poetry had a distinctive parochial or provincial flavor for a long time. The idea of India as one nation was still in the making. The matriarchal and highly patriotic passion for India and its freedom stands at the core of Suroor's poetic work.

Second, he wrote about places of natural beauty, which Indians also revere for religious reasons. Poems like *Ganga, Jamuna,* and *Prayag Ka Sangam* are good examples. Third, he wrote poems on several stories and sacred characters drawn from Indian mythology, including Lakshmi, Saraswati, and Sita.

Last, Suroor had a highly developed sensibility for feminine beauty. Therefore, he projects aspects of feminine imagery in natural subjects, like rivers and hills. For example, in his poem on the morning breeze, he presents the issue as a beautiful damsel dressed up like a bride, including great henna on her feet. Even the season of *Basant (*spring) appears as a fairy-like beloved. Maybe, subconsciously, the suppressed image of his departed wife is a source of creativity that renders his poetry mellow and heart-touching.

This chapter will mainly dwell on Suroor's two signature poems, and both the selections demonstrate love for the land. In the first case (*Gulzar-e Watan*), the poem is addressed more directly to the fellow Indians. In the second (*Bulbul O Parwana*), he uses a classical metaphoric structure to make his point.

Gulzar-e Watan is written in a free-flowing and alluring style, reminding us of Allama Iqbal, who compared India to a beautiful garden and its people as night-ingales, who have fallen in love with the garden. Suroor was ahead of many poets in using this metaphor. Since the Anjuman-e Punjab poets were also published in *Makhzan*, one could speculate whether Suroor inspired others or others inspired Suroor. In literature, influences do not operate transparently or serially. This poem is filled with metaphors. Patriotism is a plant that needs to be nourished. Its grafting can spread the sentiment of love in the land around. This love is not a made-up love; it is intuitive and pervasive. It comes from the inner depths and is mixed with blood, tears, and sacrifice. There is a visual and internal unity within a garden – between trees, plants, shrubs, and creepers to maximize its beauty. The land's allure is also enhanced if there is unity among people who inhabit it. As a garden needs care for its maintenance, the country also demands a lot of devotion to retaining its attraction, which comes only from a shared resolve. While reading this poem, let us enjoy the rhythm and flow of this delightful love-filled patriotic composition.

phuulon ka kunj-e-dilkash bhaarat mein ik banaayein
hubb-e-vatan ke paude is mein naye lagaayein
phuulon mein jis chaman ke ho buu-e-jaan-nisaari
hubb-e-vatan ki qalmein ham is chaman se laayein
khuun-e-jigar se siinchein har nakhl-e-aarzu ko
ashkon se bel-buuton ki aabru barhaayein
ek ek gul mein phuunkein ruuh-e-shamiim-e-vahdat
ik ik kali ko dil ke daaman se dein havaayein
firdaus ka namuuna apna ho kunj-e-dilkash
saare jahaan ki jis mein hon jalva-gar fazaayein
chhaaya ho abr-e-rahmat kaashana-e-chaman mein
rim-jhim baras rahi hon chaaron taraf ghataayein
murghaan-e-baagh ban kar urte phirein hava mein
naghme hon ruuh-afza aur dil-ruba sadaayein
hubb-e-vatan ke lab par hon jaan-faza taraane
shaakhon pe giit gaaein phuulon pe chahchahaayein
chhaaii hui ghata ho mausam tarab-faza ho
jhonke chalein hava ke ashjaar lahlahaayein
is kunj-e-dil-nashiin mein qabza na ho khizaan ka
jo ho gulon ka takhta, takhta ho ik jinaan ka
bulbul ko ho chaman mein sayyaad ka n khatka
khush khush ho shaakh-e-gul par gham ho n aashiyaan ka
hubb-e-vatan ka mil kar sab ek raag gaayein
lahja juda ho garche murghaan-e-naghma-khvaan ka
ek ek lafz mein ho taasiir-e-buu-e-ulfat
andaaz dil-nashiin ho ek ek daastaan ka
murghaan-e-baagh ka ho us shaakh par nasheman

pahunche na haath jis tak sayyaad-e-aasmaan ka
mausam ho josh-e-gul ka aur din bahaar ke hon
aalam ajiib dilkash ho apne gulsitaan ka
mil mil ke ham taraane hubb-e-vatan ke gaayein
bulbul hain jis chaman ke giit us chaman ke gaayein

The Garden of India

Build an alluring niche of flowers
inside India.
Plant in the ground, with our hands,
new shrubs of patriotism.
The fragrance of these flowers
should make people more patriotic.
Bring home saplings of patriotism
from this garden of ours.
Irrigate this tree of our desires
with the blood of our hearts.
With tears in our eyes, we should honor
these creepers and shrubs.
In every flower, we should inject
the fragrance of unity and oneness.
Each bud, we should nurture
with the spirit of our heart.
This niche should become
a representative piece of paradise,
manifesting flavors of the whole world.
The overcast sky of the garden
should be covered with a cloud of compassion.
Water pouring from the rain-filled clouds
should make a pattering sound.
Like birds of the garden,
we should playfully frolic.
Our melodies should be soul-nourishing
and our resonance heart-pleasing.
Life-giving songs of the love of the country
should be on our lips.
We should sing songs
in the shadow of the branches
while chirping with the flowers.
Dark clouds overhead,
the weather should be joyful.
Let the breeze run freely,
and trees quiver and wobble!

Autumn should not be allowed to capture
the alluring niche that we have created.
Every bed of flowers should look like beds
of flowers from paradise.
Nightingale in this garden should have
no fear of the bird catcher.
Happily, she will sing sitting on a branch,
without the fear of losing her nest.
Coming together, we should sing the melody
of the love of the country.
Styles might differ the way the birds
of the garden sing the song.
Each word should have the effect
of the fragrance of love.
Each story should be narrated
in a heart-pleasing manner.
The birds of the garden should have their nests
on the branches of trees
outside the reach of the captors,
like the cruel revolving sky!
The bursting of colorful flowers
and the days of the spring!
What a beautiful state of the garden
we can visualize!
Coming together, we should sing the melodies
of the love of the country.
We are nightingales of the garden;
we should sing the praise of our garden.

About the second poem *Bulbul o Parwana,* it is essential to say that some themes
in the classical Urdu ghazal poetry have possibilities of layer upon layer of metaphors. There is nightingale's love for the rose and the moth's self-destructive passion for the love of the candle. There is an object of love and a passionate desire
to express that love in both cases. In both cases, love ends tragically. The nightingale is busy singing songs for the love of the rose while the bird catcher comes
creepily and takes away the nightingale. Or the spring ends, and the flower dies.
The end of moth's love is even more tragic; the moth is attracted by the flame's
light and wants to embrace the flame, the object of its love. It is a painful death
by fire. This poem by Suroor is written as a dialogue between the nightingale
and the moth. Both are mindful of their end; both advise the other 'do not fall
in love because this love will kill you.' Behind these two meta-metaphors is the
idea of patriotic love that does not promise anything while it asks for the sacrifice
of one's life. Once again, Suroor charms the reader with his ability to create lyricism while narrating an encounter between two lovelorn creatures.

gira raha hai tira shauq sham'a par tujh ko
mujhe ye dar hai n pahunche kahiin zarar tujh ko
farogh-e-shola kahaan aur farogh-e-husn kahaan
hazaar haif ki itni nahiin khabar tujh ko
tarap tarap ke jo be-ikhtiyaar girta hai
nahiin hai aag ke shola se aah dar tujh ko
ye nanhe nanhe par o baal ye sitam ki tapish
mila hai aah qayaamat ka kya jigar tujh ko
qariib sham'a ke aa kar jo thartharaataa hai
nahiin hai jaan ke jaane ka gham magar tujh ko
milegi khaak bhi dhuunde n teri mahfil mein
sabaa uraaye phiregi dam-e-sahar tujh ko
samajh n sham'a ko dil soz aafiyat dushman
jala ke aah rahegi ye musht-e-par tujh ko
nahiin hai tu abhi soz-o-gudaaz ke qaabil
nahiin hai ishq ki arz o niyaaz ke qaabil
tapish y bazm mein faanuus par nahiin achchhi
ki aag laag ki o be-khabar nahiin achchhi
kari hai aanch mohabbat ki sham'-e-mahfil se
lagaavtein are tufta-jigar nahiin achchhi
tarap tarap ke n diiviina-vaar sham'a p gir
tapish y shauq kii o musht-e-par nahiin achchhi
ye jaan-gudaazi-e-soz-e-vafa sar-e-mahfil
kahiin n ho tire ji ka zarar nahiin achchhi
lara n sham'a se aankhein ki hai 'uduu teri
tiri nigaah-e-mohabbat-asar nahiin achchhi
ye nanhe nanhe paron ki tarap ye betaabi
hariif-e-shokhi-e-barq-e-nazar nahiin achchhi
ye par samet ke faanuus par tira girna
ye be-khudi are shoriida-sar nahiin achchhi
chaman mein chal k dikhaauun bahaar-e-shaahid-e-gul
nazar fareb hain naqsh-o-nigaar-e-shaahid-e-gul
main bul-havas nahiin samjha hai tu ne kya mujh ko
pasand shaahid-e-gul ki nahiin ada mujh ko
firaaq-e-gul mein main minnat-kash-e-fughaan huun daregh
ye daagh-e-soz-e-judaaii n de khuda mujh ko
dil-e-gudaakhta le kar azal se aaya huun
banaaya bazm mein hai soz-aashna mujh ko
jale vo bazm mein chup-chaap aur main n jaluun
ba'iid ishq se hai ho gham-e-fana mujh ko
tiri nigaah mein jaan-soz hai jo ai bulbul
vo aah aag ka shola hai jaan-faza mujh ko
khula hai tujh pe abhi aah raaz-e-ishq kahaan
tu bul-havas hai, tujhe imtiyaaz-e-ishq kahaan

The Nightingale and the Moth

Your desire is making you fall in love
with the candle.
I'm afraid this might cause you grief.
There are enchanting flames,
and there is a splendor of beauty.
Alas, you lack this awareness!
You're expressing yourself in pain,
but you're out of control.
You are not showing any fear
of the rising flame.
These young wings and feathers
and this terrible heat.
What a doomsday kind of heart
you have inherited!
You shrivel when you come close
to the candle.
You show no signs of sadness
of losing your existence.
Even your dust will not be found,
even if you try, in any meeting place.
The flowing breeze will sway your remains
in the morning, hither and thither.
Don't consider the candle
to be a compassionate enemy.
She will not rest without burning
the handful of your feathers.
You are not yet ready for burning and melting.
You are not yet ready
for the tribulations of loving.
The desire for burning
is not suitable for this meeting,
because O unaware,
the love of fire is not good.
The burning that love gives
is greater than the flame of this candle.
The attachment that will roast your heart
is not suitable for you.
Suffering great pain,
do not fall in love with the candle.
This agony of burning
of constancy in this gathering
will not be ideal for your well-being.

Falling in love with the candle
is falling in love with your enemy.
Your desire-filled loving glances
are not suitable for you.
This fluttering of these youthful wings
signifies your impatience.
The luminosity of your desire
is not ideal for you.
By closing these wings and
then falling on the light
is close to madness,
which is not ideal for you.

I have come with a molten heart
from eternity.
This gathering has made me
a friend of the pain of love.
She burns in the meeting.
Why shouldn't I burn too?
My sorrow for mortality
is beyond this love.
In your case, O nightingale,
whatever burns in your heart,
alas, that flame of fire
is life-giving to me.
You have not learned, alas,
the secret of love.
You are filled with passion,
you have no idea
about the greatness of love.

Note

1 Hukam Chand Nayyar, *Navaa-e Suroor* (Benares: Idaara-e Roznama Hindostan, 1967), p. 8.

8

JOSH MALIHABADI

Once I came from Pakistan to visit Delhi and met Pandit Nehru. He did not spare any words and told me satirically, "Pakistan was created for Islam, Islamic culture, which meant that it was created for the promotion of Urdu. But when I visited Pakistan recently, I found that I was the only person in the room wearing a pajama and sherwani. All government officials were dressed like the Britishers and were speaking in English. They addressed me in English. I was shocked and realized that all those slogans for Urdu that we heard in undivided India were empty from within. When I got up to speak, I chose Urdu, and this made many people very uncomfortable. I proved that I had more love for Urdu than your folks. Josh Sahib, please forgive me for saying this, you left your country of birth to go to Pakistan in the name of Urdu. In Pakistan, Urdu has no place. Okay, sure you can go back to Pakistan." I lowered my head in shame.[1]

Josh Malihabadi

Shabbir Hasan Khan Josh Malihabadi (1898–1982) was born in an Afridi Pathan family in Malihabad in Uttar Pradesh. His early schooling was at home under the direction of his father, and it was aimed at providing him proficiency in four languages, namely, Urdu, Persian, Arabic, and English. His family had a long tradition of producing men of learning who established themselves as poets and scholars. He got his higher education at St. Peters College in Agra and Vishwa-Bharati University, the center of integrated learning established by Rabindranath Tagore at Shantiniketan. Josh is undoubtedly one of the most talented poets of India's freedom struggle. He entered the literary scene as the struggle for freedom was gaining steam after First World War. He left behind a rich heritage of significant poetic work that consisting of poems, ghazals, rubai's, and an autobiography titled *Yaadon Ki Baaraat*, class in itself as a work of literary prose. He founded the magazine *Kaleem* that carried articles and poetry in favor

DOI: 10.4324/9781003360841-10

of the independence movement. Josh is also remembered as the early patron and a leading supporter of the Progressive Writers' Movement, along with another great poet and a friend, Firaq Gorakhpuri. He was appointed editor of *Aaj Kal,* a literary publication of the government of India, after independence. He was awarded Padma Bhushan in 1954.

Josh made a controversial decision in 1956 to move to Pakistan that shocked the literary world and puzzled his friends and admirers like Prime Minister Jawaharlal Nehru. Josh's fears about the Hindu rule and the dismal future for Urdu in India lacked understanding of the country's commitment to the ideals of secularism and democracy. Nothing good came out of Josh's migration to Pakistan. He was attacked by Hafeez Jalandhari, a leading poet, who saw Josh as a threat to his position of influence, as the lyricist of the national anthem of Pakistan, in the military government. He died a frustrated man, ignored by the people and the media. Not more than two-dozen people showed up at his funeral in Islamabad. Pakistan conferred on him the civilian honor of Hilaal-e-Imtiaz by President Asif Zardari in 2013, more than 30 years after his demise, which is a statement of how badly he was treated by the country of his adoption.

Although an Afridi Pathan of overwhelming personality, he was quite emotional and gullible. There is a story that he was lured by an acquaintance who convinced him that if he moved to Pakistan, he will be profusely welcomed. He was promised a license for a movie theater and a mansion to live. No such thing happened. He was heartbroken. He lost his muse and wrote very little, except for fun poems, such as *channa jor garam,* a refrain meaning, 'I sell roasted grams, hot and spicy.'

As a writer, Josh was called '*Shaa'yir-e Hurriyat o Shaa'yir-e Shabaab*' poet of youth and romance and revolution. He captured these titles beautifully in his poetry and couplets, such as:

> *kaam hai mera taghayyur naam hai mera shabaab*
> *mera naa'ra inqilaab o inqilaab o inqilaab*

> My work is transformation,
> and my name is youthfulness.
> My slogan is revolution,
> revolution, revolution.

> *ek diin-e nau ki likhon ga kitaab-e zar-fishaan*
> *sabt ho ga jis ki zarriin jild par Hindostaan*

> One day, I will write a shining book
> of a new religion
> On its golden binding,
> it will be embossed *Hindostan.*

Josh lived to realize this ideal quite well because when we look at the totality of his work, these two themes come out clearly and strongly.

In this chapter, we present some milestone poems by Josh on the themes of freedom, love of the land, and the beauty of the country. The poem *Shikast-e Zindaan Ka Khwaab* (A Dream of the Fall of the Jailhouse) was written by Josh in his early years as a poet. It's a short poem of 16 lines, but within this limited space he presents a metaphoric picture of India's jailhouses that were being filled by the agitators. The jailhouse was tumultuous and trembling, the chains were breaking, the prisoners were fired up, and the sky was opening to rain fire and swords. These are very powerful metaphors to describe a dream rather than what was happening inside the prison. There is a roar and a rumble of lightning throughout the poem, and in the last couplet, the uprising sounds climax as a sudden bolt of thunder. The gates are crashed, and the prisoners rush out as free persons! The over-powering metaphors are a significant feature of josh's uncontrollably power-packed creativity. Notice the din and clamor of the freedom struggle as we reach the climax.

> kya hind ka zindaan kaanp raha hai guunj rahi hain takbiirein
> uktaaye hain shaayad kuchh qaidi aur tor rahe hain zanjiirein
> diivaaron ke niiche aa aa kar yuun jam'a hue hain zindaani
> siinon mein talaatum bijli ka aankhon mein jhalakti shamshiirein
> bhuukon ki nazar mein bijli hai topon ke dahaane thande hain
> taqdiir ke lab ko jumbish hai dam tor rahi hain tadbiirein
> aankhon mein gada ki surkhi hai be-nuur hai chehra sultaan ka
> takhriib ne parcham khola hai sajde mein pari hain taamiirein
> kya un ko khabar thi zer-o-zabar rakhte the jo ruuh-e-millat ko
> ubleinge zamiin se maar-e-siyah barseingi falak se shamshiirein
> kya un ko khabar thi siinon se jo khuun churaaya karte the
> ik roz isi be-rangi se jhalkengi hazaaron tasviirein
> kya un ko khabar thi honton par jo qufl lagaaya karte the
> ik roz isi khaamoshi se tapkengi dahakti taqriirein
> sambhlo k vo zindaan guunj utha jhapto k vo qaidi chhuut gaye
> uttho k vo baithiin diivaarein dauro k vo tuuti zanjiirein

The jailhouse of India is shaking,
and there are echoes of God's greatness.
Some of the prisoners have lost their patience,
and they are breaking up the chains.
The imprisoned rebels are gathering
under the walls.
There is lightning brewing in the hearts,
and swords are reflecting in their eyes.
There is the sparkle in the eyes
of the oppressed and hungry,
and mouths of guns are getting ready
to spew fire.

There is a cracking sound
on the lips of destiny,
and all plans are at the end of their lives.
The eyes have the redness of radicals,
and the ruler's face has shed its luminosity.
The banner of impending storm
and destruction is open,
and structures of the future
are kneeling in prayer.
Those who had their hands
on the nation's pulse
have no idea that things would go
topsy-turvy suddenly.
Black snakes will appear
from the smoldering ground,
and cracking bolts will rain from the sky.
Those who were stealing blood
from the hearts of the deprived
had no idea that the portraits of their colorlessness
will turn pale one day.
Those who were putting locks
on the lips of the ruled
had no idea that from the silence
would arise a thousand rumbling roars
for liberation.
Beware because the jailhouse
is in turmoil.
Be aware because it is breaking up
and the prisoners have fled.
Arise because the walls are falling.
Run because the chains have broken
into pieces.

Another poem titled *Watan* (My Country) is a classic patriotic poem. It consists of nine stanzas of six lines each. The tone is highly personal and emotional. A large portion of the poem is devoted to describing the natural beauty of the land – the beauty of its gardens, flowers, birds, rivers, and mountains. This is an essential part of patriotic poetry. Because of his command over Urdu language, Josh really excels in capturing these elements in beautiful words that are also skillfully rhymed. The second, and equally important part, is the description of the people. Nature alone does not make a country great. The feelings and emotions that country's men and women have for the land make it truly great. Josh dwells at length on the interaction between nature and the people – how peoples' lives and their homes draw their strength from the natural attributes. Above all, how people are willing to sacrifice their lives for the love of the country and its freedom. Many poems were written on this subject by different Urdu poets during the freedom struggle, but this poem by Josh undoubtedly stands apart for its metaphoric inventiveness and lyricism.

ai vatan paak vatan ruuh-e-ravaan-e-ahraar
ai k zarron mein tire buue-chaman rang-e-bahaar
ai k khwaabiida teri khaak mein shaahaana viqaar
ai k har khaar tera ruu-kash-e-sad-ruu-e-nigaar
reze almaas ke tere khas-o-khaashaak mein hain
haddiyaan apne buzurgon ki teri khaak mein hain

paaii ghunchon mein tere rang ki duniya ham ne
tere kaanton se liya dars-e-tamanna ham ne
tere qatron se suni qira'at-e-dariya ham ne
tere zarron mein parhi aayat-e-sahra ham ne
kya bataayein k teri bazm mein kya kya dekha
ek aaiine mein duniya ka tamaasha dekha

teri hi gardan-e-rangiin mein hain baanhein apni
tere hi ishq mein hain sub-h ki aahein apni
tere hi husn se raushan hain nigaahein apni
kaj huyien teri hi mahfil mein kulaahein apni
baankpan siikh liya ishq ki uftaadon se
dil lagaaya bhi to tere hi parii-zaadon se

pahle jis chiiz ko dekha vo faza teri thi
pahle jo kaan mein aaii vo sada teri thi
paalna jis ne hilaaya vo hava teri thi
jis ne gahvaare mein chuuma vo saba teri thi
avvaliin raqs hava mast ghataaein teri
bhiigi hain apni masen aab-o-hava mein teri

ai vatan aaj se kya ham tere shaidaaii hain
aankh jis din se khuli tere tamannaaii hain
muddaton se tere jalvon ke tamaashaaii hain
ham to bachpan se tere 'aashiq-o-saudaaii hain
bhaaii tifli se har ik aan jahaan mein teri
baat tutla ke jo ki bhi to zabaan mein teri

husn tere hi manaazir ne dikhaaya ham ko
teri hi sub-h ke naghmon ne jagaaya ham ko
tere hi abr ne jhuulon mein jhulaaya ham ko
tere hi phuulon ne nau-shaah banaaya ham ko
khanda-e-gul ki khabar teri zabaani aaii
tere baaghon mein hava kha ke javaani aaii

tujh se munh mor ke munh apna dikhaayein ge kahaan
ghar jo chhorein ge to phir chhaavni chhaayein ge kahan
bazm-e-aghyaar mein aaraam ye paayein ge kahaan

tujh se ham ruuth ke jaaein bhi to jaayein ge kahaan
tere haathon mein hai qismat ka navishta apna
kis qadar tujh se bhi mazbuut hai rishta apna

ai vatan josh hai phir quvvat-e iimaani mein
khauf kya dil ko safiina hai jo tughyaani mein
dil se masruuf hain har tarah ki qurbaani mein
mahv hain jo teri kashti ki nigahbaani mein
gharq karne ko jo kahte hain zamaane vaale
muskuraate hain teri naav chalaane vaale

ham zamiin ko teri naapaak na hone dein ge
tere daaman ko kabhi chaak na hone dein ge
tujh ko jiite hain to ghamnaak n hone dein ge
aisi aksiir ko yuun khaak n hone dein ge
ji mein thaani hai yahi ji se guzar jaaein ge
kam se kam vaa'da ye karte hain k mar jaaein ge

Dear country,
the soul of the unpretentious
and the liberal.
Your gardens are fragrant
and the colorful springs.
Hidden are dreams of royalty
and majesty in your dust.
Every thistle in your way
attracts hundreds of faces.
There are pieces of diamonds
in your sticks and prigs.
Entombed in your dust
are the bones of our elders.

From your flowers,
we have found a world of color.
From your thorns,
we have learned the lesson of desire.
From your drops,
we have gained the sanctity of the oceans.
From your particles,
we have read lines of the Scriptures.
What more can we say
about what we saw in your assembly?
In one mirror, we saw the spectacle
of the whole world.

We have our arms spread around
your beautiful neck.

Hidden in your love
are our yearnings of each morning.
The sparkle of our eyes
owes itself to your beauty.
It was in your assembly
we tilted our caps with dignity.
Our adolescence learned a lot
from the passion for love.
When we fell in love,
we chose nothing other than your fairies.
The first thing that we saw
was your ambience.

The first thing that poured into our ears
was your sound.
The air that put the cradle in motion
came from you.
The air that kissed our homes and hearths
came from you.
The primal dance, the intoxicated air,
those dark clouds.
The freshness of your air moistened
the early signs of our youth.

Dear land, we have not become
your lovers today.
We have desired you
since the day we opened our eyes.
We have been watching
your spectacles for ages.
We have been your mad lovers
since our childhood.
We have liked your bearing in the world
since our infancy.
When we spoke with a stutter,
that was your language.

We learned to appreciate beauty
from your sceneries.
We woke up listening
to your morning melodies.
Your clouds, and nothing else,
rocked us in our swings.
Your flowers decked us
when we became bridegrooms.

Your tongue gave us the news
about the laughter of the flowers.
Nourished was our youth by the breeze
that came from your gardens.

If we turn our face from you,
where else could we go?
Where could we find a camp to live
if we leave our homes?
In the assembly of the strangers,
what comfort shall we find?
If we stop loving you,
what could be the target of our other love?
The written inscription of our fate
lies in your hands.
Our relationship is more robust with you
than yours with us.

Dear country, our zeal lies
in our power of conviction.
What is the fear if our boat is caught
in this deluge?
From the bottom of our hearts,
we are ready for any sacrifice.
We are busy acting
as the guardians of your boat.
Some want to sink this boat,
but those of us who are the boatsmen
have smiles on our faces.

Defiled shall not be the land
of our country.
Torn into pieces shall not be
your veil, ever.
A depressing mood
you will not slip into if we are alive.
Your elixir, your healing power,
shall never go to waste.
Determined, we are to sacrifice
our lives for you.
Above all, we shall die for you.
That is the promise.

Albeli Sub-ha (A Swinging Dawn) is unusual because it does not read like a patriotic poem on the surface. It seems to fall in the category of natural romanticism, something that was popularized by British poets like William Wordsworth

(1770–1850) and Samuel Taylor Coleridge (1772–1834). Josh writes in his individualistic style, using figurative and aesthetic diction that looks at nature through the prism of femininity. Nature is the bride that is removing tresses from her forehead. Wearing a decorative feminine rosy garb, every delicate petal in the garden, dipped in the crimson color, is drying a hem of the mantle in the fresh air. Another dimension of Josh's poetic art is his ability to reify every object, making every abstract physical thing in this natural panorama as something living, having the attributes of things that are animate. The morning star is shaking. The horizon is changing colors. Every bud is humming a tune. The gentle breeze is swinging the cradle of flowers. The deep structure of the poem becomes visible when the poet writes about hearing a voice (*havaa-e-gulshan ki narm rao mein ye kis ki aavaaz aa rahi hai,* meaning, like the tender flow of the air from the garden, whose voice am I hearing?) The poet poses a question, but he does not provide an answer. Whose voice is it? It could be the voice of the beloved that he is alluding to. Or it could be the voice of lady liberty, the icon of freedom. The ideal persona is left to the reader's imagination. The poem is a great joy to read, and its words linger on in one's consciousness long after the reading ends. *nazar jhukaae uruus-e-fitrat jabiin se zulfein hata rahi hai*

> *sahar ka taara hai zalzale mein ufuq ki lau tharthara rahi hai*
> *ravish ravish naghma-e-tarab hai chaman chaman jashn-e-rang-o-bu hai*
> *tuyuur shaakhon pe hain ghazal-khvaan kali kali gunguna rahi hai*
> *sitaara-e-sub-h ki rasiili jhapakti aankhon mein hain fasaane*
> *nigaar-e-mahtaab ki nashiili nigaah jaadu jaga rahi hai*
> *tuyuur bazm-e-sahar ke mutrib lachakti shaakhon pe ga rahe hain*
> *nasiim-e firdaus ki saheli gulon ko jhula jhula rahi hai*
> *kali pe bele ki kis ada se para hai shabnam ka ek moti*
> *nahien ye hiire ki kiil pahne koi pari muskura rahi hai*
> *shaluuka pahne hue gulaabi har ik subuk pankhuri chaman mein*
> *rangi hui surkh orhni ka hava mein pallu sukha rahi hai*
> *falak pe is tarah chhup rahe hain hilaal ke gird-o-pesh taare*
> *k jaise koi naii naveli jabiin se afshaan chhura rahi hai*
> *khatak ye kyuun dil mein ho chali phir chatakti kaliyo zara thaharna*
> *havaa-e-gulshan ki narm rau mein ye kis ki aavaaz aa rahi hai*

Eyes downcast,
the bride of nature,
is removing her tresses
from her forehead.
The morning star is shaking,
and the light of the horizon
is breaking.
In every pathway,
there is a melody of cheerfulness.
Every garden is celebrating

the season of color and fragrance.
The birds sitting on the branches
are singing melodious songs,
and every little bud
is also humming a tune.
Stories are hiding in the sparkling
and squinting eyes
of the stars of the morning.
The intoxicated eyes of the beloved,
a portrait of the moon,
are spreading the magic.
The birds,
who are minstrels of the morning,
sit on springing branches
and sing.
The gentle breeze,
which are friends with paradise,
is swinging the cradle of flowers.
A pearl of dew
is settled on jasmine's bud
and just look at its stylishness!
No, it is a fairy
wearing a necklace of diamonds
which is smiling.
Wearing a decorative feminine
rosy garb,
every delicate petal in the garden
dipped in the red color,
is drying a hem of the mantle
in the fresh air.
The stars are sparkling in the sky,
around the newly crescent moon,
like a young bride
is removing from her forehead
a shiny adornment.
Why is this inkling in my heart,
O blooming buds?
Please wait for a moment.
Like the tender speed of the air
from the garden,
whose voice am I hearing?

We conclude this chapter with selected lines from two of his landmark short poems, *Badli ka Chaand* and a legendary poem titled *Roop Mati*. Josh was known for his command of language and spontaneous idioms. The associated phrases and the rhyming of words were instantaneously piling up before him, and he simply had to touch them with his creative wand, and they got fixed in the lyrical rhyme scheme automatically. Josh's imagery and sensuality is such that we go with the flow and feel absorbed in it. Often, the individual words melt and vanish, and the scenario comes alive, and we become part of it.

Badli ka Chaand

khurshiid voh dekho duub gaya, zulmat ka nishaan lahraane laga
mehtaab voh halke baadal se chaandi ke varaq barsaane laga
parda jo uthaaya baadal ka darya pe tabassum daur gaya
chilman jo giraayi badli ki maidaan ka dil ghabraane laga
ubhra to tajalli daur gayi duuba to falak be-nuur huua
uljha to siyaahi daura di suljha to ziiya barsaane laga

The Moon and Clouds

Look, the sun has gone down and
the darkness is spreading.
The moon sailing through the fleeting clouds
is blowing silvery leaves away.
As faint grey clouds move away,
a silvery boat delicately sails across the sky.
But when gusts of wind sweep across,
the moon starts playing hide and seek.
There is a burst of light when it comes out,
but when it goes down, sudden darkness takes over.
When entangled, it vanishes;
when freed it is radiant and luminous.

Roop Mati

rukhsaar mein sham'e ka'ba ki zao
aankhon mein chiraagh-e dair ki lao
khush paikar o khush jamaal o khush-ruu
chatki huuyi chaandni lab-juu
palkon ki jhapak mein muskaraahat
sho'le ki khafiif thartharaahat
barsaat ki raagni ki raatein
ghaltiida hasiin dast o paa mein
anfaas mein kamsinii ki khushbuu
bangaal ka ankhariyon mein jaaduu
chehre pe shabaab ka talaatum
but-khaane ki sub-h ka tabassum
ras ki bondein k narm baatein
aawaaz mein maalve ki raatein

Roopmati

A radiant face,
lighted by a candle of Ka'ba
Eyes gleaming by the glow of a temple
A modest smile
as the eyebrows go down –
a quivering flame
On a rainy night,
someone singing a raagni
Hands and legs,
tender and supple
Breathing indicative of blooming youth
The Bengal magic working all over
The youth bursting from the limbs
The morning temple bells tolling
Soft speech drenched in dew drops
Whispering dreamy nights of Central India.

Note

1 Josh Malihabadi, *Yaadon Ki Baaraat* (Karachi: Josh Academy, 1970), p. 533. Translation by Surinder Deol.

9

TILOK CHAND MEHROOM

While looking at the ethical and healing tone of Mehroom's poetry, some people conclude that he was a poet of high moralistic ideals. But this was one aspect of his multifaceted genius. He was not a poet who promoted individualism; the essence of his poetic work lies in his humanitarian and communitarian outlook. Commitment to moral values is not enough. They are means to an end but not an end. In India we value progress, but it must serve the well-being of the collective. The foundation of a better life and a bright future can be laid only on highest ethical values. Slavery is a negation of this ideal. Freedom by contrast creates an environment that grows human potential. Mehroom's poetry should be looked at from the lens of love of the land and a creative yearning for freedom. This way we can recognize his true voice and reach the secret that resides in his heart.[1]

Gopi Chand Narang

Tilok Chand Mehroom was born in a small village Mauz'a Zaman Shah in Mianwali district, now in Pakistan, in 1887. When the Indus River drowned the village for good, the family moved to Issa Khail. He distinguished himself as a student and was trained as a teacher. After holding teaching positions in several schools, he achieved the distinction of being appointed as a lecturer in Urdu and Persian at Rawalpindi's prestigious Gordon College. After partition, he moved to Delhi and occupied a similar position at the Punjab University's Camp College. Mehroom's son Jagan Nath Azad grew up to be a distinguished poet in his own right.

Mehroom was born into and lived in a predominantly Muslim environment, although his family background was a conventional Hindu. He approached all religious scriptures with an open mind, and he continued to practice what was best in Islam, Hinduism, and Sikhism. Mehroom earned great respect from

DOI: 10.4324/9781003360841-11

people with diverse religious backgrounds for his lifelong pursuit of unity in diversity and love for human brotherhood.

Saraiki (Multani), a dialect of Western Punjabi, was Mehroom's mother tongue, although Urdu was the language of commerce and literary discourse. He was always conscious that how could he, who was not a resident of Delhi or Lucknow, become a credible poet of the Urdu language. This was the reason why he never adopted any younger poet as his disciple. But despite his humility and reservations, he distinguished himself in all genres of Urdu poetry – nazm, qasida, ghazal, rubai, and noha, but substantively he was a poet of nazm. As a man who learned to write poetry with his effort, he was undoubtedly inspired by the work of poets like Hali, Mohammad Husain Azad, Shibli, Chakbast, Allama Iqbal, and Durga Sahai Suroor Jahanabadi. While he was still a student in the tenth grade, he published poems in esteemed literary journals like *Makhzan* of Lahore. He started writing patriotic poetry at an early age, and this passion for expressing the beauty and diversity of the motherland continued until he died in 1966.

Sajjad Zaheer, one of the prominent voices in the progressive writers' movement, wrote the following note in his book *Roshnai* after meeting Mehroom in Rawalpindi in 1945.

> Pandit Tilok Chand Mehroom was the most distinguished literary personality in Rawalpindi. I was invited to speak at a forum organized by the Urdu Society of the Gordon College about the progressive writers' movement. I was very happy to discover that Hazrat Mehroom was presiding over the function. He was a professor of Urdu and Persian at Gordon College. He must be around sixty at that time. I was a little hesitant in saying anything in the presence of such a mature thinker and a highly respected teacher. Therefore, I opened my speech full of trepidation. When my speech ended, Pandit Ji told me that although he had different views about the progressive writers' movement, if its aims and objectives were the same as I had described in my speech, how could anyone have a different understanding of the movement. I thought his remark was a blessing for the movement as for me personally.[2]

In the long and arduous history of India's freedom struggle, there were many events in which the blood of nonviolent protestors was spilled for no reason. Still, nothing comes close to what happened in Jallianwala Bagh in Amritsar on the fateful day of April 13, 1919. A crowd of peaceful protestors had gathered to celebrate the festival of Baisakhi when acting brigadier general Reginald Dyer ordered his troops to fire on unarmed civilians, killing hundreds of people and injuring many more. It was outrageous that Dyer was allowed to resign with no punishment, although Winston Churchill, then secretary of state, wanted Dyer to be disciplined. Michael O'Dwyer, who was Lt. Governor of Punjab at the time of the Amritsar massacre and approved of Dyer's action, was killed by Udham Singh in March 1940 in London. Udham Singh had suffered injuries in the massacre. Poet Rabindranath Tagore renounced his knighthood in protest of the deaths of innocent people who had gathered for a peaceful protest. Many poets wrote poems about the genocidal massacre, including Mehroom. His poem of 12 couplets is unique because he not only ruefully captured the cruelty and barbarity in his words, but he also compared Dyer to Nadir Shah, the notorious invader and mass murderer. Let us read some of the couplets from this poem.

mela samajh ke baagh mein daakhil hua koi
jhamghat a'jiib jaan ke shaamil hua koi
nikla tha koi luutne fasl-e bahaar ko
aaghuush mein liye tha koi shiir khwaar ko
thi darmiyaan-e baagh hazaaron ki bhiir bhaar
naagaah ik taraf se chali goliyon ki baar
phir voh hua k jis se larazati hai tan mein jaan
patthar ka dil banaayuun to kuchh ho sake biyaan
daayir ke qatl-e aa'm ne khuun-e vafa kiya
lohuu se laal daaman-e bartaania kiya

One entered the garden
thinking that it was funfair.
One entered because it gave the feel
of an extraordinary assembly.
One had come to enjoy the beauty
of spring at its best.
One had come carrying a kid
who was being breastfed.
In the center of the garden,
there was a gathering of thousands.
A rain shower of bullets started
for no earthly reason.
My inner being trembles
to describe in words what happened.
If I could turn my heart into a piece of stone,
then I could say something.
Dyer murdered the meaning of fidelity, and
the emblem of Britannia was drenched
in the innocents' blood.

Lala Lajpat Rai, a highly respected leader of the independence movement, suffered injuries when the police attacked a peaceful march, and he died on November 17, 1928. A month later, Bhagat Singh, a young revolutionary, killed a British officer named Saunders, mistaking him for James Scott, superintendent of police. The latter had ordered the attack on the protesters in which Lala Lajpat Rai was a participant. While in jail, Bhagat Singh and his associates went on a hunger strike to protest terrible prison conditions. The hunger strike gave rise to popular support, and Jawaharlal Nehru visited the jail where Bhagat Singh was held. A special tribunal in October 1930 found Singh and two of his associates guilty, and they were sentenced to death by hanging. Bhagat Singh, 23 years old, Rajguru, and Sukhdev were hanged in the Lahore jail on March 23, 1931. The freedom struggle produced many martyrs, but Bhagat Singh occupies a special place. We can best explain it in the words of Jawaharlal Nehru:

> Bhagat Singh did not become popular because of his act of terrorism but because he seemed to vindicate, for the moment, the honor of Lala La-jpat Rai, and through him, of the nation. He became a symbol, the act was forgotten, the symbol remained, and within a few months, each town and village of Punjab, and to a lesser extent in the rest of northern India, resounded with his name. Innumerable songs grew about him, and the popularity that the man achieved was something amazing.[3]

Mehroom's poem about Shahid Bhagat Singh is a fitting tribute to the memory of great martyr. He is presented as a 'sardar,' which we have inadequately translated as 'leader' because it could mean many things, including the pioneer, guide, pathfinder, hero, protector, and fighter. If all martyrs are placed in a line, Bhagat Singh is not the first among equals but, more accurately, the greatest among all. It is not incorrect to say that Bhagat Singh is not one person's name; rather, he is an icon, a shining symbol of what martyrdom is all about. It is the unconditional love of the country, and when the opportunity arises, it is about sacrificing one's life for the freedom and well-being of the nation.

Mehroom celebrates Bhagat Singh's entry into the jailhouse. He didn't get into jail to spend time as a prisoner. The prison was a temporary dwelling place before execution. The best part of the poem is where Mehroom describes Bhagat Singh's state of mind. As a prisoner, he was not downcast, worried, or anxious. He was joyous, singing, dancing as if this was not hanging but a wedding, a union with a loved one. He kissed the rope used for hanging like a garland of flowers. Mehroom ends the poem while putting a curse on the oppressors for the evil deed of taking the life of a patriot like Bhagat Singh.

zindaan mein shahiidon ka vo sardaar aaya
shaida-e-vatan paikar-e-iisaar aaya
hai daar-o-rasan ki sarfaraazi ka din
sardaar bhagat-singh sar-e daar aaya
ta daar-o-rasan shauq se ithlaa ke gaya
to shaan-e-shahadat bhi vo dikhla ke gaya
tukre hota hai y dil tire maatam mein
laashe ka ang ang vo katva ke gaya
pi kar mai-e-shauq vo jhuumana tera
be-parvaayaana vo ghuumna tera
hai naqsh tira ahl-e-vatan ke dil par
phaansi ki rasan ko vo chuumana tera

jaam-e-hubb-e-vatan ke ai matvaale
ai paikar-e-namuus hamiyyat vaale
ho aalam-e-arvaah mein shaadaan k nahien
ab tere vatan mein vo hukuumat vaale[4]

Lo, the leader of the martyrs,
has entered the prison house.
The lover of the land and
an icon of sacrifice itself has arrived.
This is the day to celebrate and
exalt the stake and the rope.
Lo, the leader Bhagat Singh has arrived!
His passion for walking the gallows is
like simply walking in the air.
He demonstrated the glory of martyrdom.
Our hearts are shattered into pieces when
we grieve for him.
He left only after each part of his body
was slashed into pieces.
Dancing after drinking the wine of passion
and natural dance movements,
they left a mark on the hearts of patriots,
the way he kissed the rope of the gallows.
The champion of the cup
of the wine of the country's love.
The symbol of honor and courage itself.
Wonder whether in the world of the dead,
You must be proud and fulfilled.
The oppressors who tortured you
have been made to quit lock stock and barrel.

Another poem *Phuul Barsaao Shahiidaan-e Watan Ki Khaak Par* also deals with the theme of martyrdom and including all martyrs. Mehroom uses two interconnected metaphors of 'flowers' and 'ashes.' Honoring the dead with flowers is an old Indian tradition. Garlands are placed on the dead bodies, and flower petals are tossed in the air as the body is taken away for cremation. The poem starts by praising the bravery of these martyrs. They are eulogized in the second stanza for their constancy, their oath of allegiance to protect their motherland's honor. They were the best among the best. Their hearts were filled with the love of all humanity, not limited to their country. Their presence was a source of delight and inspiration for others. Such was the strength of their commitment to the motherland that they made even death to be afraid of them while it succeeded in taking away their lives.

jin sar-afraazon ki ruuhein aaj hain aflaak par
maut khud hairaan thi jin ki jur'at-e-be-baak par

naqsh jin ke naam hain ab tak dil-e-ghamnaak par
rahmat-e-iizad ho daa'im in ki jaan-e-paak par
phuul barsaao shahiidaan-e-vatan ki khaak par
phuul barsaao k phuulon mein hai khushbu-e-vafa
thi sarisht-e-paak in ki aashiq-e-juu-e-vafa
maut par un ki gae jo ruu-e-dar-ruu-e-vafa
kyon na hon ahl-e-vatan ke ashk-e-khuun juu-e-vafa
phuul barsaao shahiidaan-e-vatan ki khaak par
chashm-e-zaahir-biin samajhti hai k bas vo mar gae
dar-haqiiqat maut ko faani vo saabit kar gae
jo vatan ke vaaste katva ke apne sar gaye
khuun se apne rang tasviir-e-vafa mein bhar gaye
phuul barsaao shahiidaan-e-vatan ki khaak par
dekh lena khuun-e-naahaq rang ik din laaega
khud-gharaz zaalim kiye par apne khud pachhtaaega
raah par daur-e-zamaan aakhir kabhi to aaega
aasmaan is khaak ki taqdiir ko chamkaaega
phuul barsaao shahiidaan-e-vatan ki khaak par

The souls of all those who gave their lives
for the land now live in heaven.
Even death was shocked
at the audacity of their braveness.
Their memories are etched forever
in our grieving lives.
May the mercy of God
be specially reserved for their holy lives!

Shower flowers on ashes
of martyrs of our land!

Shower flowers because they carry
the fragrance of constancy.
They had a sacred form,
these lovers seeking constancy.
They looked upon death with
the power of the lover's perseverance.
Why shouldn't the tears of the people
appear like blood drops of endurance?

Shower flowers on ashes
of martyrs of our land!

The outer eye looks upon them
and thinks that they died,
but in reality

they made death itself to perish.
Those who gave their lives
to the country, they filled
the portrait of constancy
with the color of their blood.

Shower flowers on ashes
of martyrs of our land!

You should wait and see
that the blood of the innocent
will show its vengeance one day
and the selfish oppressor will feel sorry
for his draconian deeds.
This cycle of the movement of ages will,
at last, find some respite to correct itself.
The heavens will take pity on
the dust and particles of this land.

Shower flowers on ashes
of martyrs of our land!

The following poem *Khaak-e Hind* is a celebration of India in terms of its *khaak*, *dharti*, which can be translated narrowly as soil, dust, grime, or more broadly as the earth, farms, fields, and land. The poet does not spare a beautiful attribute that is not used to describe land's beauty. It is more than a star; each particle of the land is radiating light. From its splendor, we can see eternal beauty. The beauty that we see steals our hearts. It cannot be found anywhere else. The land of India is the pride of the world. Even when it is passing through a difficult time, it stays as majestic as the sky. The poem honors explicitly those who fight to protect the land from aggressors. The sceneries overflowing with nature's bounty make our hearts captives of this land.

The poem was written when the country was still under the control of the colonialists. This fills the poet's heart with sadness, but he points out that the people have not lost their spirit to fight for the country's freedom. Although misery caused by slavery has crossed all limits, this has not diminished the perpetual beauty and elegance of the land. It is a matter of time before this land's bounties will be revealed for the world to witness.

anjum se barh ke tera har zarra zau-fishaan hai
jalvon se tere ab tak husn-e-azal a'yaan hai
andaaz-e-dil-farebi jo tujh mein hai kahaan hai
fakhr-e-zamaana tu hai aur naazish-e-jahaan hai
uftaadgi mein bhi to ham-auj-e-aasmaan hai
ai khaak-e-hind teri azmat mein kya gumaan hai
manzar vo jaan-faza hain aur dil-paziir tere

jaanein hain tujh pe shaida aur dil asiir tere
shiiriin o saaf dariya hain juu-e-shiir tere
hain dasht-o-koh-o-sahra jannat-naziir tere
ankhein jidhar uthaao firdaus ka samaan hai
ai khaak-e-hind teri azmat mein kya gumaan hai
tujh ko mita diya hai har-chand aasmaan ne
phuunka hai aah dil ko soz-e-gham-e-nihaan ne
chhori na taab apni par husn-e-dil-sitaan ne
jauhar bhare hain tujh mein sannaa'-e-do-jahaan ne
fasl-e-khizaan hai teri phir bhi tu gul-fishaan hai
ai khaak-e-hind teri azmat mein kya gumaan hai
go had se barh gayaa hai ranj-o-malaal tera
ab tak mita nahien hai naqsh-e-jamaal tera
aakhir kabhi to hoga zaahir kamaal tera
hoga kabhi to aakhir daur-e-zavaal tera
kab ik ravish pe qaa'im ye daur-e-aasmaan hai
ai khaak-e-hind teri azmat mein kya gumaan hai

More than a star,
each particle of yours
is radiating light.
From your splendor,
we can see eternal beauty.
The style that steals our hearts,
where else can we find it?
You are the honor of the time,
and the pride of the world.
Even in your distress,
you are compared to the sky.
O Land of India,
who can doubt the majesty
of your being?

Life-giving and heart pleasing
sceneries of yours.
Our being is deeply in love with you and
our hearts are your captives.
Your river waters are sweet and
unblemished like milk.
Your deserts and wilderness for us are like
those found in paradise.
Wherever you raise your glances,
there is the atmosphere of heaven.
O Land of India,

who can doubt the majesty
of your being?

You have been diminished by
the angels of the skies.
The heart is blown apart by
deep sadness that lies within.
People who possess the beauty of
the vexations of their heart have
not given up.
You're filled with the jewels
chiseled by artisans —
masters of two worlds.
You're passing through the autumn,
yet you're sprinkled with flowers.
O Land of India,
who can doubt the majesty
of your being?

Although misery has crossed all limits,
this has not devoured your
endless beauty and elegance.
Your glory will be revealed one day.
The cycle of your downward spiral will end.
The order of the angels of the sky is
not limited to a single mode.
O Land of India,
who can doubt the majesty
of your being?

The above selections are excellent examples of patriotic poetry, but they do not fully present the variegated rainbow-like spectrum of Mehroom's literary excellence and legacy. His range of subjects was much more comprehensive than many of the other contemporary poets. We conclude this chapter with a famous historical poem *Noor Jahan Ka Mazar*, frequently studied as a classic poem in school textbooks. Noor Jahan (1577–1645), also known as Mehr-un Nissa, was the twentieth and the last queen of the Mughal emperor Jahangir. It is said that she was the most beautiful of the Mughal queens. Gold coins were struck in her name. But now, her mausoleum is found in a dilapidated condition, standing utterly neglected on the banks of river Ravi. Selected stanzas of the poem are reproduced below.

din ko bhi yahaan shab ki siyaahi ka samaan hai
kahte hain ye aaraam-gah-e-nuur-jahaan hai
muddat hui vo sham'a tah-e-khaak nihaan hai
utthta magar ab tak sar-e-marqad se dhuaan hai

tujh si malika ke liye baara-dari hai
ghaaliicha sar-e-farsh hai koi na dari hai
kya aa'lam-e-bechaargi ai taaj-vari hai
din ko yahiin bisraam yahiin shab-basri hai
hasrat hai tapakti dar-o-diivaar se kya kya
hota hai asar dil pe in aasaar se kya kya
naale hain nikalte dil-afgaar se kya kya
utthte hain sharar aah-e shararbaar se kya kya
duniya ka ye anjaam hai dekh ai dil-e-naadaan
haan bhuul na jaaye tujhe ye madfan-e-viiraan
baaqi hain na vo baagh na vo qasr na aivaan
aaraam ke asbaab na vo aish ke saamaan
tuuta hua ik saahil-e-raavi pe makaan hai
din ko bhi jahaan shab ki siyaahi ka samaan hai

Noor Jahaan's Mausoleum

Even during the daytime,
it feels like the darkness of the evening.
They say this is the final resting place of Noor Jahaan.
It has been ages, but the candle burns
from under the dust.
Smoke is seen rising from the top of the grave.

This summer house with twelve doors
is meant for a queen.
There is no carpet to cover the floor,
not even an ordinary floor covering.
What a state of helplessness.
O, what kind of kingship is this?
You rest here during the day.
You rest here during the night.

What kind of longing is seen
falling from the doors and windows.
How the heart is touched by the elements seen here!
Lamentations pour out from the broken heart.
Sparks are seen rising from the rain of gleaming flashes.

Look my innocent heart;
this is how the world ends!
You should not forget this grave in a deserted place.
Gardens remain no more,
nor there are mansions and meeting places.
There is absolutely nothing here for relaxation,
no pleasure-inducing devices.

A broken building stands on the banks
of the river Ravi near Lahore.
Even during the daytime,
it feels like the darkness of the evening.

Notes

1 Gopi Chand Narang, 'Mehroom Ki Qaumi Shaay'iri' in *Afkaar-e Mehroom*, ed. Malik Ram (New Delhi: Mehroom Memorial Committee), p. 106. The year of the publication is not mentioned. Translated by Surinder Deol.
2 Gopi Chand Narang, ed. *Aasaar-e Mehroom* (*Pagdandi* of Amritsar's Mehroom Number), (New Delhi: Maktaba Jamia Ltd., 1968). Back of the title page.
3 S.K. Mittal, Irfan Habib (June 1982), 'The Congress and the Revolutionaries in the 1920s,' *Social Scientist*, 10 (6): 20–37.
4 Ali Jawwad Zaidi, *Urdu Mein Qaumi Shaa'yri Ke Sao Saal* (Lucknow: Uttar Pradesh Urdu Academy, 1982), p. 238.

10

FIRAQ GORAKHPURI

In the death of Firaq and Josh Malihabadi, a few days ago, Urdu and Hindusthani have suffered two grievous blows ... Firaq Gorakhpuri appealed to and affected our people at many layers of consciousness. It was a privilege for me to have known Firaq for long years. He wrote to me now and then as he wrote to my father. In recent months, one could see from his letters, that he was feeling that his end was near. Yet, when I saw him, I was told that he was much better and would soon be discharged from the hospital. Such are ways of life and death.[1]

Indira Gandhi

Raghupati Sahay Firaq was born in 1896 in Gorakhpur, Uttar Pradesh, in a reputable Kayastha family. Firaq inherited from his father the qualities of humanism, pacifism, universalism, and secularism that became hallmarks of his poetic philosophy. As a high-achieving student, he mastered several languages – Hindi, Sanskrit, Urdu, Persian, and English – at an early age. The family was deeply religious, and it observed all Hindu customs and traditions with meticulous care. Firaq gained spiritual knowledge from the Vedas, the Gita, epics like Ramayana and Mahabharata, and the works of saint poets like Kalidas, Surdas, and Tulsidas that influenced his thinking in later years. The traces of these rich traditions are found in the totality of Firaq's poetic work, so much so that some people labeled him a 'Hindu poet of Urdu language' as a compliment. Firaq rejected this description and considered it an attack by fanatical elements to pigeonhole his standing as a great Urdu poet. It was a limiting view of the diversity of ideas in Firaq's verse. It is more accurate to say that he combined three primary influences of his life in his poetry – ancient Hindu India and its scriptures, the Indian Islam concerning the Sufi tradition of the subcontinent, and the contemporary Western philosophy.

DOI: 10.4324/9781003360841-12

In 1914, he fell victim to a deceitful act in which he was married to a woman named Kishori Devi, who was a good person, but intellectually she was no match to Firaq. This event in his life led to ruinous consequences such as marital unhappiness, separation, and pain that lasted until the last day of his life. He expressed his frustration in a couplet.

gham-e firaq to us din gham-e firaq hua
jab unko payar kiya main ne jin se pyaar nahien

My sadness became despair on that day
when I was made to love someone
for whom I had no feelings.

Firaq received his higher education in Allahabad. In 1918, he was selected for the prestigious Indian Civil Service. He gave up that career track to work for the District Congress Committee and went to prison with other Congress Party members. As a young party worker, he was a frequent visitor to the Anand Bhavan and worked closely with Pandit Jawaharlal Nehru. He got to know Indira Gandhi when she was a young girl, and this association lasted for the rest of his life. He ended his political aspirations in 1927 when he took up teaching as a profession, first at Lucknow and then at Kanpur. After earning his MA degree in English from Agra University in 1930, he was hired as a lecturer in English at Allahabad University. He spent the rest of his life teaching English literature. He was awarded Padma Bhushan in 1968, Jnanpith Award in 1969, and Sahitya Akademi Fellowship in 1970. He died in 1982 at the age of 85 at the New Delhi residence of advocate R.K. Garg, one of his students. Thousands of Allahabad residents showed up to bid farewell at his public funeral. Firaq had contemplated the day of his death, and he had written a couplet about it.

aaj allahabad hai suuna shaa'yir ke uth jaane se
sadiyon sadiyon dhuundo ge lekin kahaan firaq ko paao ge

Today, Allahabad is forlorn and bereft
because of the poet's demise.
You will search for Firaq over centuries,
but you will not find anyone like him.

Firaq's accurate epithet can be a full-blooded poet of 'Indianness.' However, the diversity of India and Urdu's *Ganga-jamuni* paradigm makes it difficult to delineate what this 'Indianness' means precisely. In this context, we recall Indigenous flavors found in poets like Amir Khusrau, Mohammad Quli Qutb Shah, Mir Taqi Mir, Ghalib, Iqbal, a host of others. Given India's vastness and variegated cultural roots, the 'Indianness' of each one of these has its specific characteristics. We shall speak of Firaq's approach in the light of selections we have presented in this Chapter. Firaq claimed that a poet's hands are meant to praise the bells of the temple of humanity and the symphony of creation.

Firaq grew up to be the most respected and prolific poet of the twentieth century, and his name is mentioned along with other major poets of the past century, like Iqbal, Josh, and Faiz. Besides ghazal, he wrote beautiful rubais on Indian domestic life and womanhood. He did not write many nazms, but his nazm poetry occupies a special place in Urdu literature, even with the output he left behind. He also took pride in his achievement, as modesty was not a part of his temperament.

> aane vaali naslein tum par rashk karein gi ham-a'sro
> jab ye dhyaan aaye ga un ko tum ne firaq ko dekha tha.[2]

> The coming generations will envy you,
> my contemporaries
> when they will come to know
> that you saw Firaq in person.

We start with an exceptional poem titled *Hindola* (The Cradle). This remarkable epic poem encompasses 5,000 years of Indian history, from the great scriptures like Ramayana and Mahabharata to modern poets like Ghalib and Tagore. Firaq weaves his personal story into the more remarkable account of his motherland and ends the poem with a plea for better opportunities for India's younger generation, who would one day become guardians of this great nation. As the poem is very long, we present an abbreviated version that includes the most substantial parts of this masterpiece.

> dayaar-e-hind tha gahvaara yaad hai hamdam
> bahut zamaana hua kis ke kis ke bachpan ka
> isi zamiin pe khela hai raam ka bachpan
> isi zamiin pe un nanhe nanhe haathon ne
> kisi samay mein dhanush-baan ko sambhaalaa tha
> isi dayaar ne dekhi hai krishn ki liila
> yahiin gharondon mein siita sulochana raadha
> kisi zamaane mein guriyon se khelti hongi
> yahi zamiin yahi dariya pahaar jangal baagh
> hua zamaana k siddhaarth ke the gahvaare
> mohanjodaaro harappa ke aur ajanta ke
> banaane vaale yahiin ballamon se khele the
> isi hindole mein bhavabhut o kaaliidaas kabhi
> humak humak ke jo tutla ke gungunaaye the
> sarasvati ne zabaanon ko un ki chuuma tha
> yahiin ke chaand va suuraj khilaune the un ke
> inhiin fazaaon mein bachpan pala tha khusrav ka
> isi zamiin se utthe hain tansen aur akbar
> rahiim nanak o chaitanya aur chishti ne
> inhien fazaaon mein bachpan ke din guzaare the
> ahalyabaaii daman padmini o raziya ne

yahiin ke peron kī shaaḳhon mein daale the jhuule
inhien nazaaron mein saavan ke giit gaaye the
inhien fazaaon mein guunji thi totli boli
kabir-das tukaaraam suur o miira ki
isi zamiin ke the laal miir o ghaalib bhi
aniis o haali o iqbaal aur vaaris-shaah
yahiin ki ḳhaak se ubhre the premchand o tagore
yahiin se utthe the tahziib-e-hind ke me'aamaar
isi zamiin se utthe vo desh ke saavant
ura diya tha jinhein company ne topon se
isi zamiin se uthi hain an-ginat naslein
pale hain hind hindole mein an-ginat bachche
is arz-e-paak se utthiin bahut si tahziibein
yahiin tuluu huiin aur yahiin ghuruub huiin
isi zamiin se ubhre kaii uluum-o-funuun
faraaz-e-koh-e-himaala ye daur-e-gang-o-jaman
aur in ki god mein parvarda kaarvaanon ne
yahiin rumuuz-e-ḳhiraam-e-sukuun-numa siikhe
nasiim-e-sub-h-e-tamaddun ne bhairviin chheri
vo din ke barhte hue saaye sah-pahar ka sukuun
sukuut shaam ka jab donon vaqt milte hain
gharaz jhalakte hue sarsari manaazir par
mujhe gumaan paristaaniyat ka hota tha
har ek chiiz ki vo khwaab-naak asliyyat
mere shu'uur ki chilman se jhaankta tha koi
liye rubuubiyat-e-kaaenaat ka ehsaas
har ek jalve mein ghaib o shuhuud ka vo milaap
har ik nazaara ik aaiina-khaana-e-hairat
har ek manzar-e-maanuus ek hairat-zaar
kahiin rahuun kahiin khelon kahiin parhuun likhuun
mere shu'uur pe mandlaate the manaazir-e-dahr
main akasr un ke tasavvur mein duub jaata tha
vafuur-e-jazba se ho jaati thi mizhah pur-nam
mujhe yaqiin hai in u'nsuri manaazir se
k aam bachchon se leta tha main ziyaada asar
kahaaniyaan jo sunuun un mein duub jaata tha
inhien fasaanon mein pinhaan the zindagi ke rumuuz
unhien fasaanon mein milti thiin ziist ki qadrein
rumuuz-e-besh-baha theth aadmiyat ke
kahaaniyaan thiin k sad-dars-gaah-e-riqqat-e-qalb
har ik kahaani mein shaaistagi-e-gham ka sabaq
vo u'nsur aansuon ka daastaan-e-insaan mein
vo nal-daman ki katha sarguzasht-e-savitri

shakuntla ki kahaani bharat ki qurbaani
vo marg-e-bhishm-pitaamah vo sej tiiron ki
vo paanchon paandavon ki sovarg-yaatra ki katha
vatan se rukhsat-e-siddhārth rām ka ban-baas
vafa ke baa'd bhi siita ki vo jalaa-vatani
vo raaton-raat siri-krishn ko uthaaye hue
bala ki qaid se vasdev ka nikal jaana
vo andhkaar vo baarish barhi hui jamuna
gham-aafriin kahaani vo hiir raanjha ki
shuau'ur-e-hind ke bachpan ki yaadgaar-e-aziim
k aise vaise takhayyul ki saans ukhar jaaye
kahaaniyon ki ye daulat ye be-baha daulat
fasaane dekh lo in se nazar bhi aati hai
fasaanon se mere bachpan ne sochna siikha
fasaanon se mujhe sanjiidgi ke dars mile
fasaanon mein nazar aati thi mujh ko ye duniya
gham o khushi mein rachi pyaar mein basaaii hui
meri sarisht mein ziddain ke kaii jore
shur'uu hi se the maujuud aab-o-taab ke saath
mere mizaaj mein pinhaan thi ek jadaliyyat
ragon mein chhuutte rahte the be-shumaar anaar
nadiim ye hain mere baal-pan ke kuchh aasaar
vafuur o shiddat-e-jazbaat ka ye aalam tha
nadiim zikr-e-javaani se kaanp jaata huun

The Cradle

The land of India was once
a swinging cradle, my friend.
A long time ago.
It's a story of the childhood of many.
Ram spent his boyhood
playing here and there.
In this ancient land,
with his small youthful hands,
he managed to hold in balance
arrow and arch.
This very land witnessed
Krishna's divine play.
In nest like shelters here,
Sita, Sulochana, Radha,
sometime in the past,
must have played with dolls.
These very fields, these rivers,
hills, forests, gardens,

in the times past,
were home to Siddhartha.
The builders of Mohanjodaro,
Harappa, and Ajanta
played here with arrows and lancets.
In this very swinging cradle once,
Bhavabhuti and Kalidas
must have uttered melodies
in their stammering voices.
Sarasvati cuddled words
as they poured out of her mouth.
The moons and suns of this place
were their playthings.
In these environs,
Khusrau grew up to be a man.
From this dust, once rose
Tansen and Akbar.
Rahim, Nanak, Chaitanya,
and Chishti too gained consciousness
in this very environment.
Ahalyabai, Daman, Padmini, and Raziya
placed their swings
on the branches of native trees.
In these spectacular valleys,
they sang melodies of Savan.
The echo of their lisping tongues
was heard here.
Kabir Das, Tuka Ram, Sur, and Mira too.
Mir and Ghalib, the loved ones of this soil.
Anis, Hali, Iqbal, and Waris Shah.
Premchand and Tagore rose from this soil.
Also, the builders of the Indian civilization.
Great thinkers were produced by this dust.
And those brave ones who were blown away
by the company's guns.
Generations came after generations, countless.
The cradle of India made boundless kids grow up.
From this sacred land came many civilizations.
They saw the light of the day and,
their nightfall.
Arts and sciences saw the first light
of the day here.
Great heights of the Himalayas,
the vast spread of rivers Ganga and Jamuna.

And in their lap,
caravans found nourishment,
and they grasped paths of peace
and tranquility.
The morning breeze of civilization
streamed notes of Bhairvi.
The lengthening shadows and afternoons
filled with quietness.
The stillness of the evening
when two time zones come together.
When I faintly looked
at the typical views around me,
I felt that I had been transported
into a fairyland.
Things showed reality
as if it was just like a dream.
From the screen of my consciousness,
someone looked down,
feeling the providence
of the whole existence.
In each spectacle, in each demonstration
there was a union of the unseen
and the witnessed.
The panorama was a mirror-house
of wonders.
Every familiar view was part
of the wonderland.
Wherever I lived, wherever I played,
wherever I studied,
scenes of the whole world circled
my consciousness.
I used to drown myself
in the contemplation of these things.
My eyelashes used to get teary
with these emotions.
I put my trust in these elemental views
as I was much more sensitive
than other kids.
I used to lose myself in the stories
that I heard because they had hidden
in them the secrets of life.
From these stories,
I learned the norms and values of life.
There were many mysteries

about how to be a good human being.
These were not stories, tales or myths.
They were a hundred ways
of gaining richness of knowledge.
Every word gave the lesson
of the secrets of sorrow.
Those elements showed up
as tears in the narrative of humankind.
That tale of Daman and an account of Savitri.
The myth of Shakuntla and the sacrifice of Bharat.
The death of Bhisham Pitama on a bed of arrows.
Recite the incident of how the five Pandavas
reached paradise.
Siddharth saying farewell to his dominion
and Rama's exile.
With her fidelity beyond reproach,
how Sita was still made to exit.
How carrying Krishna in his fold
in the darkness of the night,
Vasudev's escape from that dreadful prison.
That pitch darkness, the flooded Jamuna.
That heart-rending story of Heer and Ranjha.
These are great memories of ancient India's
cumulative consciousness
that would confound ordinary minds.
This is the wealth of stories,
this limitless treasure trove of stories.
Look at these stories; you can see them,
and they are visible.
My childhood learned to think
after reading these stories.
They gave me lessons
about sobriety and contemplation.
I looked upon the world
through the prism of these stories.
Mixed up in agony and happiness,
situated in love.
My temperament learned to live
with contradictions.
Present from the beginning
with brightness and grandeur.
In my disposition was present
the quality of dialecticism.
In my veins exploded

several firecrackers.
My friend, these were some of the influences
of my childhood.
There was such a gush of feelings and emotions
that I'm afraid of talking about my youth.

Firaq was fully involved in the freedom struggle in his youth, and he spent a year and half in prison with Jawaharlal Nehru. The following couplet is a visual echo of the agony of those solitary and lonesome nights. Note the way the sound of syllables pierces the dread of darkness.

ikka dukka sadaaye zanjiir
zindaan mein raat ho gaaii hai!

The lonesome sound of the jingle
of chains now and again.
A dreadful night has fallen
on the prison!

The theme of *Aazadi* (Freedom) is an undercurrent in the poetry of the freedom movement. Many Urdu poets wrote poems using the title *Azaadi*, but as their approaches and skills differed, they brought various thoughts to this subject. Firaq, too, wrote a poem with this title. Some lines of this sensitive poem were already presented in Chapter 5, but we offer the complete poem here. In these 16 couplets, the poet introduces several qualifying metaphors to define freedom's meaning and implications. While using the word *aazaadi* as a *radiif*, he carefully selects *qafiyas* that make the concept come alive. But as the dream of independence was still a dream, the picture that emerges is somewhat formidable. The words evening and darkness are used repeatedly to denote freedom, and the end of slavery is blended with the dawn. This is understandable because there were times of hope in the long struggle for freedom, and there were times of great suffering. The poem asserts that the workers and farmers will usher in a new world by their sacrifices. We presume that the poem's overall creative flavor had to do with the difficult times when it was written.

meri sada hai gul-e-sham'a-e-shaam-e-aazaadi
suna raha huun dilon ko payaam aazaadi
lahu vatan ke shahiidon ka rang laaya hai
uchhal raha hai zamaane mein naam-e-aazaadi
mujhe baqa ki zaruurat nahien k faani huun
meri fana se hai paida davaam-e-aazaadi
jo raaj karte hain jamhuuriyat ke parde mein
unhein bhi hai sar-o-sauda-e-khaam-e-aazaadi
banaaeinge naii duniya kisaan aur mazduur
yahi sajaaeinge diivaan-e-aam-e-azaadi
faza mein jalte dilon se dhuaan sa uthta hai

are ye sub-h-e-ghulaamī ye shaam-e-aazaadi
ye mahr-o-maah ye taare ye baam-e haft-aflaak
bahut buland hai in se maqaam-e-aazaadi
faza-e-shaam-e-sahar mein shafaq jhalakti hai
k jaam mein hai mai-e-laala-faam-e-aazaadi
syaah-khaana-e-duniya ki zulmatein hain do-rang
nihaan hai sub-h-e-asiiri mein shaam-e-aazaadi
sukuun ka naam na le hai vo qaid-e-be-mii'aad
hai pai-ba-pai harakat mein qayaam-e-aazaadi
ye kaarvaan hain pasmaandgaan-e-manzil ke
ki rahravon mein yahi hain imaam-e-aazaadi
dilon mein ahl-e-zamiin ke hai niiv us ki magar
qusuur-e-khuld se uuncha hai baam-e-aazaadi
vahaan bhi khaak-nashiinon ne jhande gaar diye
mila na ahl-e-duval ko maqaam-e-aazaadi
hamaare zor se zanjiir-e-tiirgi tuuti
hamaara soz hai maah-e-tamaam-e-aazaadi
tarannum-e-sahari de raha hai jo chhup kar
hariif-e-sub-h-e-vatan hai ye shaam-e-aazaadi
hamaare siine mein shole bharak rahe hain Firaaq
hamaari saans se raushan hai naam-e-aazaadi

I lend my voice to the rose-like candle
of freedom's evening.
I am presenting to the hearts of the listeners
the message of freedom.
The blood of the martyrs
has given us its reward.
The echo of freedom, its name,
is being heard everywhere.
I don't need immortality
because I'm a mortal being.
From my death is born
the immortal spirit of freedom.
Those who rule the country
under the veil of democracy
do not know the true meaning
of real freedom.
The farmers and workers
will make a new world.
The magisterial court of freedom
will be arranged here.
Our surroundings are filled
with the smoke of burning hearts.

Bemoan this morning of slavery!
Hail this evening of freedom!
These suns and moons and the stars
in the seven layers of the sky
are marvelous and the place of freedom
is majestically high.
In the environs of the morning and evening,
we find twilight.
The spirit of freedom that has the color
of tulips is in our wine glasses.
The blackness of the world
has two colors of darkness —
hidden in the morn of slavery,
there is an evening of freedom.
Don't talk of peace of mind
because it is a limitless prison;
the order of freedom is in motion
without a stop.
These caravans belong to those
who are tired and dispirited,
but among the travelers,
there are leaders of freedom.
The dome of freedom is higher
than the fault-ridden paradise.
Even there, the lowly of the earth
have put up their flags.
Alas, the rich, did not find
the resting place of freedom.
With our strength, we have broken
chains of darkness.
It is our passion that keeps shining
the moon of freedom.
The melody of the morning is inviting
from its secret place.
The country's chained morning is blocking
the evening of freedom.
In our bosom, flames are rising, Firaq.
The name of freedom is luminous
with the force of our breath.

Countries or nations come into being in one of the two ways: either the natives who have lived in land for a long time come together and form a political entity that eventually becomes a country; or people migrate from other places and over time they evolve a shared culture and learn to live together. India is an example of both these outcomes. People in South India have lived together for times immemorial, with minimal outside inflows. Still, most of North India is made up of people from Central Asia, Persia, and other places, either as conquerors or as migrants looking for a better climate and productive resources. These people did not originate from one place, allowing a great diversity of cultures, languages, and religions to flourish. While historians can talk about these things based on facts, politicians use the same information to create divisions and attack the concept of diversity. On the contrary, the poet uses his imagination to create a picture inspired by the vision and filled with metaphors, neither pure history nor politics. The poet's objective is to produce durable literature and reach his readers creatively and aesthetically. In the following ghazal poem, Firaq uses the metaphor of *kaarvaan* (caravans) to demonstrate how the country came into being, one caravan at a time. It was a long and complicated process, but the underlying thesis holds. India was not created at one point in time. What we see today is the result of a long evolutionary process. And that is the secret of India›s everlasting beauty and inner strength.

> *ziir o bam se saaz-e khilqat k jahaan banta gaya*
> *ye zamiin banti gaii ye aasmaan banta gaya*

Slowly and gradually,
with ups and downs,
the magic of creation unfolded.
Land emerged
and the sky opened.

> *daastaan-e jaur-e behad khuun se likhta raha*
> *qatra qatra ashk-e gham ka be-karaan banta gaya*

Someone continued
to write the tale
of extreme agony.
Each drop of suffering
was transformed
into a boundless ocean.

> *ishq-e tanha se huii aabaad kitni manzalein*
> *ik musaafir karvaan dar kaarvaan banta gaya*

The lonely love
created and settled
many points of disembarkation.
One traveler
joined others
and it made caravan
after caravan.

> *main tere jis gham ko apna jaanta tha vo bhi to*
> *zeb-e unvaan-e hadiis-e diirgaan banta gaya*

The sorrow
that you gave me
was solely my possession.
It became beautiful part
of stories
that others shared.

baat nikle baat se jaise vo tha tera bayaan
naam tera daastaan dar daastaan banta gaya
One thing always
led to another —
that was your narrative
of sharing dialects and languages.
Your name became part
of a rich and riveting story.

ham ko hai maaluum sab ruudaad-e ilm o falsafa
haan har iimaan o yakiin vahm o gumaan banta gaya

I know the convoluted origin
of knowledge and philosophy.
With passage,
they became the basis of faith,
doubt, conviction,
and evolution.

main kitab-e dil mein apna haal -e gham likhta raha
har varaq ik baab-e taariikh-e jahaan banta gaya

I wrote the tale
of my painful life
in the journal of my heart.
In time, every page —
it was like a chapter
in the history of the world.

bas usi ki tarjmaani hai mere ash'aar mein
jo sukuut-e raaz rangiin dastan banta gaya

My couplets are a representation
of the essence of silence
which slowly and gradually
became a chronicle of colorfulness.

meri ghutti mein pari thi ho ke hal urdu zabaan
jo bhi main kahta gaya husn-e bayaan banta gaya

The Urdu language was part
of my genetic make-up.

Whatever I had to say
blossomed into a
delightful lyrical style.

sar-zamiin-e hind par aqvaam-e aalam ke firaaq
qaafle baste gaye hindostaan banta gaya

Masses of people from other homelands
chose this soil, Firaq.
Caravan after caravan set up homes
at a leisurely pace and with time
India emerged as one nation.

Firaq was primarily a poet of ghazal and ruba'i, although he wrote some land-mark nazms too. His collection of ruba'is titled *Ruup* is unparalleled in Urdu literature. It contains three eternal themes – *Sundaram, Satyam, Shivam* (Beauty, Truth, and Creation). He described the beauty of an Indian woman in her many facets, like being a daughter, sister, wife, mother, as no one else had. She is not merely someone with a charming face and an attractive body, she is a multifac-eted being and plays many roles. Firaq creatively dwells on the ancient Indian concept of *jagat maata* or *janani,* 'the universal mother.'

Interestingly Firaq was encouraged to write ruba'is by his friend, Josh Mali-habadi. But the decision to make ruba'i a mirrorwork of *Hindustaaniyat* (Indian-ness) was his own. He ventured to capture the smell of the soil found earlier in Mir, Nazeer Akbarabadi, and in the early verse of Iqbal. Once Firaq got on this task, he included flavors reminiscent of poets like Tulsidas, Surdas, Mirabai, and Tagore. Most of his ruba'is are an exposition of what is known as *shringaar ras* (one of the core *rasas* of the nine *rasas* established by the ancient Indian *aestheticians*). We present here four rubaais as samples of Firaq's work, but this topic requires a separate chapter to address its myriad embellishments fully.

amrit vo halaahil ko bana deti hai
ghusse ki nazar phuul khila deti hai
maan ladli aulaad ko jaise taare
kis pyaar se premi ko saza deti hai

She can change the nectar into venom.
Flowers blossom on seeing her anger.
Like a caring mother watches her kids.
She punishes her lover with great fondness.

aankhein hain k paighaam mohabbat vaale
bikhri hain latein k niind mein hain kale
pahlu se laga hua hiran ka bachcha
kis pyaar se hai baghal mein gardan daale

Are these eyes or intimations of love?
Are these scattered tresses or black snakes asleep?

By the side is glued a baby deer.
With great love, she lowers her neck in an embrace.

doshiira faza mein lehlahaaya huua ruup
a'aiina-e sub-h mein chalakta huua ruup
ye narm nikhaar, ye sajal dhaj, ye sugandh
ras mein kuvaare-pan ke duuba huua ruup

The beauty that shines and glitters
in this virgin atmosphere,
the beauty that reflects in the mirror
of the morning.
This soft glow, impressive disposition,
and aroma —
the beauty drowned in the essence
of innocence.

hai biyaahata par ruup abhi kunwaara hai
maan hai par ada job hi hai doshiiza hai
wo mod bhari, maang bhari, god bhari
kaniya hai, suhaagan hai, jagat-maata hai

She is married,
but her beauty is angelic.
She is a mother,
but her elegance is maiden.
That honey-filled lass,
married and mother.
The young beauty, wedded,
a mother of the universe.

Firaq was an astonishing ghazal poet with an Indigenous tone and temper. He took great pride in being a ghazal writer, as we can notice from one of his couplets.

dhuundein ge mujh ko bazm-e sukhan mein agar kahien
paayein gi mujh ko baa'd ki naslein ghazal ke biich

If they try to find me in the gathering of verse,
the coming generations will find me
amid the assembly of ghazal.

Firaq wrote long-form ghazals, sometimes each containing more than two-dozen couplets. Within those ghazals were hidden some precious gems – couplets that were counted as masterpieces of Urdu poetry, each one narrating a complete story in two lines, each one making the reader to stop and reflect. We present below five such couplets that are often shared in the assemblies of ghazal loving friends.

ek muddat se teri yaad bhi aayi n hamein
aur ham bhuul gaye hon tujhe aisaa bhi nahien

My memory has not stopped over
to see you for a very long time.
And I forgot to remember you,
that is not the case either.

is daur mein zindagi bashar ki
biimaar ki raat ho gayi hai

The life of human beings
in the present times
seems to have become like
a patient's unending lonesome night.

ye nigaah-e ghalat andaaz bhi kya jaadu hai
dekhne waale tere ji n sakein mar n sakein

There is some magic hidden
in your bewitching glance of looking at others.
Those who encounter you
are caught in a dilemma.
They find it hard to die and equally hard to live.

tum mukhaatab bhi ho qariib bhi ho
tum ko dekhuun k tum se baat karuun

I am speaking with you
and you are close.
Do I look at you
or speak with you?

kis liye kam nahien hai dard firaq
ab to who dhyaan se utar bhi gaye

Why has the pain
not lessened, Firaq?
Now that she has gone away
from my thoughts.

We end this chapter with few couplets from one of Firaq's signature ghazals.

kisi ka yuun to hua kaun u'mr bhar phir bhi
y husn o i'shq to dokha hai sab magar phir bhi

No one belongs to anyone for life,
then again …
This beauty, this love –

these are all deceptions,
then again ...

hazaar baar zamaana idhar se guzra hai
naaii naaii si hai kuchh teri rahguzar phir bhi

People have trampled this pathway –
it seems one too many times.
Then again,
this promenade that belongs to you —
it looks new and fresh.

teri nigaah se bachne mein u'mr guzri hai
utar gaya rag-e jaan mein ye neshtar phir bhi

I spent my life trying to save myself
from the charms of your eyes.
Then again, I couldn't protect
my heart
from your piercing lancet.

agarche bekhudi-e i'shq ko zamaana hua
firaq karti rahi kaam vo nazar phir bhi

Love's rapture ended
a long-time ago.
Then again, Firaq,
her eyes continued
to pull and allure me.

Notes

1 Ajai Mansingh, Gopi Chand Narang, Foreword. *Firaq Gorakhpuri: The Poet of Pain and Ecstasy* (New Delhi: Rolli Books, 2015). Kindle digital edition.
2 The second line was also written as: *jab un ko maa'luum ye hoga tum ne firaaq ko dekha tha.*

BIBLIOGRAPHY

Abdulhaq, Maulvi (Muallafa), *Nusrati*, New Delhi: Anjuman'e Tarraqi Urdu.

Akbarabadi, Nazeer. 1951. *Gulzar-e Nazeer*, Compiled by Salim Ja'far, Allahabad.

Arshi, Imtiaz Ali. 1958. *Divan-e Ghalib, Nuskha-e Arshi*, Aligarh.

Azad, Muhammad Husain. 1982. *Aab-e Hayaat*, Lucknow: Uttar Pradesh Urdu Academy.

Bary, Theodore De, Stephen N. Hay, Royal Weiler, and Andrew Yarrow. 1958. *Sources of Indian Tradition*, New York: Columbia University Press.

Deol, Surinder. 2019. *SAHIR: A Literary Portrait*, New Delhi: Oxford University Press.

Faiz, Faiz Ahmad. 1953. *Dast-e Saba*, Delhi: Azad Kitab Ghar.

Forché, Carolyn and Duncan Wu, eds. 2013. *Poetry of Witness*, New York: W.W. Norton & Company.

Gilmartin, David. 2010. 'Sufism, Exemplary Lives, and Social Science in Pakistan' in *Rethinking Islamic* Studies: *From Orientalism to Cosmopolitanism*, Columbia: University of South Carolina Press.

Golkandvi, Tab'ii. 1999. *Masnawi Bahram o Gul-e Andam*, New Delhi: Qaumi Council Bara-e Farogh-e Urdu.

Hali, Altaf Husain. 1897. *Yaadgaar-e Ghalib*, Lahore: Sheikh Mubarak Ali Tajir-e Kutb.

Hasan, Sibte. 2006. *Aazaadi Ki Nazmein*, New Delhi: National Council for Promotion of Urdu Language.

Hashim, Shah. 1088 Hijri. *Divan Zaadah*, Manuscript, Patna: Kutab Khana Khuda Baksh.

Hashmi, Nurul Hasan, ed. 1954. *Divan-e Wali*, Karachi: Anjuman Press.

Husain, Ehtisham. 1947. *Rivayat aur Baghavat*, Lucknow: Idara-e Ishaa'at-e Urdu.

Husain, Ehtisham. 1948. *Adab aur Samaaj*, Bombay: Kutab Publishers.

Husain, Ehtisham. 1952. *Tanqiid aur Amli Tanqiid*, Delhi.

Jafri, Sardar. 2013. *Taraqqi-Pasand Adab*, New Delhi: Anjuman Taraqqi Urdu Hind.

Kaokab, Tafazzul Husain, ed. 1863. *Fughaan-e Delhi*, Vol. I, Delhi.

Malihabadi, Josh. 1970. *Yaadon Ki Baaraat*, Karachi: Josh Academy.

Mansingh, Ajai. 2015. Gopi Chand Narang, Foreword. *Firaq Gorakhpuri: The Poet of Pain and Ecstasy*, New Delhi: Rolli Books.

Mas-hafi, Ghulam Hamdani, 1211 Hijri. *Third Divan of Mas-hafi*, Manuscript, Rampur: Raza Library.

Metcalf, Charles, ed. *Ghadar Ki Sub-h o Shaam, Daily Dialy Diary of Moenuldeen Hasan Khan and Jivan Lal* (Publication information is not available.)

Mir, Taqi Mir. Compiled by Abdulbari Aasi. 1941. *Kulliyaat-e Mir*, Lucknow: Naval Kishore.

Mittal, S.K. and Irfan Habib. 1982. 'The Congress and the Revolutionaries in the 1920s,' *Social Scientist*, 10 (6): June 1982.

Mohani, Hasrat, ed. *Intikhaab Urdu-e Mualla*, 1903–1908, Aligarh.

Narang, Gopi Chand, ed. 1968. *Aasaar-e Mehroom* (*Pagdandi* of Amritsar's Mehroom Number), New Delhi: Maktaba Jamia Ltd.

Narang, Gopi Chand. 2016. trans. Khurshid Alam, *Bharatiya Lok Kathaon Par Aadharit Urdu Masnaviyan*, New Delhi: Bharatiya Jnanpith.

Narang, Gopi Chand. 2017. trans. Surinder Deol, *Ghalib: Innovative Meanings and the Ingenious Mind*, New Delhi: Oxford University Press.

Narang, Gopi Chand. 2020. trans. Surinder Deol, *The Urdu Ghazal: A Gift of India's Composite Culture*, New Delhi: Oxford University Press.

Narang, Gopi Chand. 2021. trans. Surinder Deol, *The Hidden Garden: Mir Taqi Mir*, New Delhi: Penguin India.

Narang, Gopi Chand, ed. Undated. 'Mehroom Ki Qaumi Shaay'iri' in *Afkaar-e Mehroom*, ed. Malik Ram, New Delhi: Mehroom Memorial Committee.Nayyar, Hukam Chand. 1967. *Navaa-e Suroor*, Benares: Idaara-e Roznama Hindostan.

Panigrahi, Devendra N. 2004. *India's Partition: The Story of Imperialism in Retreat*, London: Routledge.

Prigarina, Natalia. 1997. trans. Osama Faruqi, *Mirza Ghalib*, Hyderabad.

Qureshi, Abdur Razzaq, ed. 1957. *Nawaa-e Aazaadi*, Bombay: Adabi Publishers.

Raza, Kalidas Gupta, ed. 1995. *Divan-e Ghalib Kamil, Nuskha-e Raza*. Mumbai: Saakaar Publications Pvt. Ltd.

Sauda, Compiled by Aasi. 1932. *Kulliyaat-e Sauda*, Vol. I., Lucknow: Naval Kishore.

Savarkar, Veer. 2019. *The Indian War of Independence 1857*, New Delhi: Abhishek Publications.

Shefta, Mustafa Khan. *Divan-e Shefta*, Lahore: Akademi Punjab.

Siddiqi, Abu-aliis, ed. 1955. *Lucknow Ka Dabistan's Shaa'yiri*, Lahore.

Suroor, Ale Ahmad. 1946, *Naye aur Purane Chiragh,* Lucknow: Lucknow University.

Ul-aa'm, ed. 1264 Hijri, *Divan-e Munir*, Vol. 1., Rampur: Syedi.

Zachariah, Benjamin. 2004. *Nehru*, New York: Routledge.

Zafar, Bahadur Shah. 1876. *Kulliyaat-e Zafar*, Divan I. Kanpur: Munshi Nawal Kishore.

Zaidi, Ali Jawad. 1957. *Naghma-e Azadi*, Lucknow: Publications Bureau, Department of Information.

Zaidi, Ali Jawad. 1975. *Zabt-Shuda Nazmein*, New Delhi: Majlis-e Jashn Ali Jawad Zaidi.

Zaidi, Ali Jawad. 1982. *Urdu Mein Qaumi Shaa'yri Ke Sao Saal*, Lucknow: Uttar Pradesh Urdu Academy.

INDEX

For Product Safety Concerns and Information please contact our EU
representative GPSR@taylorandfrancis.com
Taylor & Francis Verlag GmbH, Kaufingerstraße 24, 80331 München, Germany